Allison Akene Ayida

Nigeria's Quintessential Public Servant

Allison Akene Ayida

Nigeria's Quintessential Public Servant

edited by

Femi Kayode & Dafe Otobo

m a l t h o u s e 

Malthouse Press Limited

Lagos, Benin, Ibadan, Jos, Oxford, Port-Harcourt, Zaria

&

Foundation for Economics Education

Malthouse Press Limited
11B Goriola Street, Off Adeola Odeku
Victoria Island, Lagos
E-mail: malthouse_press@yahoo.com
malthouse_lagos@yahoo.co.uk
Tel: +234 (01) -773 53 44; 613 957; 0802 364 2402

and

Foundation for Economics Education
Ibadan

First Published 2004
ISBN 978 023 185 4
ISBN-13: 978-978-023-185-9

Distributors:
African Books Collective Ltd

Tel: +44 - (0) 1865 -726686
Fax: +44 - (0) 1865 -793298
Email: abc@africanbookscollective.com
Website: http://www.africanbookscollective.com

Dedication

Dedicated to my loving wife,
Mrs Oluremi Victoria Ayida
and her darling children
Mrs Alero Aboyowa Otobo
Mrs (Dr) Gbubemi Anire Ayida-Akerele
Mr Omatseyin Akene Ayida
Mr Abidemi Allison Ayida
and
Mr Maje Amaju Ayida
for their endurance and loving care and support
in my "planning and development days".
We thank God for the life he has bestowed on us.
May His name be praised.

Acknowledgements

This landmark book is the outcome of collaborative effort by many committed specialists who have worked hard and long, often in several roles simultaneously, to ensure its efficient and successful completion. We express our deep appreciation of you all, starting with the subject of the book himself.

Mr Ayida's candour and meticulous attention to detail ensured, from the outset, that the project would be a big, challenging and rewarding venture. He readily turned over to the team of researchers and interviewers all of his rich collection of published and unpublished records and gave valuable leads to other sources of relevant information. We are grateful for his unflinching support throughout.

Four refreshingly complementary perspectives of the extraordinary subject of this book have been provided by four eminent personalities in Nigerian society: Chief Tayo Akpata, Professor Akin L. Mabogunje, Dr Michael Omolayole and Chief Philip Asiodu. We are grateful for their insightful and enriching contributions.

We express our special gratitude to Professor Emman C. Edozien for making the initial contacts in his inimitable way.

Finally, we salute the courage and sacrifice of core members of the technical team, comprising Professors 'Femi Kayode, Dafe Otobo, Demola Oyejide, Mark Nwagwu and 'Bode Aiyepeku, who carried out the project design and management, research and interviews, writing and reviewing, and editing. Others included Dr Ayo Odusola, A.A. Fajingbesi, E.C. Obioma, A.I. Ayodele, P.A. Olomola, S. Edo and Olu Oluwasola, and Messrs I. F. Olaniyan and G.O. Falokuun.

Research assistance was provided by Yemi Olabiyi and Muyiwa Ola, and Sola Balogun did all the typing. We acknowledge your diligence and patience throughout all aspects of the project.

Foreword

On my way to the Kaduna Airport to fly to Lagos to take over as Permanent Secretary, Federal Ministry of Information, on 12 July 1967, I called on my bosom friend, confidant and boss, the late Alhaji Ali Akilu, Secretary to the Military Government of Northern Nigeria to say farewell to him and his family. As we shook hands in good-bye he drew me aside and advised me to as soon as possible after arriving in Lagos, I should call on two men - Allison Ayida and Philip Asiodu, both Permanent Secretaries in the Federal Government. He advised that I should work closely with both men. They, he said, were good and loyal Nigerians and very intelligent.

At Lagos Airport, I was met by an official driver and taken to an empty, but fully furnished flat at 36 Glover Road, Ikoyi. It occurred to me that I would need to eat dinner and considered how best to get one. I began to inquire about Ayida and Asiodu and was led to Mr. Ayida's house at 11, Ikoyi Crescent. Although we may have met once or twice at official meetings, since the military take-over of Government, we had not as yet become familiar with one another. So I introduced myself as the "new chap from Kaduna, just come to take over the Federal Ministry of Information" and thought I should call on him and convey Akilu's warmest regards. After a while I rose to say good night, but his wife Remi invited me to stay and have dinner. I needed no persuading. Soon afterwards. Asiodu walked in and we all had dinner together and talked until early the next day. So began a long, happy and very rewarding association.

From that night until now and forever, one of the most enduring personal and official relationship in Nigerian Government circles was born. This was at the beginning of the Nigerian Civil War, which lasted thirty whole months, in which many Nigerians died, were maimed or impoverished. Both Ayida and Asiodu were from the Mid West and I from the North East. Ayida and Asiodu went to the same educational institutions in Nigeria and Great Britain. As I write this Foreword, I cannot help but feel how remarkable it is that these men of three different backgrounds and upbringing could so unite and feel the same on almost anything in both their official views and private lives. But it happened. The three of us and our families have remained close friends. We celebrate and commiserate together.

All throughout the civil war and after, we worked together, travelled extensively together in Nigeria and around the world, even some time, having to stay together in the same room and cook our meals. In all this Ayida played a very central role. He was the most patient among the three of us. He has a gift of defusing tension and saving very explosive situations, even at Cabinet and Supreme Council meetings, at which we used to be in attendance and occasionally allowed to explain situations and answer questions.

Throughout the civil war, Mr. Ayida, was Permanent Secretary, Federal Ministry of Economic Development. Immediately following the end of the Civil War, the Ministry of Economic Development was renamed, Federal Ministry of Economic Development and Reconstruction. The three 'Rs' was immediately launched - Reconciliation, Rehabilitation and Reconstruction. It was recognised that reconciliation at this point was key to Nigeria's future. So the "No Victor, No Vanquished" slogan was launched in one united effort.

When the civil war ended with the departure of Ojukwu on 10 January, 1970, I was myself in Enugu and had participated in writing the early morning broadcast for Mr. Ukpabi Asika, then

Administrator of the East Central State, the theatre of the war with General T. Y. Danjuma. The broadcast had included instructions to Federal troops on how to treat civilians and advising civilians to approach Federal Forces for assistance, etc. In the aircraft on my way back to Lagós, I reflected on the events of that day and wondered whether we had not preempted the broadcast of the Head of State considering that he had just put down a mammoth revolt. On arrival at the airport, a military vehicle took me directly to Dodan Barracks where an all day meeting was still going on and the broadcast the Head of State was to make was in preparation. I drew Ayida aside and told him of the "blunder" we had committed in Enugu. As usual he calmed my concerns and said: "do you know what we should do?" "No," I said. "We should capture parts of salient features of the Asika's broadcasts into General Gowon's speech." When he had finished his broadcast, I told General Gowon the full story. His response was, "Honestly I trust you boys. Our thinking is now the same."

Ayida went on to become the Secretary to the Federal Government on the sudden death of Mr. Abdul Aziz Atta. He held that position with distinction and was retained by the Murtala Administration, until 1977. Asiodu had been retired by the incoming administration in August 1975. With his departure, I suddenly felt alone and uncomfortable in the service. Nearly all of my colleagues whose ways I understood had disappeared. But my life-long friend and school classmate and colleague at work both in the Northern Region and the Federal Public Service, the late Liman Ciroma, had been named his successor. I could not desert him. So I stayed one year and left in 1978.

In public service, Mr. Ayida along with Asiodu and I had come under public lime light and consequently controversy. Many things any of us said were magnified, reported, analyzed and commented upon in the media. This almost certainly led to the retirement of both Asiodu and Ayida.

Upon his retirement, Mr. Ayida, called from Dodan Barracks and broke the news to me. I was speechless and headed for his house. In the case of Asiodu, we all knew that the July 29 1975 revolution would sweep him away and so we were not surprised.

In private life, in the true spirit of service, Mr. Ayida, has continued to make himself available for the service of this country. He has developed wide business interests and connections and his always sought to involve me and many of his former civil service friends.

Mr. Ayida continues to show his concern for the future of the country for which he has devoted his entire working life and worked so hard to defend and to preserve. In this I will continue to associate myself.

This book will fill a wide gap in the political and social history of Nigeria. I commend it especially to the younger generation of Nigerians, who although aware that there had been a civil war in their country, do not know or have access to the true causes of the war, how it was fought and how eventually Nigeria was preserved. I hope there will be more of this kind of book in the bookshelves of reading Nigerians.

Ahmed Joda
Abuja, 2004

Contents

1

The Nigerian public service in perspective

Antecedents of Nigeria's public service

The evolution of modern humans follows the path of the evolution of society. How society develops within the context of nations and their global interests or dominance determines the course of human history. In this process, there seems a virile conflict - if not antagonism - between the individual on the one hand and the inclusive society in which the individual is supposed to seek full development, on the other. Tradition, the hallmark of civilizations, seeks to place humans within the context of a particular culture which, it is believed, helps advance human life, leading to progress. Thus, tradition is at one and the same time an instrument of conservatism and change - conserving what is great and useful that it may become greater and more useful as an instrument of change. According to Soyinka, "the fundamental problem for the African intellectual who struggles for cultural renewal continues to be that of reconciling tradition and progress." And as Ajayi pointed out, "the proper role of tradition as a living reality and an important factor in politics and social change remains to be adequately studied. Unfortunately, so little is known or said about traditionality, "the substance of tradition itself," as

Munoz has observed.

Colonialism had insidiously replaced the autochthonous virile traditions and cultures of the diverse communities and nations that were later to become Nigeria, with a strange set of rules which emasculated them of their vigour and nobility. Okonkwo, of *Things Fall Apart* fame, captures this mood on his return from Umofia. While he was away, His Majesty's obedient servants had introduced a new system of government with its new system of justice and maintenance of the law, and he wonders:

> Perhaps I have been away too long...I cannot understand these things you tell me. What is it that has happened to our people? Why have they lost the power to fight? (Achebe, 1958:124)

Obierika answers him:

> How do you think we can fight when our brothers have turned against us? The white man is very clever. He came quietly and peaceably with his religion. We were amused at his foolishness and allowed him to stay. Now he has won our brothers, and our clan can no longer act like one. He has put a knife on the things that held us together and we have fallen apart. (Achebe, 1958:124)

When, therefore, one thinks of tradition in Nigeria one must consider not only the indigenous ways of the people, but also the new traditions brought by the white man in the form of public service, or, as we say, the civil service. What is the justification for this? Admittedly, the civil service served the purpose of colonialism by providing the tools and principles and philosophy of governance. The people had little or no voice in how they were governed. In a way, the service can be considered to be inimical to their interests since, it could be argued, whatever was good for the white man must be bad for the black man. But this is true only up to a point - up to the point as perceived by an ill-educated class. When we move into the world of learning, then the argument can be turned on its head and made to serve the purpose of the black man. Had Winston Churchill not boasted in Parliament, "*Let us therefore brace ourselves to our duties and so bear ourselves that if the British Empire and its Commonwealth last for a thousand years, men will still say, 'This was their finest hour*" (18 June, 1940)?

The British Empire collapsed under the weight of its apparent strengths, namely, colonialism and empire-building: when the colonies sought, and gained, independence from the imperial powers. The Commonwealth collapsed under the weight of the selfsame colonialism: the new nations of Africa and India were not comfortable in the same "club" with their erstwhile lords who supported apartheid in South Africa... What are the lessons? Freedom is an essential, unconquerable attribute of humans and a non-negotiable feature of their humanness. People must be free and all equal or society cannot survive. The military domination of Nigerian life, with excessive coercive power without cogent participation of the people in governance, was not significantly different from Nigeria's experience under colonialism. Why does Nigeria seem heedless of this aphorism? So much for the antecedents of Nigeria's public service...

Nigerians expect their public servants to be saints - learned and knowledgeable, faithful, genteel and prudent, in one word, perfect. Unfortunately, or perhaps, fortunately (we cannot, of course, help it), our public servants are just like ordinary Nigerians: they have faults and failings, weaknesses and ordeals. They suffer like anyone else, bear pain and abuse with a smile like some people do. They can be efficient and deliberate, expert at what they do, like the best of us, of which there are not so many. Moreover, the civil service is, unquestionably, the epitome of the Nigerian public service.

While workers in Nigerian parastatals, such as the Central Bank of Nigeria, and the federal and state universities may, correctly, be referred to as 'public servants,' by far the most visible Nigerian public servants are the civil servants in the federal and state ministries and their agencies. Consequently, the 'ideal public servant' in Nigeria is, rightly, perceived by most Nigerians as the 'ideal civil servant.' It is an onerous responsibility that has been borne quietly and honourably by Nigerian civil servants for many decades.

The Civil Service is the most visible, most powerful component of Nigeria's public service. But, what do we understand by 'the ideal civil servant'? And, by inference, who is 'the ideal civil servant'?

The ideal civil service

In 1975, in a lecture entitled, *The New Style Public Service,* delivered at the Public Service Forum of the former Western State of Nigeria, the unflappable and debonair public servant, Jerome Udoji, gave us the following prescriptions as to what the civil service *ought* to be:

> The new style public service is nothing but a result-oriented public service. It is public service with a purpose, a Service that is out to achieve certain well-defined and well-articulated objectives; a Service whose performance can be measured and assessed. It is a Service that is run by specialists and professionals and not by amateurs... a Service where concrete performance in the achievement of predetermined departmental or organizational goals and targets is the main criterion for advancement and not the ethnic group, language, or sex of the officer concerned...It is a service that takes pride in excellence and jobs well-done...a Service where professionalism is extolled and amateurism

> discouraged...a Service which is modest enough to recognize that modern government is big business and therefore requires the use of experts both in the formulation of policies and in their implementation. It is a Service that does not ask for conditions that are not applicable in other walks of life, a Service that does not surround itself with protective regulations and orders against any removal for incompetence, obsolescence, or any other cause... In short, the new style public service is one that adopts modern methods of management in three key areas: in the definition of its objectives and programmes, recruitment and development of staff to carry them out, and the execution of projects that constitute the programmes (Udoji, 1999).

We look up to our civil servants. They should work behind the scenes. We expect them to perform excellently and yet, we do not expect to hear from this top class of professionals. And, as Udoji clearly enunciates above, they work in "a Service that does not ask for conditions that are not applicable in other walks of life." Civil servants are not known to be great speakers who hold you spellbound with words, perhaps because they are not allowed to open their specialized mouths in public. They deal with papers and files and yet more files; they send files up and down with apparently very little being accomplished. They should be brilliant, discreet, genteel, thorough, apolitical, able to study a problem dispassionately, identify all its different perspectives, analyse the merits and demerits of each possibility, and give sound, impeccable advice when this is sought. Otherwise, they should just keep quiet with their mouths well zipped up. God bless the Nigerian civil public servant who is keen to speak up; he will surely be damned. The civil servant appears little more than a closet masterpiece, brought out for the show and then stowed safely away till the next meeting!

But it would be a great pity if this were the only return we expect from the rich resources invested in the production of our civil servants, especially members of 'the top civil service.' Why must they only be seen and not heard? And if and when they are, indeed, heard, what manner of 'hearing,' one might justifiably ask?

In a 1995 address entitled, "The Civil Service in the Year 2000 and Beyond," delivered to the Delta State Public Service Forum, Udoji made the following remarks on the function of the Nigerian civil servant:

> The civil service structure and functions in any country depend on that country's political system of government. *After all, the job of a civil servant is to carry out the legitimate wishes of his political master.* How he carries them out depends not only on the country's political system but also on the tenure of government as well as on whether the executive power of government is single or collegiate, that is to say, whether executive powers are vested in one person as in the presidential system, or on a group of persons as in the parliamentary system ((Udoji, 1999) (emphasis added).

Thus, the Nigerian civil servant may not show striking initiative; his abilities for originality and innovation may not be called to the fore - it all depends on what his masters want from him or determines as his role.

Civil servants spend long hours attending meetings, at least that is the impression given by their messengers who rattle off "*oga* de meeting," even before the visitor has finished the sentence, 'Is the *oga* in?' You might then wonder, what a civil service meeting is like. Is it the arena where the civil servant exerts maximum influence and can, therefore, do the most good or damage through either his thoroughness or ineptitude? Is it where the fate of a public servant is decided by those who may be indifferent, or are simply ethnic bigots, consumed by their exalted sense of self? Is it where those present are encouraged to bare their minds and speak the truth by seeking appropriate answers to the questions confronting them? As the word itself implies, 'a meeting' is an occasion for people to get together and try to come to some agreement on the issues they wish to consider. It is inconceivable that a meeting could ever be called for the participants to decide how to come to blows and beat each other up: you do not need a meeting for violence, you just go out and do it, Mafia style. Although a civil service meeting may not be called to decide how best to shoot one another, it is, nonetheless, where those who come to deliberate on important issues of state may tear one another to pieces, or try to say nice things they do not really mean; where participants may do everything possible to stop a decision being taken that does not go along with their own favoured position. No, a civil service meeting is not really a 'meeting': it is a war, and participants should always attend with their weapons well charged, that is, weapons of intrigue, beguilement, and treachery. The less you say or do at such meetings, the greater the heights you are likely to ascend in the estimation of your superiors, who may not really want you to do much except support whatever their position might be. The more befuddled your contribution to such meetings, the better....

But this impression would not be quite correct. Allison Ayida would find this notion of a civil service meeting both rude and offensive. Why? He is brilliant, charming and pleasant, impeccable and genteel, refined and astute, a perfect gentleman. To Allison, a civil service meeting is where sincerity and clarity carry the day; where truth reigns supreme and facts are bared; where the scoundrel speaks his mind and is then forgotten; where rancour is doused with a large dose of sophisticated wit; where good men and women show the stuff of which they are made; where the national interest is debated, scoured, scrubbed, and rendered spotless.

Allison Akene Ayida (all As) has remained an open question till now. From now on, we shall know him better, as he really is. He could easily have become a professor, but the subject of his choice was not taught at the (then) University College, Ibadan. It is true that, in the words of Spender (1986), he sometimes "had the sensation of being in a library... reading a history and coming to a chapter left unwritten that blazed nothing... nothing except him... nothing but his great name and his great deeds." But the history had not been written till now. It was a blank page, no ink, no words. And as he well knows, you cannot write your own history. Allison Ayida may be hated by some and loved by many, hated for what he said and did, for his guts and indefatigable style, and loved for his brilliance of thinking, tenacity of purpose and humility of accomplishments. We shall continue the story from his entry into the Nigerian civil service, but before then, a summary of Ayida's vision of the Service, as enunciated in his public lecture entitled, the Federal Civil Service and Nation Building, ends this opening chapter.

Ayida's vision of the Nigerian civil service

- The Public Service is, indeed, one of the central pillars in the foundation of the Third Republic.

- The execution of government policy, once this is settled by the Cabinet or Minister or Commissioner as political head of the Ministry or the top echelon of the Higher Civil Service... is, to a large extent, determined by the efficiency and competence of the civil service."

- The second traditional primary function of the Higher Civil Service is the initiation of public policy and advising Government on the full implications of policy options open to Government.

- In a dynamic and unstable situation with sudden and abrupt or frequent changes in Government, the Civil Service plays a vital role in providing continuity and serves as the store of knowledge of past government decisions and procedures. The Service also plays an educative role in assisting new Ministers or Commissioners in adapting themselves to the realities of power and giving up some of their 'opposition' ideas of Government. Our recent experience has shown that the continuity and educative influence of the Higher Civil Service in times of serious political crisis resulting in a power vacuum can be critical in determining the course of events, at least in the short run.

- In a Federation, the Federal Civil Service...provides one of the main unifying factors.

- The Civil Service is one of the visible arms of Government and a source of stability. As an embodiment of Government in the day-to-day life of the people, the Civil Service helps to preserve the mystique of Government and authority, through the daily contacts of officials at all levels, with the general public.

- The Higher Civil Service is sometimes called upon to act as the custodian of public conscience.

- The Higher Civil Service is part of the elite and therefore has a leadership role to play both within the Service and in the community as a whole.

Part I

The man and his career

2

The early years

A man was born
among many
who were born.
He lived among many men
who also lived, and that alone
is not so much history
as earth itself... (Neruda, 1964)

Allison Akene Ayida was born on late Sunday/Monday, June 16, 1930 in Gbelebu, an Ijaw village near Siluko, in present day Edo State. But both parents are from Ugbege in present Warri North Local Government Area in Delta State. His mother Christiana Ejurewa, had a bitter-sweet week-end from Friday evening to Sunday night before his birth: bitter for pain, sweet for the anticipated birth. Allison was a man among many also born on that day, but who knows what may have happened to all those others? Are they alive, how have they fared, where are they now? Nature quenched our thirst with the wine of his birth which we, the labourers, awaiting his entry into life managed to tap from the palms of Gbelebu. Yes, since then we have known nothing but joy, for we were all there. Allison fills the earth, in fact, is earth itself.

The colonial setting of his birth

The first and only son of his parents, young Allison came into life in the thick of British colonial rule in Nigeria – at a time when the Nigerian could not be expected to take charge of his own destiny, being regarded as unfit and unqualified to rule. The Governor of the Colony and Protectorate of Nigeria was Sir Graeme Thompson (1925-31), soon to be followed by Sir Donald Cameron (1931-35). Before this, Sir Hugh Clifford (1919-25), the immediate successor of Lord Lugard, had denigrated the possibility of Nigerians conducting their affairs themselves in these disparaging terms:

> It can only be described as farcical to suppose that ... continental Nigeria can be represented by a handful of gentlemen drawn from a half-dozen coast towns - men born and bred in British-administered towns situated on the seashore who, in the safety of British protection, have peacefully pursued their studies under British teachers, in British schools, in order to enable them to become ministers of the Christian religion or learned in the laws of England, whose eyes are fixed, not upon African native history or tradition or policy, nor upon their own tribal obligations and duties to their Natural Rulers which immemorial custom should impose on them, but upon political theories evolved by Europeans to fit a wholly different set of circumstances, arising out of a wholly different environment, for the government of peoples who have arrived at a wholly different stage of civilization...*(Crowder, 1962: 255)*.

Worse, Sir Clifford could not possibly imagine that there could really be a Nigerian nation. One might then wonder what was the objective of Lugard's amalgamation of the Protectorate of Northern Nigeria and the Colony and Protectorate of Southern Nigeria Protectorate into the Colony and Protectorate of Nigeria if this new amalgam was not supposed to grow and mature into a full nation. Sir Clifford's remarks on this bear recalling:

> Assuming ...that the impossible were feasible – that this collection of self-contained and mutually independent Native States, separated from one another, as many as there are, by great distances, by differences of history and traditions, and by ethnological, racial, tribal, political, social and religious barriers, were indeed capable of being welded into a single homogeneous nation – a deadly blow would thereby be struck at the very root of national self-government in Nigeria, which secures to each separate people the right to maintain its identity, its individuality, its own chosen government, and the peculiar political and social institutions which have been evolved for it by the wisdom and by the accumulated experience of generations of its forbears (Crowder, 1962:255-6).

Curiously enough, it was this same Sir Hugh Clifford who introduced the 1922 Constitution which, for the first time in British Africa, provided for elected African members on a Legislative Council – a development that fuelled the engines of Nigerian nationalism.

> The universal belief among the British rulers in Church and State was that Nigerians were unable to govern themselves; their existence as thinking and intelligent men was unrecognized. As colonial rule strengthened and lengthened, the *bien oui oui* collaborators ought to have seen through the veil, that the policy in vogue was that of British heads and Nigerian hands. They ought to have perceived that the British would not relinquish power unless they were forced to do so. Nigerians, it was believed by a few extremist white rulers, lacked the power of inductive character. '*Bien oui oui*' is a French term meaning 'Yes men' in English or 'His Master's Voice'

> to describe unabashed protégés of the French masters who endorsed everything done by their masters by repeatedly saying 'very well', the literal meaning of '*bien oui oui*' (Ayandele, 1974).

This was the Nigeria of educated men like Herbert Macaulay, regarded as the father of Nigerian nationalism, Henry Rawlinson Carr (1863-1945) who was appointed Resident for Lagos Colony immediately after the First World War, Dr. Abubakir Ibiyinka Olorunnimbe, a product of the University of Glasgow, 1930 to 1937, and later the first Mayor of Lagos, Dr. Nnamdi Azikiwe, the first Igbo graduate, Kitoyi Ajasa, the first Lagos indigene to be trained as a lawyer, A.W. Howells, Isaac Oluwole and T.A.O. Ogunbiyi, who were trained by the CMS, and Sir Adeyemo Alakija who hailed from a wealthy family. Thomas Adesina Jacobson Ogunbiyi had founded the Christian Ogboni Society in 1914 - which later transformed into the Reformed Ogboni Fraternity - and had sought to right the wrongs of imported, 'white man's' Christianity. Remarkably, this elite group of Nigerians owed great loyalty to the British Crown. As Herbert Macaulay himself asserted in an interview granted to a delegation on the fight against slavery, at Government House on February 26 1913, "We are, to a man, proud today, Sir, that we are subjects of the British crown for the British Government administers justice without fear or favour" (Ayandele, 1974:59).

A blossoming father/son relationship

> From the dusty boom of the country
> they took me, still an infant
> into the rain of Araucania.
> The boards of the house
> Smelled of the woods,

> Of the deep forest.
> From that time on, my love
> Had wood in it
> And everything I touched turned into wood
> (Neruda, 1964)

Allison's father, Jones, was a teacher and was fondly called 'Teacher' by everybody in his community. An ambitious and energetic man, the 'teacher' left teaching and ventured into trading and timber business at a time when private enterprise required daring, good timing and a large dose of luck. After an initial period of sporadic success, the business fell on hard times, owing to the depression in the world economy of the 1930s. We might attempt to situate this unfortunate change in fortunes within the context of the commercial trade of the time, which was beginning to witness a stormy Urhobo dominance. This effort has some merit because Jones Ayida, being formerly a teacher and well educated and sophisticated, would be expected to grasp what makes a business succeed and to follow it faithfully, being well disciplined, astute and hard-working.

Clearly, the Itsekiri had dominated the trade in the Western Nigeria Delta from the time of the Portuguese in the late sixteenth century to the colonial times. Urhobo nationalist activities began very early in colonialism, with the avowed purpose of wresting from the erstwhile dominant Itsekiri direct contact with the British colonialists and become themselves the main middle-men in trade and politics. It was at this time that the Urhobo Progressive Union and its leader 'Mukoro Mowoe came into prominence and succeeded in securing for the Urhobo their cherished autonomy. By 1938 the relations between the two ethnic groups, Itsekiri and Urhobo, had deteriorated immeasurably. This crisis was to reach gigantic proportions in 1952 when, under the dominant party in Western Nigeria, the Action Group, with Chief Obafemi Awolowo as the Premier of western Nigeria, the title of *Olu of Itsekiri* was restored to the original title of *Olu of Warri*, and Warri province was changed to Delta province.

But Allison, by 1952, was well on his way to great things at Oxford.

Returning then to Mr. Jones Ayida, we find that the collapse of his business venture left him devastated but not hopeless. Gathering heroic courage, Ayida left Gbelebu and migrated to Lagos to seek employment. This called for uncommon courage and determination; for going to Lagos in those days was more like going overseas. In fact, many provincials who had been sent off to the United Kingdom, to the white man's land, to learn the white man's ways, and to be completely transformed into an educated and civilized man, got no further than Lagos. Those who succeeded in going farther often spent a long period in Lagos securing the required passport and other papers. Lagos, to all intents and purposes, was perceived by the locals as the land just next door to England. Mr Ayida, in spite of his doggedness and education, still could not find employment in Lagos. His little son, Allison, who not yet in school, travelled with his father. So inseparable were they. Not long after they arrived in Lagos, little Allison, who was not at all used to life in the big city, once missed his way, got lost and simply had no clues as to how to get home! Wailing and totally miserable, he was taken by some fatherly gentleman to a near-by police station. The police were prepared to help, but Allison did not know the address where he lived with his father. They did manage to get him home, however, perhaps by some vague description which the hapless little boy was able to convey to them. Mr. Jones Ayida, totally distraught, was now relieved at the recovery of his only son.

Things were no easier for Jones Ayida in Lagos. In spite of a huge effort and a relentless search for opportunity, he could not find a job. Consequently, he packed his bags and, with his little son, returned to Gbelebu. One can imagine what his detractors would say on his return: expressions like, ‘a failure’, ‘a stupidly ambitious man’, ‘a dreamer whose dreams never come true’, etc. However unfriendly and unwelcome his homecoming environment may have been, Jones Ayida was determined to get on with his life and to put those years of disappointment behind him. Ever and unrepentantly ambitious, he wanted his son to see the world. Whatever may have been the disappointments he endured, he was determined that his son would not suffer his fate; the son would ride on, borne on his father's horse, though it be withered and broken.

But young Allison had not even started school. His star was still being formed in the firmament of the heavens.

Allison started school late, judging by today's standards when children are already in primary school at age four. Not so in his days: before you went to school, you would keep your head straight, raise your right hand and bend it over the head to touch your left ear. If the hand and ear made contact, it meant you could go to school; if not, you were homeward bound. If, in addition, you had a doting and loving grandmother who would not let go of her ‘baby’, as was the case with Allison, then you were homebound for several years, anyway, the acrobatics that determined the proximity between your right hand and left ear notwithstanding.

This had its advantages, though. You see, in Allison's days, children went to primary school not so much to learn ‘book’ but to play, run, and learn ABC and 2 plus 2 equals four, or 2 times 2 equals 4 and so on - all of which the lad learned at home from his ‘teacher’ father. So good was he in learning that his father would show him off when friends visited. He would call on his bright son to recite some passage he had recently taught him and, to his great delight and pride, his son would not let him down: he would recite everything correctly without missing a word or phrase. At this stage, young Allison precociously knew the difference between a phrase and a sentence – the former was a statement which did not have a verb and did not make complete sense; the latter had a verb and made sense. Wow! One wonders how many of our students in primary six today know this. What was even more commanding was that the elder Ayida exposed young Allison to the world of literature, of novels and story-telling. Allison's future career as a man of letters was being forged in the furnace of his family background. With the loving care of his maternal grandmother, he was developing a stable, vibrant and confident personality.

Primary and secondary school life

At the age of seven going to eight, Allison had not yet started school. By the time he was finally enrolled at the United Nigeria African Church School in Gbelebu, young Allison was living with his aunt and her husband and, when they were transferred to Ubiaja, in Edo State, his father agreed that they could take Allison along so that he might be further exposed to the world and gain a wider knowledge of different Nigerian cultures. At Ubiaja, Allison attended Roman Catholic Mission School and, by his own admission, nearly became a Catholic. His earlier upbringing in a tradition of basic values and discipline was further reinforced by sound Catholic teaching. This was a time of duty and devoted service. Young Allison would get up by 4.30 hours in the morning and go down the hill to fetch water for daily use in the home, there being no pipe-borne water in Ubiaja in those days, long before the great Anthony Enahoro and his group were to change things and make life more comfortable for their people. He would make two such trips before going to school and, on the second trip, would have his bath and then bring the second bucket of water home. This would last the family till the next day when the early morning water-fetching routine would be repeated....

Was this time of day not too early and somewhat frightful

for youngsters? "Not so", Allison replied, and he continued when interviewed on the subject,

> You see, there were a number of us in the household and we all went together to the stream. Moreover, other boys from other compounds also came to fetch water, so there were many of us and we played as we went along. It was a lot of fun. And in late moon, this was even more enjoyable. This was a chance to see and play with my friends. This was a remarkable time of day for me and I looked forward to it everyday because it gave me a chance to see and play with my friends.

Indeed, this was the age when children did a lot of housework and provided assistance to their parents and guardians who relied on their responsibility and sense of duty. A child could be sent on an important errand and be expected to conduct himself or herself with great decorum and get the job done well. Good conduct was deeply imbued in the character of growing children who were expected to reflect the good name of the family: the family name was everything. Young Allison was exemplary, mild of behaviour and genial of conduct. He took great pride in doing well whatever he was asked to do and his only joy was the satisfaction of his parents.

After spending a year and a half at Ubiaja, Allison returned with his aunt and uncle-in-law to Warri and became a student of Ogitsi Memorial School in Okere, Warri. Good teachers were in short supply in primary schools in Gbelebu and young Allison, being of superior intellectual ability, far above the level of his peers, was given the distinguished responsibility of teaching his classmates Spelling (that is, English Language) and Arithmetic by his teacher, Mr. S.E.I. Cole. He remembers his teacher with singular fondness:

> Mr Cole was a great teacher and very smart. He took about four classes at a time. One of his

> innovations in the village school was to get some of the pupils in each class to teach their mates in those subjects in which they excelled and, in the process, pupils could learn from their fellows. And this was under the supervision of Mr. Cole.

What could be a greater confidence booster than being chosen from your own peer group to be their teacher, their leader? This was the age when you knew where you belonged, you worked hard to improve your lot and made your family proud of your success; and excellence was acknowledged, cherished and rewarded.

Allison left Ogitsi Memorial School on graduation, for Collegiate School, Warri for six months. While at the Collegiate in Warri, young Allison sustained an injury on his left leg, just below the calf close to the ankle, while playing in the streets... The scar is still visibly there for all to see, if only he would just lift up his trousers for you - a not so usual act, though. The wound would not heal and he was taken to Gbelebu for treatment. He was then asked to come to Lagos to complete his education. It was at this time that he sat for the entrance examination to King's College, Lagos, the school without peer in its class, though some 'rascals' from Government College, Umuahia, might quarrel with this appellation. Believe it not, this young boy, brought up in the remote crannies of Gbelebu and Okere, excelled and was admitted into King's. Can you imagine how Allison felt, how proud his father was, how elated his grandmother was, how all of Okere and environs must have basked in the reflected glory of their son's success? Let's capture the mood of the occasion in the words of Allison himself:

> I took the entrance examination to King's in 1946 together with a group of boys in Lagos. One of them was young Achuzia who became the Col. Achuzia of

> the Biafran Army. On the third day at King's College, a student in Class II gave me an imposition of twenty lines of Shakespeare, for bouncing a football I carried for the captain of the football team. It was an illegal imposition as "fagging" had been abolished but I had to write it up for him. The irony is that when I became a school prefect, the young man became one of the boys I had to supervise because he lost a year by repeating Class III while I got double promotion to Class IV. We were in the same House. I never retaliated for the imposition.

It follows as night the day that Allison, even before 1949, was already one of the best pupils in Nigeria's primary schools of his day.

At King's he got double promotion, skipping one of the years by going from Class II to Class IV, further evidence that he was much better than his peers and that he was able to handle difficult stuff, if it could be taught. His guiding principle must have been, "Tell me what you want me to do and I shall do it." Or, put differently, "Give me a place to stand and I will move the world." Put even more positively, "If it can be done, I shall do it." This was a lad whom nature blessed with a large dose of intellect, with brain power. How did his new classmates receive him? He would say, with characteristic simplicity:

> Oh, they were quite receptive and understanding and I got along well with them. I easily merged with the new class and they accepted me as one of them. The only trouble, if you could call it that, was with my former classmates who were somehow envious, you would say.

Allison was in Hyde Johnson House, the hall noted for punctiliousness and no-nonsense bravado. Coming from a superior family background, he was already instilled with humility, discipline and would later fully blossom into the exquisite public officer that he became. He is exceedingly proud of his years at King's. It was the age of innocence, of simplicity, of lively mirth, of effortless delight. In his own words,

> Those days were the best; they had everything that one required; we can't deny that. In terms of innocence, sweet innocence, King's was on top of the world and we were riding high; in games we were everything; in academic work everything was smooth; there was no problem.

Listening to Allison Ayida talk about his life then, one is immediately transported to another world reminiscent of Wordsworth's "the hour of splendour in the grass, of glory in the flower, the glory and freshness of a dream."

In secondary school, Allison studied all the subjects in both science and arts - English, English Literature, Mathematics, Additional Mathematics, History, Geography, Latin, Chemistry, and Biology, but not Physics. Asked why he did not sit for Physics in the Cambridge School Certificate examinations, he replied:

> I wanted to study engineering but I didn't have Physics. I didn't like the Physics teacher, so I didn't do Physics. Up to the School Certificate level, you had to study all the subjects, including the ones you were not offering for the exam. So I had to do Physics up to that level and when they did the test before the School Certificate exam, I came third and one boy in our class started talking. The Physics teacher then taunted the class, 'Mr. Ayida came third without offering Physics, so what are you all doing?' One naughty boy stood up and said, "Sir, it shows the teacher is not teaching us very well, if somebody who does not attend classes could come third". That was a really naughty boy!

The teacher was probably not all that good, but surely, that Allison came third showed that he was gifted and put his talents to great use, even at such early age. For the Higher School Certificate examination, which he sat for in 1952, Allison offered Latin, History and British Constitution. Of course, he also did General Knowledge, which was really English and compulsory. He passed all the subjects with distinction. He had earlier sat for the GCE Advance Level in English, History and British Constitution and passed with Distinction in June 1951. As a pioneer student he had to sit for the HSC for the benefit of King's College. For Allison, his King's College years (1947-1952) were formative, memorable and glorious.

As would be expected of King's men of their time, some of Nigeria's notable personalities were Allison's contemporaries, including His Royal Highness, Oba (Dr.) K.A.O. Sansi, the Okulu of Esure, who gave up his practice as a veterinary surgeon to wear the noble, ancestral crown of his forbears; engineers and architects, such as T.A. Makanjuola, F. Santos and T. Anyalaja. Amongst the medical doctors were Dr. Ben A. Oni-Okapku of the hospital in Benin eponymously bearing his name, Prof. J.T.K. Duncan, Dr. W.O. Gbajumo, Dr. J. Ade Idowu, Dr. L.B. Oshin, and Dr. (Chief) O. Ade-Onojobi. The legal luminaries of his set include Gally Brown Peterside (SAN), Chief O. Oyewole, Ireto Sagay and N. Nwanodi. Of particular interest are his contemporaries who, just like him, had a career in the public service and rose to the prestigious level of federal Permanent Secretary: Otunba C.A. Tugbobo and Izoma Phillip Asiodu who remains, till today, a very close and warm friend of Allison's, their somewhat different personal characteristics and ways of life notwithstanding.

After the rich experience at King's what does one do? If one was brilliant and gifted, one might seek to ascend greater intellectual heights, discover the vastness of life, forge one's mettle in the furnace of challenges and love. This is the stage when one's spirit comes to the fore, when one confronts the big questions of life, such as: Why am I here in this world? What purpose does my life serve? Do I live only in the realities of the human body? What am I made for? What is my ultimate end? Saint Josemaria aptly captures the spirit thus:

> You are more than a treasure,
> you are worth more than the sun itself:
> you are worth all Christ's Blood!
> How can I fail to take up your soul
> - pure gold –
> and place it in the forge,
> and fashion it with fire and hammer,
> until that gold nugget is turned
> into a splendid jewel
> to be offered to my God,
> to your God?
>
> (Josemaria, 1988)

3

Uncommon grooming for High Service

Oxford and preparation for Public Service

It was at Oxford that Allison, now fully mature, but not yet tested, came to his own. He puts it simply thus: "In those days, when you come out of school you are already a man. You are ready to move ahead." Yes, he was ready to take on the world with a strong presence of God's guidance in his soul. He was 'gold', but not yet 'splendid jewel'. He was ready to move ahead. And now, at Oxford in 1953, he would really 'move ahead.' From the standpoint of innocence, of elegance, of splendid delight, the King's years were unsurpassed. Oxford was, however, the fantastic years of life that would set Allison apart from his peers and distinguish him as one of the best public servants Nigeria ever had, certainly amongst the top five of Nigeria's finest civil servants, ever. How did he get to Oxford?

Having demonstrated superior scholastic abilities in his Higher School Certificate examination, Allison earned a Western Nigeria scholarship for studies overseas. Actually, he had wanted to read Economics in Nigeria, but the University College, Ibadan, did not have an Economics department in the early 1950s and so Allison was admitted to read History instead. He was good at History, yes, and well liked recalling events of the past, telling tales, and relating to cultural events of his experience and as told him by his father and grandmother. He did not, however, read History at UCI; the Government, instead, sent him to the University of Oxford to read the trio of Political Science, Philosophy and Economics (PPE).

What set him on the path of PPE?

To find an answer, at least in part, we go back to King's. There was this teacher, an Oxford graduate, Mr. R.M. Elphick, who made a tremendous impact on him. On one occasion that turned out to be decisive for Allison, Mr. Elphick decided to teach his class PPE instead of History, normally scheduled for the period. As Allison tells it, *"Mr Elphick was an Oxford graduate himself and had read PPE, sometimes known as Modern Greats. He told us all about it and we became convinced that the field was more relevant to our needs."* Young Allison was so fascinated and the occasion made such an indelible impression on his youthful mind that he decided there and then that he would read PPE, if he ever had the chance. The chance surely came, and soon.

Allison was at Oxford for three years, 1953-1956, resident at Queen's College. Phillip Asiodu was to accompany him to Oxford where they both read the same subjects. His other contemporaries at this time included the late Professor Oje Aboyade, long time professor of economics at the University of Ibadan, one of Nigeria's most distinguished development economists and an indefatigable associate of Allison over the years in the Ministries of Planning, Economic Development, and Finance and Professor H.M.A. Onitiri who made his name as Director of the Nigerian Institute of Social and Economic Research (NISER). He went on to do his master's degree in Money and Banking at the London School of Economics (1956-1957), but had to return home before he could complete the programme when his father died. He never returned to LSE.

At this time, in the early 1950s, only some 210 students had graduated from Nigeria's only university, UCI, about the time Allison was graduating from Oxford. Today, at the University of Ibadan, a majority of courses would routinely register over 200 students. Yet, it took all of eight years to graduate 210 students from the entire university! And the list of graduates was a who's who of Nigeria's academic personalities of later years. It would be invidious to select just a few names for mention for one is sure to miss out many who are, perhaps more distinguished than those chosen. Our examples, no matter how carefully chosen, would reflect some bias for which no apologies need be offered. Among the best known of UCI graduates of this era are some of Nigeria's first and most distinguished novelists and dramatists, ambassadors, teachers, public servants, professors and outstanding scholars, including Professors Chinua Achebe and Wole Soyinka (literature), Jacob Festus Ade Ajayi (history, 1951), Akinlawon Ladipo Mabogunje (geography,1953), James Okoye Chukuka Ezeilo (mathematics,1953), Cyril Agodi Onwumechili (physics,1953), Akpanolu Ikpong Ikpong Ette (physics,1954), Caleb Olawole Olaniyan (zoology,1954), Emmanuel Urvumagbunmwum Emovon (chemistry,1955), and Olumuyiwa Awe (physics,1955). The unforgettable wizard of words, polyglot and astute politician, Chief Ajibola Ige, of blessed memory, graduated in 1955 and Nigeria's celebrated, genial poet, brave of mind and purpose, Christopher Ifekandu Okigbo in 1956. Leslie Otseweyinmi Harriman, an Itsekiri like Allison, and also an ex GCI man, a zoologist, who later became one of the first Nigerian ambassadors, an exquisite and refined gentleman in the manner of Allison, graduated in 1955. Who says Nigeria is not blessed?

Entry into the Civil Service

Allison Ayida returned to Nigeria in 1957 with a Bachelor of Arts (Hons.) degree from Oxford University, graduating in political science, philosophy and economics. He was appointed Assistant Secretary in the Federal Ministry of Education on 27 October that year, barely two days after returning from the United Kingdom. Having been trained at Oxford and LSE as a Western Nigeria Government scholar, it was incumbent on him to serve either that Government or the Federal Government, which by this time was bracing for independence and required the best Nigerian brains for the Herculean task of nation-building ahead. His personal choice was an academic life at the University College, Ibadan, as lecturer in the Extra-mural Department, then headed by Ayo Ogunsheye. But the path of his life was already cut out for him and he followed his star into the Federal Civil Service, there to serve his country at an epochal period of national history.

He remembers, with sweet fondness the interview for the job thus:

> The interview was a formality. The Chairman [of the interviewing panel] was an Oxford man. The only question he asked me was about the controversy over the new urban clearway in Oxford as to whether it should pass through Christ Church meadows or the High Street. As a Queensman (that is, from Queen's College), I preferred the former but as lover of beauty, the meadows had to be preserved from iconoclasts! The Chairman was obviously impressed...The Northern member of the Commission asked why I was not returning to the old Western

Region, my home state! I was irritated by the question, but I answered as politely as I could that I specialised in Money and Banking which was an exclusive Federal responsibility. He surprised me by asking why one of the Dantatas should be sent to jail for printing his own currency as part of his fundamental human right? I asked if he wanted a technical answer or the layman's. He answered both. I explained that if anybody was allowed to print his currency notes, I would not be there for the interview for a job and he would not be a member of the Public Service Commission. Each person's notes would be worthless as none would gain general acceptability. As I delved into the theory of aggregate supply and demand and the Quantity Theory of Money, he interrupted me that I was talking over his head and he was more than satisfied with the layman's answer I had already given. He was particularly happy that I knew so much about the Dantata case although it happened six months earlier while I was in England. Incidentally, the Northern member of the Commission was Alhaji Yahaya Gusau who, ten years later, became the Federal Commissioner for Economic Development with me Allison Ayida as his Permanent Secretary.

Allison was there at the transition from colonial rule to independence. He was there at independence at the inception of Nigeria's national identity. He was there during the first years of parliamentary government when Nigeria was first run by Nigerians for Nigerians. He was there when the 'khaki boys' struck in January 1966, displacing the politicians of the First Republic. He was there in July 1966 when the military struck again, this time among themselves, and almost precipitated the break-up of the nation. He was there when the military struck yet again in an effort to regain some measure of public confidence and end the rudderless, misdirected ebb and flow of military power. The military struck once more in 1976 by dealing a deadly blow to the Military Head of State, and Ayida was there to suffer it all before finally bowing out in 1977. What a career! What an experience! What a life!

What manner of a country did Allison return to in 1957? The amiable Sir John Macpherson had left office in 1954 and was replaced by Sir John Robertson, who was to oversee the 1957 and 1958 Constitutions for an independent Nigeria and was Governor-General at Nigeria's independence in 1960. In 1957, Gold Coast became the first country of British colonial Africa to gain independence and it was felt that Nigeria, too, would have gained independence at the same time, but for the North which appeared unprepared for self-government. The East and the West, under their respective Premiers, Nnamdi Azikiwe and Obafemi Awolowo, were already self-governing by 1956. When the Sardauna of Sokoto and Premier of Northern Nigeria announced that the North would, in fact, become self-governing in 1959, all was clear for Nigeria to speak with one voice on national independence.

By 1957, the British colonial backbone had been broken by persistent nationalist agitation and Nigerian independence was now simply a matter of time. The most complex issue dogging delegates to the 1957 Constitutional Conference was the ever-intractable minorities problem. In the North, the East, and the West, minority ethnic groups not included in the Hausa, Igbo, and Yoruba majorities sought the creation of new states where they would gain control of their lives and be freed from the domination of the major tribes. The Conference referred this matter to a special commission, headed by Sir Henry Willinks. Although it admitted that minority fears of tribal domination and discrimination were real and needed to be resolved, the Willinks Commission declined to recommend the creation of new states in addition to the three existing Regions.

The thinking of the Commission was made clear by one of its members, Mr. Philip Mason in a series of articles in the highly influential, weekly journal, *West Africa*. He argued that for Nigeria to develop and survive as a united nation it was important that none of the three major parties, the NPC, the NCNC, and the AG would be so powerful as to dominate the others. This, of course, could be translated to mean that none of the three major tribal groups would be in a position to lord it over the others on national issues, since each region and political party had a strong tribal support at this time. It would follow that a party seeking such national domination within the existing political structure had to seek support from outside its regional stronghold which, in essence, meant that it had to appeal to a minority group in another Region. Thus, it was argued, the minorities would have a crucial role to play in nation-building. This issue would always be immanent in Nigerian political life.

In preparation for independence and to assure as wide a support as possible for the Federal Government, a national government was formed with four ministers from the NPC: Alhaji Abubakar Tafawa Balewa, as Prime Minister and Minister of Finance, Mallam Bukar Dipcharima, Minister of State, Alhaji Muhamadu Ribadu, Minister of Lagos Affairs, Mines and Power and Alhaji Inua Wada, Minister of Works and Surveys. The NCNC contributed Chief Kola Balogun, Minister of Research and Information, Mr. J.M. Johnson, Minister of Internal Affairs, Dr. K.O. Mbadiwe, Minister of Commerce and Industry, Mr. R.A. Njoku, Minister of Transport, Mr. Aja Nwachukwu, Minister of Education, and Chief Festus Okotie-Eboh, Minister of Labour and Welfare.

In the 1959 federal elections, the NPC and its allies won 143 seats, the NCNC 89, and the Action Group 73, with 7 seats going to Independents. Thus, no one party had enough seats to form a majority government. After a week of intense negotiations, the NPC and the NCNC agreed to form a coalition government. This time the spoils belonged to the winners: the

Federal Government at Independence in 1960 was composed of ministers from only members of the coalition, the NPC and the NCNC. This time around the Minister of Finance was Chief Festus Okotie-Eboh, with the sobriquet, *Omimi Ejo*. A new ministry, the Ministry of Pensions, had Mallam Shehu Shagari as its Minister, the man who was to become Nigeria's first Executive President in 1979. Notable also was Mallam Waziri Ibrahim, Minister of Health, with whom Allison later worked in the Ministry of Economic Development.

What manner of civil service awaited Allison on his return to Lagos, the city of King's College? Allison himself tells us in his own words as follows:

> Historically, before the attainment of national independence in 1960, the Nigerian civil servant at the policy level was neither a Nigerian nor a civil servant, even if he was sometimes civil. The expatriate district commissioner or the administrator at headquarters was like Shelley's Ozymandias, master of all he surveyed:
>
> "..king of kings
> Look on my works, ye mighty, and despair."

After independence, however, the Nigerian civil servant became the servant of all and sundry. The departing expatriate senior servants contributed in a great way towards debasing the image of the top senior servant as the adviser and confidant in the decision-making process. They pampered the new Nigerian political master, *but he gradually came to look on the disciplined civil servant as the major obstacle in his exercise of absolute power*.

> Many of the top Nigerian civil servants themselves were not equipped for their new role of advising the politician on the running of modern government, particularly in the context of national economic

> development. Many top Nigerian administrators, brought up in the tradition of the colonial civil service, were more interested in routine administration. Many of them did not have the vision required for the imaginative task of nation-building in many areas of governmental economic activities.
>
> There was, therefore, an administrative vacuum at various levels for purposes of plan administration. One is not thinking of lack of academic qualifications as such when referring to the inadequately equipped. *Not all civil servants had the courage and moral fibre to present their advice objectively at all times* (emphasis added)

These are particularly striking statements by one who was later disparagingly referred to as one of the "super perm-secs" by those who showed little or no appreciation of the immeasurable power of the human mind and intellect and their evocation and manifestation in commanding acts of the highest degree of rectitude and fortitude, even in the civil service. We shall have good reason to return to this subject later in the book.

In 1958, Allison was moved to the Ministry of Finance where he spent five years, rising to the position of Senior Assistant Secretary. This was the time of the preparation of the *First National Development Plan, 1962-68*, in which he himself did not play a leading role. Still, like the unique person he is, he made his mark: his ideas were sought and his input, particularly into budgets, was original and ingenious.

There was this occasion when the Minister of Finance, Chief Okotie-Eboh, called him at about 7 p.m. one evening, just a few days before a budget presentation to Parliament, and said to him, "This is the budget, you read it and let me know what you think." There and then, Allison studied it and agreed with its main thrust and content. He explained to the Minister (if he did not already know this) that the budget was the most important statement of Government's planned activities and should, therefore, enjoy the full support of the Prime Minister. He identified five striking omissions. The Minister asked him to write them down and send them to the Permanent Secretary for inclusion in the budget. In those days, the budget completely guided Government's programmes and everybody followed its implementation faithfully.

Ayida was, in those days, far and away ahead of his peers; he was clearly in a class by himself. Generally, senior civil servants are supposed to be administrators, not experts on the affairs of the ministry over which they preside. They are, however, required to avail themselves of the expert knowledge provided by the technical and professional cadre, within and outside their respective ministries and parastatals, in order to make appropriate recommendations as a basis for government policy. But Ayida is special as an administrator, a professional and an expert on Economics and Finance, all rolled up in one, and the civil service was the richer for having him. During the period 1958-1959, Ayida spent fruitful time at the Chase Manhattan Bank and at the Federal Reserve Bank, both in New York. On his return to Nigeria, he wrote his Permanent Secretary as follows (with editorial remarks in parenthesis):

> I am reluctantly bothering you with this 'shorthand' Report on my stay with the Chase Manhattan Bank and the Federal Reserve Bank of New York because:
>
> (i) it might be of general interest;
>
> (ii) Mr. Lee might be interested in the section on the Federal Reserve Bank of New York esp. the appendices;
>
> (iii) it might serve as a record to indicate what to expect when considering whether to accept future offers from

American banks or the Reserve Bank to arrange training programmes for officers from this Ministry or the Central Bank (the Bank of America has standing offers!); and

(iv) consequent upon (iii) I have enclosed an extra copy, in case Mr. Fenton might want some of his experts to have a glance at parts of the report. (Though I surmise the appendices may be of some interest as well).

Ayida must have felt that his visit was a successful one and that Nigeria stood to gain immensely from his first-hand experience in these two banks in New York. He displayed great confidence in his abilities, as illustrated in *(iii)* and *(iv)* above, especially in regard to the possibility of his report providing useful guidance on what could be expected from the training programmes offered by American banks to their Nigerian counterparts. His status as a financial expert was well served by his remark that Sir Fenton's experts at the Central Bank might do well to read aspects of the report. His Permanent Secretary, in his hand-written response, dated May 9, 1960, described Ayida's Report as a "first class report which shows most clearly that you have derived very great benefit from your stay in New York." This was a time when civil servants derived great satisfaction from doing their duty here in Nigeria and overseas - particularly overseas - where they served, of course, as Nigeria's respected ambassadors. Ayida made Nigeria proud then and still makes Nigeria proud today.

Ayida also recalls, with contented glee, an incident when he was selected to take a special seat during a flight to London as a junior finance official in the Federal Government delegation, led by Sir Abubakar Tafawa Balewa, to Nigeria's first Commonwealth Prime Minister's Conference as an independent state. He recalls the occasion in his own words as follows:

> The late Sir Abubakar used to travel by scheduled [commercial] flights and the only courtesy the Nigeria Airways extended to him was to leave the seat next to him vacant. Even then, he regarded that as wasteful! That was certainly low profile administration, as we knew it before the advent of petro-Naira. (Nigerian leaders of today now have a Boeing 707 or an executive jet to themselves with an entourage of some thirty functionaries!) While the men in the corridors of power waited anxiously to see whom the Prime Minister would select for the vacant seat by his side, we, the baggage boys, checked on the luggage tags, immigration and customs formalities, and so on. The men of timber lined up like school children for the roll call – Chief Festus Okotie-Eboh, Minister of Finance, Alhaji Inua Wada, Minister of Works, late Zanna Dipcharima, Minister of Commerce and Industry, Dr. Jaja Wachukwu, Minister of Foreign Affairs and Commonwealth Relations, not to mention the seven Permanent Secretaries, led by Mr. S.O. Wey, as Secretary to the Prime Minister. They were all in the race for the coveted seat. I could not believe my ears when the late Prime Minister announced to the Ministers-in-waiting that he would like Mr. Ayida to occupy the seat next to him. There was consternation! I was stunned. But I took my seat quietly and the great Nigerian leader chatted quietly with me, an Assistant Secretary, as we dined. Then he fell asleep. I kept vigil, not even a wink lest I touched the Prime Minister! When we arrived in London the next morning, I heaved a sigh of relief that the 'heavy burden' was gone.

Ayida's star was clearly in the ascendancy. In 1963, on the recommendation of the Prime Minister, Sir Abubakar Tafawa Balewa, the President, the Right Honourable Nnamdi Azikiwe appointed him Permanent Secretary in the newly created Ministry of Economic Planning. In a 1974 speech at the 4th Annual Re-Union Dinner of the Institute of Administration, University of Ife, Jerome Udoji characterized Ayida's leadership of the new Ministry in the following words:

> The one lesson to learn from these stories is the importance of *establishing one's acceptability*. It is not something that we can lay claim to, no matter how erudite and eminent we may be. It is something *that has to be earned and demonstrated*...Take the example of the Ministry of Economic Planning. When this ministry was about to be created, there was a strong resistance from officials of the Ministry of Finance who argued that there was no need for such a ministry because planning was inherent in all it did. The ministry was eventually created and it has *justified its existence such that today it has become one of the most important ministries of government*. In some countries it has swallowed the Ministry of Finance (Udoji, 1999) (emphasis added).

It would, thus, follow that Ayida made a huge impact at Planning and gave it a robust standing and acceptability. How did this come about? Let us hear Allison himself:

> The first thing I was told by the then Secretary to the Prime Minister was that Government was embarking on the experiment which involved giving young officers relatively higher positions and responsibilities to ascertain their ability to cope and learn on the job. Regarding the Ministry itself, the Government had launched a Development Plan and its coordination and implementation became its major challenges. In addition, there were areas such as technical assistance projects and agricultural research institutes which we had to coordinate and harness. *I*

> *felt I was on trial, and the most important thing was to justify the confidence reposed in me so that other young men would be given a chance* (emphasis added).

Ayida succeeded on account of a combination of several exquisite qualities: he is brilliant and erudite, humble and prudent, with an unparalleled sense of service. He uses all necessary means to accomplish whatever he sets out to do. He sees his way clearly through difficulties and readily unties any Gordian knot with adroit hands of excellence and purpose. His interaction with Professor Ojetunji Aboyade, whom he had met in the UK at that seminal conference at Hull, will probably be reckoned as one of the truly masterful collaborations in Nigerian history. Aboyade played a distinctive part in Allison's life, as Tunnji Olaopa tells us in his expansive writing on Aboyade as follows:

> The recommendation which set Ayida on a permanent professional path in the policy environment came in 1963. Allison Ayida was, until 1963, a young officer (Senior Assistant Secretary) in the Federal Ministry of Finance. He was posted that year to head the Ministry of Economic Development as a Permanent Secretary. With this posting, he jumped the post of Deputy Permanent Secretary. This was a professional challenge to him. He did not consider the task a simple one and was *determined not to approach it alone.* He went to the University of Ibadan to explain to the late Professor Kenneth Dike, then Principal of the University College, his new responsibility. *He felt that there should be an interaction of ideas and practice between economic planners in the university and in government. His objective was to make a Nigerian effort, using largely Nigerian professional manpower. As he wanted the best, he had in mind involving in this programme either Aboyade or Onitiri,*

both of them teachers in the College ((Olaopa, 1997) (emphasis added).

We can readily see, in this example, an extremely valuable and endearing quality in Allison, a quality that marks great leaders: out of great confidence in themselves, they seek the best for the job in hand; use the best brains available; attack issues from the best vantage point; and succeed with what they have, knowing only too well that one must row with the oars one has in one's hand. Allison was not, however, in a good position to evaluate the two economic giants, Aboyade and Onitiri, whose services he needed and was, therefore, guided by Professor Dike's recommendation. Ayida recalls Professor Dike's very incisive assessment of the two, "I would prefer you work with Aboyade because he is stronger on policy... He is the man you should work with. He is particularly gifted. The nation has a lot to tap from his solid policy and management genius." Ayida and Dike, there and then, worked out an arrangement that would enable Aboyade to continue with his academic work at University College and, at the same time, serve as a consultant to the Ministry of Economic Development.

This arrangement was in place until 1968 when Aboyade became Head of the Central Planning Office during the war and rehabilitation years - all owed to Ayida's faith in, and great regard for, Aboyade's scholarship, discipline, accountability, honesty and, above all, genius. Thus was to begin one of the earliest, most imaginative and fruitful collaborations between academia and government in Nigerian history. It was synergy at its best. This marked out Ayida as a truly enthusiastic intellectual ready to test his ideas in the crucible of the new, emergent political economy enunciated by Aboyade. This was Ayida's first step in planning: compose the team and bring in the best minds right from the beginning so that they not only clearly identify with national objectives but, given a free hand, can actually determine what these objectives should be and how best to achieve them. In this regard, his ingenuity was extraordinary. More than this, he had superb confidence in his abilities, seasoned with striking humility. Allison was to spend eight years at Planning, 1963–71, a period covered by the momentous civil war and its immediate aftermath.

An analysis of some aspects of development financing should help to set the stage for a deeper appreciation of Ayida's unusual gifts and abilities. Many countries, such as Nigeria, need a large measure of foreign capital for projects, equipment and services considered of great importance to development and which cannot be readily financed from local resources. This often leads them to embark on some form of borrowing and project-financing with foreign capital. The structure and composition of the foreign indebtedness of a developing economy is, consequently, one of the most significant phenomena of its development profile. Accordingly, foreign capital may be profitably channelled towards investment in growth-sensitive areas on the assumption that such investment could not be made using domestic resources at the particular time without compromising investment in basic infrastructure. Of course, the money would have to be paid back and the pattern and distribution of the maturity of such external debt often determine the extent of the financial burden of servicing the debt over time. As important as the absolute level of the indebtedness may be, for a developing economy, it is really this schedule of debt-servicing and debt re-payment that affects the health of an economy, both short and long term, especially if the arrangement was poorly and corruptly negotiated.

Ayida consistently and irresistibly argues the case for Nigeria, always putting the interests of Nigeria first, second and last, relentlessly and steadfastly. His 1964 lecture to the Nigerian Economic Society entitled, "Contractor Finance and Supplier Credit in Economic Growth", bears clear testimony to this. He affirms that,

> Contractor finance, supplier credit and other deferred payments arrangements are usually 'short-term' credit although a few of them spill over into the 'medium-term' range when there are special considerations. The cost of these forms of foreign indebtedness to the recipient economy is, *ipso facto*, very high.

Ayida takes his audience through a cost/benefit analysis of foreign indebtedness, as a percentage of annual budget and gross domestic product, based on data from three countries, Nigeria, Ghana and Liberia, and seriously questions whether debtor developing countries should rely on short-term credit as a source of capital formation for their long-term development initiatives. He goes further to treat his audience to a detailed analysis of the pattern of international flows of capital and the nature, *modus operandi* and the economic consequences of forms of short-term credit, namely, contractor finance, supplier credit, and guaranteed investment. Having studiously demonstrated awareness of what could go wrong with negotiating debt-servicing and debt re-payments, he drops the bombshell in the following words:

> Would the Nigerian Government not be justified in not honouring such guarantees unless the foreign partner meets part of the debt from his group's resources outside Nigeria where it is subsequently shown that the contractor-cum-consultant-cum-technical partner-cum-machine peddler-cum-lender acted in bad faith in preparing the project? This question is the more pertinent where there is subsequent evidence to prove 'collusion' with vested Nigerian interests whose actions cannot be said to be *bona fide* at the relevant time. Should Nigeria's international credit-worthiness be called to question if she subsequently repudiates such guarantees unilaterally? These are real and not academic questions (emphasis added).

Whenever and wherever the subject is Nigeria, Ayida confidently bares his mind, without making apologies to anyone. The remarks cited above, as he himself admits, "raised a storm in official and diplomatic circles, with interesting repercussions." Since West Germany was the source of the sort of contractor finance addressed in the lecture, their Ambassador to Nigeria took great exceptions to the statement and sought official guarantees from the Federal Government to protect the interests of his country. The (then) Federal Minister of Finance, the late Chief Festus Okotie-Eboh, had to make a statement in Parliament assuring the international community that Ayida's address merely reflected the academic views of its author and no more. This would not be the last time that one of Ayida's publicly aired views on important national issues would fray official and journalistic nerves; his 1973 presidential address to the same Nigerian Economic Society would have a similar impact, as narrated elsewhere in this book.

The Second National Development Plan

The *Second National Development Plan (1970-1974)* was an Ayida masterpiece, and he received genuine encomiums for it. Dotun Okubanjo, President of the Association of Advertising Practitioners in Nigeria, in his congratulatory letter of 7th April, 1972 wrote thus,

> This is one of the boldest Budget [sic] ever announced by any Government of this country. It is dynamic, natural and down to earth in its objective. It is now left to the Nigerians to seize the opportunities that are now created. When the history of the economic emancipation of this country comes to be written your part will be written in letters of gold.

The indomitable, gregarious and usually loquacious Dr. K. O. Mbadiwe was at a loss for words in expressing his exuberance for the Budget. He wrote Ayida to say, "The Budget which has just been published is excellent in many ways. To achieve this means very hard work on your part. I want to congratulate you and your whole team." Perhaps the highest praise came from Dr. Pius Okigbo, an extremely intelligent and versatile man, who exulted as follows in a letter to Ayida, dated 5th April, 1972:

> I do not usually write this type of letter; but I it would be dishonest of me not to tell you that studying the present year's budget has filled me with excitement and joy. I have accordingly so informed your Commissioner. The budget is sound, realistic and forward looking; it is so eminently sensible in perspective and so patently right in approach. All of you who have worked on it, and particularly your Commissioner and yourself, deserve the highest praise for it. Furthermore, for all the mud it is now so fashionable to cast at the public servants, it is redeeming to see a job so well done.

The *Second National Development Plan* contained nuggets of both short- and long-term declarations of economic intent, such as the following:

> An unregulated activity of the mining sector could lead to a situation where, because of current limited absorptive capacity, the country misses the opportunity to optimize the returns from a process of rapidly extracted mineral resources, while in the future with better absorptive capacity, the returns are then no longer there because the resources have been exhausted. The Government would strive for an optimal trade-off between the desire for an immediate utilization of the commercially valuable mineral

> resources and their rates of extraction...*This is particularly true of crude oil mining. Unless a judiciously formulated policy is adopted and followed, the country will suffer seriously from what is fast becoming an oil illusion*...It is often forgotten that oil is an expendable resource, and that the more it is exploited, the less there is for use in future (emphasis added).

Unfortunately, what had been feared was exactly what had happened: the country missed the opportunity to optimize the returns from oil because, in large part, it lacked the absorptive capacity.

Despite its excellence, *The Second National Development Plan* suffered perniciously in its implementation due, in large part, to a weak institutional framework and a poor executive absorptive capacity. The unanticipated 'oil boom' yielded relatively huge revenues that only produced a profligate and insidious pattern of expenditure, thereby creating an illusion of wealth. This had a disastrous effect on other sectors of the economy which suffered, in particular, because the cost of exports became expensively non-competitive since the economy was apparently buoyed by the large influx of foreign exchange earned from oil export. This precipitated the dreaded 'Dutch disease phenomenon.'

The 1970s might, arguably, be considered 'Ayida's decade.' As he himself sees it, his generation was born in the economic depression years of 1929-33, hard at work during the Nigerian civil war economic measures years of 1966-70, and even harder at work during the post-war rehabilitation and reconstructing years, as well as during the relatively minor economic and financial crises of 1972 and 1978. Ayida might even be considered as belonging to the period which has been dubbed 'the *Wasted Generation*'. In *Illusions and Social Behaviour*, one of the great inaugural lectures to come out of the University of Ibadan in 1978, Professor Oyedunni Teriba attempted to provide an insight into the nation's poor economic performance, especially in the 1970s. As he saw it, illusion would be one of the key factors. He illustrated his point with the concept of the 'money illusion' by which an individual feels better off when she has more money in her pocket, causing her to spend more in order to confirm the feeling of being 'better off', regardless of the price of commodities. Teriba drew attention to the interplay of many illusions which had featured in the Nigerian economy - the *buoyancy* illusion, the *planning* illusion (with apologies to Ayida and Aboyade), the *naira* illusion, the *manpower* illusion, the *foreign exchange* illusion, and the illusion of *figures* - all of which had plagued the effective performance of the economy since political independence.

The 1970s were also the age of the 'Udoji awards' of huge salary increases to Nigerian public servants, ostensibly arising from the recommendations of the Udoji Commission. But, the Gowon Military Government had gone overboard to please Nigerians in an apparent attempt to shore up its waning level of popular support and, perhaps, 'bribe' or inveigle Nigerians into accepting a deferment of the promised return to civilian rule. Government, thus, upped the Udoji recommendations with such stupendous arrears that workers literally went on a spending spree. Predictably, phenomenal price increases followed and all was back to the ante-Udoji situation in real terms. But the 'money illusion' had already been ingrained in the people's psyche and was not about to die a quick death: it transmogrified as corruption.

4

In the eye of a storm

No event is isolated from other events of the past. The makings of the Nigerian civil war can be found in certain factors, some somewhat remote, others more immediate. Of the latter, the precipitating factors have to be sought in the massacre of ordinary civilians of Eastern Nigeria origin, the vast majority of whom came from amongst the Igbo, on May 29, 1966, followed by the assassination of the Supreme Military Commander, Major-General Aguiyi Ironsi, and his host, Lieutenant-Colonel Adekunle Fajuyi in Ibadan, on July 29 and the killing of Nigerian military officers, of mainly Igbo extraction in Abeokuta and Ikeja on the same day. By far the most atrocious, however, were the pogroms in Northern Nigeria visited upon ordinary Nigerian citizens whose only sin was that they came from Eastern Nigeria, most of them, the Igbo. These massive massacres, however, trace their origin and seek justification in the first coup in Nigerian history, on January 15, 1966, organized and executed by a group of Nigerian Army Officers, most of whom were Igbo. The North lost two of its most illustrious sons, the Prime Minister, Sir Abubakar Tafawa Balewa, and Sir Ahmadu Bello, the Premier of Northern Nigeria and President of the Northern Peoples Congress (NPC), the majority party in the coalition government of the Federation, made up of the NPC and the NCNC, the National Council of Nigerian Citizens. It was felt that the Igbo of the

East had wrested power from the Hausa-Fulani of the North, a situation that could, apparently, not be tolerated.

One could go farther back and seek the factors that led to the first coup and subsequent events. One could even see the amalgamation of the protectorates of Northern and Southern Nigeria under Lord Lugard as an ingredient in the makings of the coup of 1966. The Nigerian nation that stood on the shaky tripod of North, West and East, with the North being larger than the East and the West put together, was almost doomed from the beginning to political instability and inter-regional violence. Moreover, there is no intention here to examine either the details of the immediate cause of the Nigerian civil war or the events of that war. Our focus is to draw attention to certain critical roles played by Ayida in 1966 and early 1967, before the war broke out.

One such incident was a meeting between His Excellency, the Governor of Eastern Nigeria, Lt.-Colonel Odumegwu Ojukwu, with a number of high-level federal civil servants, Messrs. S.O. Williams, E.O. Ogbu, H. Ejueyitche, N. Ade-Martins, A.A. Ayida, P.C. Asiodu, and A.A. Atta at State House, Enugu, on Thursday, October 27, 1966 at 1.30 p.m. His Excellency opened the meeting by welcoming the visitors to Enugu. Though he had had only a short notice of the visit, the Governor was prepared to listen to the delegation's views on "ways and means of lessening the tension which is in the country today."

Mr. H.E. Ejueyitche, the serving Head of Service and Secretary to Government commenced by tendering his apologies for encroaching themselves upon His Excellency and continued as follows:

> We are civil servants and we justifiably claim that we really do not belong to any tribe. Most of us feel as Nigerians and that is why we have thrown ourselves upon you as a surprise packet because all

> these came out of own heads only yesterday morning. We said, 'why can't we go to Enugu, meet the Governor of the East, hear what he is thinking, and see also some of the people and what they are suffering and, perhaps, find out what is in the minds of you here and what we can do to help keep this country together as one Nigeria. We have no real programme because we feel that when we become less formal in our discussions we shall get something better. We have made some notes and I think our Secretary will go into details.

At this point, Ayida who must have been the Secretary mentioned, made his remarks. He said the problems with Nigeria could be divided into three separate fields, military, political and economic, but that they could not discuss the military field. With regard to the political field, the major problem was the withdrawal of the delegation from the East from the on-going Conference of Leaders of Thought. We quote exactly his further contribution as follows:

> Many of us became very agitated when the Eastern Delegation did not turn up in accordance with your statement. So, problem No. 1 is whether, in fact, there is any message we can carry back in that field. We know that the delegates in Lagos from the other Regions did send a letter to Professor Eni Njoku, but we did not wait to get the reply; we thought this is an area where we can provide help. Also, in this field, we do feel strongly that the whole thing is that there must be some dialogue which must produce a political solution acceptable to all Nigerians and that *we remain as one country whatever the difficulties. So on the political level, the immediate object is what can be done for discussions to be resumed.*
>
> On the economic level, we feel there have been a few developments and that for the first time, owing to the sad turn of recent events, we may be entering

> a field where it may be difficult for Nigeria to go back. [One might ask, 'go back to what?' This is construed to mean that it might be difficult for Nigeria to go back to being what it used to be, to go back to being one united indivisible country.] We have just been to the Chairman of the Rehabilitation Commission and he has told us about the wonderful work the Commission has done. Maybe Mr. Atta, Permanent Secretary, Ministry of Finance, will speak later on the question of compensation. so I will not touch on it.
>
> But we feel that there is an area in which Your Excellency can help us and Nigeria – it is this question of *the exodus of civil servants of Eastern origin from Lagos, the Western Nigeria and, to a lesser extent, the Mid-western Nigeria*. We feel this is an area where your Excellency can take steps to arrive at a kind of settlement, a kind of solution satisfactory to everybody. Everyday, we find some of our relatives from Eastern Nigeria going back to their region. We know why they are leaving – they are afraid. We have personal friends, they leave us, some leave to go home and persuade their families that they are still alive and come back. But usually we get telephone calls from them saying they are sorry they can no longer return because their people will not allow them to go back. From our personal knowledge, some of these people love to come back because they know that they are safe in Lagos, but usually their relatives make it impossible for them to come back. *So this is an area where we think something can be done to lessen the tension* (emphasis added).

Ayida made it quite clear that, as civil servants, they could not take any political initiative and that it was up to His Excellency and his military colleagues who were charged with the reigns of government as to how to solve this problem. On the economic front, however, where they thought they were more competent, what was happening in all the towns in Nigeria was beginning to adversely affect the ordinary man in the street. And soon it would get worse in the rural areas. They felt that if the situation was not arrested, "it will become increasingly difficult for the ordinary man in the street (or) in the village to be a law-abiding citizen he has been all along." Without food and shelter it would be impossible for people to control their instincts, he continued. He also observed that it was very difficult for businesses to stay operational and soon the private sector would react to the adverse conditions. But before all these mishaps came to pass, they hoped there would be an answer to the political problems one way or another. Ayida continued,

> We have no vested interests as such in our official capacity and whatever vested interests we have as Nigerians we have learned to keep within ourselves, *but we are fully convinced that the consequences of trying to split would be far greater than anything we can face in staying together* (emphasis added).

Ayida expressed the feeling that though they could not make comments on the military field, they knew that dialogue was going on between the military leaders and he hoped that as the discussions continued His Excellency would be able to give them "some encouraging thing" to take back to Lagos. He continued,

> In all these areas, we know what the problems are, in many cases we think we know the solution, but the *important thing is to lessen tension and somehow those of us who have come are firmly convinced that Enugu can provide the answers* (emphasis added).

His Excellency responded by recalling all the events of the

immediate past, beginning with the chaos which ensued after the election in Western Region to the gruesome massacres of 15 January, 29 May, 29 July, and 29 September 1966, affirming that "Without mincing words, I believe and maintain that the only force which has kept this country together is myself." He pointed out that everyone, including his visitors, had welcomed the military coup of January 15, adding that after the May 29 riots when over 3,000 of his people had been killed, he had pleaded, begged his people for restraint by arguing that one could accept the event as a final sacrifice for the unity of Nigeria, and reminding his people that, over the years, they had made sacrifices for the unity of the country. He concluded by observing that a commission of inquiry had been set up on the May 29 riots, but that before it even had the opportunity of getting on with its task, the affairs of July 29 had compromised its mandate.

One may argue, with some justification, that Ojukwu had pleaded with his people for restraint because the serving Head of State at the time came from amongst his people, the Igbo, who would surely be expected to give him as much support as possible, especially after he had instituted a commission of inquiry to examine the riots and killings of May 29. After July 29, and with the assassination of the same Head of State, Major-General Aguiyi Ironsi, however, it would be expected that the Igbo had just about had enough and would no longer stomach any plea for peace or restraint. But the federal civil servants who came calling were a non-tribal group; their only tribe was a united Nigeria. In this, they were and are eminently believable, as the following episode illustrates.

On another occasion, during the four days when there was no Federal Government of Nigeria, from July 29 to August 2, 1966, the same group of senior federal civil servants who were on their way to Ikeja Army barracks to meet with the military leaders to try to extract a military-ordained leadership for the nation, were accosted by army security guards. When ordered to declare their tribe they responded in one voice, "we are civil servants," and were given free and safe passage to proceed on their way.

His Excellency recalled how he himself had escaped the 'events' of July 29 and what had happened at his end in those four days when there was no Federal Government. His exact words were captured by the astonished civil servants as follows:

> When the July 29 episode started, the only thing that saved the East was the presence of mind of one soldier who, as soon as he escaped from Abeokuta, rather than phone anywhere else, phoned directly to this House and told me what was happening in Abeokuta. He phoned at about 3.30 a.m. I left this place to the barracks, got hold of the Commanding Officer and told him what was happening. We moved into barracks. Gentlemen, by the time we got into the barracks in Enugu, next door to my house, most Northern soldiers were already out in their battle dress and moving. By that act, if I had delayed for 30 minutes, they would have got their arms and ammunitions and I would not have been here talking to you.
>
> For the first 24 hours when this thing was happening, nobody in Lagos thought it necessary to contact me here in Enugu. That makes me start doubting whether in fact the effort at controlling the thing was in fact a genuine one. At a certain stage, a colleague of mine, Lt. Col Ejoor was so incensed that he said, 'you have got some troops here, let us descend upon them.' I said, no, if you do that, this country would be no more. On your way back, you can branch to Benin and ask Ejoor about this. Later, Brigadier Ogundipe got here on the phone and told me briefly what was happening. By the next day, we were not seeing our way through. From here, I advised him to get on the air and at least say that in

the absence of the Supreme Commander, he was controlling things, but he was sceptical of that. I said that as soon as he says that, in 30 minutes I would announce that the totality of Eastern Nigeria is behind him. Anybody can find Ogundipe and he will confirm this. That was my advice to him.

He complained bitterly that he was being pressured by the Northern troops to hand over the state to them and that he was not willing to do so. At this point, an element now comes in to confuse the whole issue. It was at this stage that I spoke to Lt. Colonel Gowon. I understood from him that he was to take over. Once you get back to Lagos you may ask him. I told him that it was not the mere taking over of power that mattered. I asked him if he was capable of holding the responsibility because anything that happens from the minute he announces that [he's the head of state) becomes his responsibility. Gentlemen, that is the reason why I blame every single day on Gowon.

His Excellency then went into the details of military secession and why he would not recognize Gowon; how the officers who returned to their posts in response to Gowon's appeal were gunned down; and how civilians, notably one Achilefu of Nigeria Airways, was mowed down. As he saw it, the only solution was the separation of the forces. His Excellency went into some gory details of the massacre in Oturukpo of Easterners stranded there in 18 train coaches because there was no fuel and His Excellency was unable to get fuel to them in time for the train to head eastwards from Oturukpo. He then proceeded thus,

If you do not recognize anything, you should recognize that I have reason not to trust the assurances of Gowon...Our people went to this meeting...The meeting dragged on indefinitely, none

> of our delegates in Lagos could go out throughout the three weeks they were there. Those in hotels had to keep changing rooms. Can you really wonder why people do not want to go to Lagos? ...Let us be honest with ourselves. *As long as Northern troops are in Lagos, our chaps cannot go there.* Indeed that is true for Ibadan or Abeokuta. Just like saying to me, go to Kano!... A lot of them fear that the Northerners might kill them. A few certainly fear that the East might do something and they might be caught in the cross-fire. But fear is not a thing you tackle with reason. Once fear gets in the mind reason does not have a place there. The only effective weapon against fear [are] gestures of confidence... I must be brutally frank, I do not think you have done your duty, you Permanent Secretaries in Lagos. Certainly you should have advised Gowon on a number of issues. *We are amateurs in Government, we trust the Permanent Secretaries a great deal* and your responsibility is to guide us, to advise us. I honestly do not think you have given the best advice. I know everyone of you and I know your potential (emphasis added).

It is instructive to note that this was before the era of the 'super perm-secs' who were seen as the real power behind government. It is also instructive to hear the Governor of the East admit the commanding role of the permanent secretaries and how much the Military Government looked up to them for guidance and advice. Here, the Governor is seen castigating them for not pulling their weight as they should in giving the right advice to the military government of the day!

His Excellency, having presented in graphic detail the justifiable fear of Easterners in returning to Lagos, either to their jobs or to any conference, concluded his remarks by reiterating his position as follows: "We are more than anxious to find a settlement, but the settlement must be an equitable one. We are prepared to go anywhere to keep talking provided you create the necessary atmosphere for talks."

As soon as His Excellency had finished speaking, Mr Ayida came in, once again, by requesting His Excellency to clarify further the conditions of safety that the East would need to return to Lagos and the conference table. His Excellency stated that what mattered most was the effectiveness of any guarantee of safety, adding, "If you move the troops out of Lagos and the West, I am absolutely certain my men will leave this afternoon."

Atta spoke of the financial problems of the Federal Government and how difficult it was to offer financial assistance to the East. According to him, "We have gone through the list of projects to cut down all unnecessary expenses to save money to give immediate assistance to the East and you can take it from me that any amount of money that can be saved by any means will be used to give support to the people of the East." Atta went further to address the knotty political issue in his remarks as follows:

> The question I really want to ask is, I agree that some kind of temporary separation should be established in order to ensure that confidence returns. It is a question of, 'What is the means of restoring the confidence?' This, I think, we would very much want in the form of concrete proposals. The difficulty in the course of advising Government is that we are not quite sure of these things which we have said ourselves. If more ideas could come from you, so much the easier; it will make our work easier. If you can even tell us that the East would continuously use all means within her powers to try and find solutions to these problems which you yourself have expressed very strongly, without taking any unilateral action at this critical time, then I think there is a great deal of hope for this country.

> It will give everybody sufficient time for reflection and consideration in the course of establishing confidence. This is really the basic problem that I can see. *Can we say that we can go back with assurance from you that you strongly believe in the peaceful solution of the Nigerian problem and in the interest of everybody concerned without at any time acting unilaterally?* (emphasis added)

Responding, His Excellency then asked if he could be assured that Lagos and the North would use every power at their command in finding a peaceful solution to the problems of the country, and that at no time would they, either collectively or singly, take unilateral action which would have the effect of visiting on Easterners the types of action perpetrated in the past. With laughter all round, Atta replied that they could assure His Excellency that they would so advise.

One can readily appreciate His Excellency's concern. Here he was talking with people who, at best, could only advise, as they have discussed, on the pressing and burning problems of the day. The evidence suggests that the civil servants actually believed they could change the course of events and steer it towards a resolution of the serious conflict, even in the face of a seemingly total breakdown in communication and trust between the East and the rest of the country. In doing so, they probably overestimated their own capabilities because they were working in circumstances over which they had little control. But this is usually the fate of any peacemaker in attempting to bring together disparate groups that are at loggerheads, with seemingly irreconcilable differences. The action of the permanent secretaries was noble and praiseworthy.

Sir Francis Ibiam, on the Eastern side, then spoke passionately of the plight of Easterners and the unspeakable atrocities they had suffered at the hands of Northerners. He strongly expressed the view that, in fact, the civil servants should have gone to the Northerners first to ensure that they would seek peace and ease the tension, arguing that the East was not in a position to lay down the terms for peace and reconciliation. He enumerated all the unilateral actions of the Federal Military Government, without giving due consideration to the position of the East, actions which demonstrated that they did not care much for the thinking of Easterners and their sufferings. He lamented, "Our people were not killed in the way people are killed." It was apparent from the questions the civil servants were asking, however, that there was a genuine fear among the rest of Nigerians of what might happen if the Northern soldiers left Lagos or Western Nigeria.

It had been vital to persuade His Excellency to allow Easterners to attend a peace conference at which all issues of conflict and discord would be laid on the table for discussion, and much had already been said on it. To help assure His Excellency of the safety of Easterners at the peace conference being proposed, Bishop Kale who, together with Akintola Williams, had come into the meeting after it had started, made a passionate plea for the peace conference to be held somewhere in Nigeria. In his own words,

> I came with a map of Nigeria to show you a place [where] I think you can safely meet because, personally, I do not think it will be nice for us to meet outside Nigeria. I will call my fellow bishops and *we shall police the place and there will be no soldiers.* The place will be a neutral ground and I promise, on behalf of the whole clergy, that we shall robe like this and if you want us to guard you for a week or more, we shall do so, provided you meet and discuss these things. Please, allow it to be said that about 90% of this arrangement rests upon you. If this thing is not done, we shall all feel that in the end you have not lived up to the expectations of all Nigerians (emphasis added).

Surprisingly, the option was not taken up. His Excellency thanked the Bishop and asked that they have a "quiet chat" after the meeting. His Excellency went on to provide yet more evidence of the lack of trust by referring to a certain remark credited to a Northern Nigerian spokesman in the *New Nigerian* daily newspaper of October 25, 1966, to the effect that the proposed conference "was to resolve, either by negotiation or otherwise, the areas of disagreement in the memoranda submitted by delegations to the conference." His Excellency took great exceptions to this and said he had sent a telegram to General Gowon seeking his clarification of the Northern spokesman's statement.

Matters had reached such a pass that it would seem as if everybody was seeking one form of clarification or another; nothing could be taken at face value any longer. No one could be trusted to be acting in good faith. There just .was no atmosphere for credulity and the civil servants had come to help bring about the easing of tensions so that things could then begin to happen and take a normal course, eventually.

Ayida lamented that the publications in the Nigerian press had tended to add more heat, rather than light, to the tensions in the country. He, in the true traditions of an exquisite administrator, then added this incisive inquiry:

> Supposing you eventually did meet, because we are all convinced there is going to be a meeting sooner than we think, is it possible to give some kind of preview about the kind of problems because you hinted that a meeting is useless unless there is a full preparation for it? We can do some of the things [in preparing for such a meeting] and would like to know whether there are more problems we can tackle as civil servants before we report faithfully [to our political superiors] and thereby provide the final bridge for further communication.

But His Excellency was not about to be drawn into any speculative arrangement and simply answered that the East did not have any preconceived plan of action.

Ayida, in an apparent attempt to draw as much truth and specifics out of His Excellency as possible, then asked:

> When you were speaking, you did say that many people were running out of Lagos because of genuine fear. But you added the second reason. It is that many people were also leaving because of the fear that if the East is doing something they might be caught in the cross-fire. For the first one the action lies in Lagos, but for the second one, may I suggest that the initiative will rest here?

His Excellency's reply was that he had accepted such responsibility right from the beginning and had said as much in his 'Crisis '66' speech in which he had repeated that the East was not preparing to do anything inimical to the interests of other Nigerians.

Guaranteeing the safety of Easterners in Lagos and elsewhere in Nigeria was, clearly, a major task that the civil servants could not, on their own, provide. The best they could agree to would be to advise and guide Gowon of the necessity for some guarantees to be in place in order to persuade the Easterners to return. Judging by the mood of the meeting, however, it did not seem likely that the civil servants thought it would be possible or practical. Furthermore, the point which His Excellency had raised about the fear of some Easterners being caught in a possible cross-fire became an albatross that put a dent in his argument for the safety of Easterners and he did not quite know how to rid himself of this nuisance. As the meeting drew to a close, Sir Francis observed that it was not for the East to make the next move; the East had already made all the moves they could and it was up to the "other section" to give Easterners the fairness they deserved, Sir Francis concluded.

Surely, the civil servants had acted in good faith and had thought they could use their "tribal neutrality" to obtain some assurances from Ojukwu, the first of which was for him to persuade Easterners to return to their posts and then to the conference table. But they did not realize the extent to which the pogroms which the Easterners had suffered had so hardened their resolve that they just could not see how they would be expected to cooperate with the Northern-dominated Gowon government, especially after the assassination of Ironsi. Peace would come at a huge price to the Easterners and the East did not seem prepared at that stage to make any more sacrifices. The feeling was very strong that it was "the other side," the Nigerian side, that had to provide the necessary security guarantees and show sufficient remorse before Easterners could consider sitting in one room with other Nigerians at a negotiating table. On this crucial issue, the civil servants could not be as helpful as the East would have liked.

It is important to note that many of the civil servants at the crucial meeting had come from Nigeria's minority ethnic groups. Their vested interest was the survival of Nigeria, for it was in 'One Nigeria' that they could have substantial existence. If Nigeria were to break up into the former four Regions, the ethnic minorities would really have had a hard time living with their 'majority' neighbours. It was, therefore, understandable that the federal civil servants who had met with Odumegu Ojukwu, the Military Governor of the Eastern Region on that historic afternoon of 27 October 1966, were there to use all of their persuasive genius to try and save Nigeria from the impending doom.

This dogged effort of the civil servants did not end with the Enugu meeting. Ayida and Asiodu later wrote to Ojukwu when the war drums were already beginning to be heard. On May 11, 1967, Ayida and Asiodu, both ex-Oxford students like Ojukwu, wrote a long, 24-paragraph letter to Ojukwu from 16 Cameron Road, Ikoyi, Lagos. The significance of the issues raised in the letter, its timing, and the expectations of the writers were all so far-reaching that the entire letter is quoted in full as follows:

> We are presuming on our long-lasting bonds of comradeship and personal friendship to write to you in our private capacity at this most crucial stage of the history of Nigeria. We do so in confidence and because of your undoubted sense of history and occasion and in genuine admiration for the courageous role and skill you have displayed so far in riding the storms which have rocked the country and the Eastern Region in particular, for the last several months.
>
> 2. We are profoundly anxious that the genuine, lasting goals for which you have struggled so successfully should not be lost or compromised through any tragic misconceptions of the real intentions of people on all sides in the country's difficulties.
>
> 3. From reading between the lines of your public pronouncements, we believe the genuine goals for which you have stood can be summarised as follows:
>
> i. Equality of status and voice in ordering the affairs of this country. This entails the removal of the actuality or the threat of Northern domination – without, of course, substituting a new form of domination.
>
> ii. Full commitment by all to the concept of Nigeria as one country with equality, freedom of movement of peoples, equal opportunity in business, etc., as a long-term goal to be patiently realised.
>
> 4. In pursuance of these goals, we discern that you have outlined certain basic principles as regards

immediate and medium-term institutional arrangements necessary in the present circumstances of Nigeria. These appear to include:

i. A looser political framework than the 1963 republican Constitution. This is often described by many without giving any details as 'Confederation' and, lately 'loose-federation'.
ii. The abolition of a Central Authority which is sovereign and independent of the Regions in a number of matters, however few, although this Authority is supposed to be responsible for external affairs, common infrastructural services, currency, customs, etc.
iii. The fuller control of revenue resources by the Regions.
iv. The removal of any "subsidies" from any Region to another.
v. The organization of the army into regional units with a Central Headquarters composed of equal regional representatives essentially for data collection, standardisation of equipment and planning in the event of external emergencies.
vi. Ways and measures for allaying the fears of minorities should be left exclusively to the Regions.

5. We believe that the goals set out in paragraph 3 (i) and (ii) are what really matter. We also believe that provided the genuine desire is to salvage and preserve a Nigerian Union there is already a large measure of consensus on the principles enumerated in paragraph 4. We further consider that just and equitable solutions to these basic problems can be found only in the context of honest negotiation in good faith with all sides quite clear about the issues involved.

6. From what we know of you, we believe that you have no intention of taking the East out of Nigeria. If that is the case, the logic of this situation demands that sooner and not later, representatives of Eastern Nigeria will have to negotiate with spokesmen from other parts of the country. We know that compromise is now a dirty word, but where there is a genuine difference of opinion as we have in Nigeria today, the end product cannot be unilaterally determined by any one party to the dispute in advance. However just a case is, it must be clearly stated and adopted at a properly arranged Conference. In this context, it seems quite clear to us that if there are elements scheming to push the East out of the Federation, there are much stronger progressive forces in all Regions fully committed to preserving the Federation in a new framework. It will be a tragedy not to recognize the emergence of these new forces for equity and stability everywhere in the country.

7. We have pondered for a long time the principles described above. From our unexalted positions we still preserve contacts with all sections of society and with all tribes and we offer the following considered comments on the principle.

(A) Looser Political Framework

8. With regard to the need for a looser political framework, we believe this is acceptable to all provided there remains a Central Authority, however named. What is needed now is a clear definition of the powers and organs of this Central Authority. Above all, there is need for detailed indication of the working of its machinery. As regards its functions, the central responsibilities should be limited to currency, customs, common infrastructural services, external affairs, and consultative arrangements for economic matters essential for sustaining one integrated market and attracting foreign capital on a

substantial scale. All other powers can go to the regions.

(B) The States Question

There is need however for the orderly creation of states as a basis for stability and in order to remove the fear of domination of one section of the country by another. Structural imbalance in the Federation will always threaten its continued existence however loose the form of political association. The structural imbalance in the Nigerian Federation can be redressed only in an emergency situation. It is on record that the Mid-West Region was established in such circumstances.

All that may be required now is a clear admission in principle and the identification of new states boundaries. This admission could be embodied in a solemn declaration by all leaders. The physical installation of a new state apparatus could be achieved later but only with the cooperation of the regional authorities and peoples involved. This could be a compromise position between the Programme accepted by all your colleagues and your own oft-repeated position on the States issue.

But we believe that there is no other way to contain large minorities within any Region. The history of many countries such as the Soviet Union and India reinforces us in this conviction. The dissipation of resources and effort in security and military containment will be too costly for any Region or indeed the whole of Nigeria, let alone the economic dislocation through sabotage, suspicion, apathy, and group frustration.

(C) Need for a Basis for Political Stability

A looser political framework is not sufficient for stability whatever the current degree of readiness and organization and temporary internal cohesion in any Region. Chaos in any other Region will lead to border friction. No Region will be so poor or isolated that it cannot find arms somewhere to cause mischief. You may recall the current example of Somalia, with only 3.5 million people, in its military confrontation with both Kenya and Ethiopia. You will agree therefore that statesmanship and even military requirements dictate the avoidance of long-term rancour or envy amongst geographical neighbours.

We would wish you to consider further the implications of the absence of a Central Authority. Each Region will acquire de facto sovereignty, and foreign "protectors" and in due course the tragedies of the Congo and Vietnam will be re-enacted in different ways in this part of the world at present called Nigeria.

(D) Revenue Allocation

With regard to revenue allocation we honestly believe that a formula can be found for allocating revenue to Regions on the principle of derivation. The crucial question is that in spite of the application of this principle, the Central Authority should be given sufficient independent revenue to discharge its agreed responsibilities. The principle of the minimum responsibility of the Central Authority must therefore be applied as well if we are to retain the semblance of one country. How much money does the Centre keep from each Region? This can only be resolved by detailed negotiations and maybe by the appointment of an independent commission made up of non-Nigerians, unless there are Nigerians acceptable to all sides to the dispute.

On other matters relating to revenue allocation, we have tried very hard but it is almost impossible statistically to attribute most of the items in the general Merchandise category, with respect to customs duties, to Regions of origin. BUT any proven cases of subsidy from the East or any other Region to another can be removed in a new revenue allocation formula to be recommended by an

International Commission which can be established immediately a political base is agreed.

You will agree that this is the most orderly and the most desirable way of achieving revenue allocation. May we plead that there is a need to avoid creating a dangerous precedent of revenue allocation revisions by the unilateral acts of individual Regions. BECAUSE the only logical consequence of this attitude is that each Region would keep all its revenue and erect its own customs barriers against inter-regional and non-Nigerian trade, raise its own taxes and manage its own currency independently. These sovereign and completely disintegrating developments have been rightly ruled out by you yourself. One cannot overstress the fact that no Region will come off better in absolute terms economically than continuing our present "defective" system, even unchanged, though some Regions may suffer more than others. But this is not a positive basis for lasting policy. One should also add that the free flow of raw materials for industry on a countrywide basis is one of the most important benefits of modern Governments and of a Federal Government.

The only answer therefore is the immediate resumption of discussions and negotiations by all, including your representatives. Decree No. 8 which in many ways has de-centralised Nigeria much further than the 1963 Constitution need be no obstacle; it would be on the law books, so to speak, with or without amendments only as long as it takes to conclude the discussions envisaged. We earnestly plead with you to send trustworthy representatives to such discussions. The conclusions of the discussions will only become valid when they have been confirmed and accepted by you and members of the Supreme Military Council. This can be done by correspondence to save time or at a suitable meeting with adequate preparatory work and written memoranda on the issues to be resolved.

(E) Placing the Shocking Killings in Some Perspective
Much has happened since January 1966. Please do not doubt that everyone, including many Northern leaders, are deeply aggrieved and profoundly sorry for the shocking personal tragedies of May and September. In a not very different context you will also grant that (whatever the original motives of January 15) for the masses of Northerners to wake up one morning and find their two principal civilian leaders and senior military officers killed by what appeared to be "others" was in its own way a traumatic experience. But let us consider the over 600,000 people already killed in Indonesia in the current post-Sukarno disturbances amongst one Malay tribe; the millions slaughtered in the 1947 communal riots in former British India; and let us take some faith in the ultimate future of this country.

19. So much indeed has happened since January 1966. Allow us to recall the original ambition entertained by you and other patriots to "liquidate" the excesses of regionalism. We believe that most Nigerians took January 1966, despite the shock, as an opportunity to build anew. Even in the depths of the moment, we must still take this view. We recall without regret that in those days we spoke about you to our foreign friends as the likely "Nasser" of the Nigerian revolution because of our lengthy period of exposure to your abilities and character. Our passionate plea is that you use your outstanding talents to save not only Eastern Nigeria but the Federation as a whole.

(F) International Reactions
The E.C.A. [Economic Commission for Africa] Conference in Lagos last February was a unique occasion for exposure to African and other international opinion. One of us has also just

returned from visits to America and the United Kingdom on ordinary business. We are not in any position to know what your emissaries who travel abroad report to you, but we are sad to register the shift in attitude in international circles from admiration and sympathy over the tragedies of last September to anxiety and apprehension lest the latest phase of Eastern initiative crystallise in a Katanga situation. We know that the game would not be worth it – not because U.D.I. cannot be declared or sustained but because, like Katanga and the American Confederacy, etc., it is against the grain of modern history. Because we also know that the economic consequences in an absolute sense will be worse, and in the short term there would be chaos and bloodshed and Africa's one hope would be destroyed. You therefore have a unique OPPORTUNITY to maintain a permanent and noble name in our history.

(G) Settlement Would Embrace Re-Instatement of Officials

21. We appreciate that your difficulties are enormous; that you have many human problems to cope with. But the destinies of a nation and the duty of a hero in its history are clear and paramount. We recognise that a major obstacle to be removed in the course of a political settlement of the type we envisage is the future of refugees and the public officials displaced from their jobs. The problem of refugees generally can be dealt with by the reallocation of resources and long-term development. As regards Federal officials, those who left Lagos can be fully reinstated promptly as part of a settlement and it will be left to them to return when they feel it is safe enough. People like us will only be too happy to make way for others in furthering a just quota system of official appointments to the highest positions. You can also demand and obtain

for any individuals you care to name, who may feel hunted because of alleged past acts and associations.

(H) An Historical Role

22. You can claim inestimable credit for compelling this re-examination of the true basis for preserving a Nigeria of equals and for demonstrating the true basis of viability of the country. We hope that you can take the decisive step of arresting further deterioration by permitting the immediate resumption of talks on the lines suggested here. The important thing is to get away from shibboleths and sit down to talk about the concrete details of the arrangements desired. Already there is a large area of agreement which tends to be obscured by the use of vague terms. Therefore any immediate institutional arrangements proposed should be compatible with the search for a permanent solution guaranteeing stability and equality.

23. The world will applaud you. Generations of Nigerians will forever be grateful if you can once again take the initiative for a settlement starting with some gestures indicating your faith in the continued existence of Nigeria. We are in our own humble way trying to get your other colleagues to do likewise.

24. We have dared to write thus in full confidence justified only by the companionship of school years, and College days. We trust that you will consider our views and reciprocate our confidence.

Yours sincerely,
(signed)
P.C. Asiodu & A. A. Ayida

Gogo Nzeribe and some others took this letter to Enugu and delivered it in person to Ojukwu, meeting with him from 10 a.m. to 6 p.m. on that eventful date, May 11, 1966. There is little doubt that this is one of the most important letters in Nigerian history for a number of reasons: for the unusual initiative of two unheralded individuals holding "unexalted positions" in demonstrating their unqualified and unalloyed faith in the oneness of Nigeria; for what it dared to accomplish, even at the late hour of the imminent disintegration of the Nigerian body polity; for the latent and persuasive power of friendship; and for the positive use of power and influence in an attempt to preserve the unity of Nigeria.

Ojukwu had responded by taking Nzeribe and his colleagues to hospitals filled with the maimed from the massacres of September 29, 1966 and the earlier ones of May, and July and had insisted that a condition for the East to relent and return to the negotiating table was for the Head of State, Lt. General Gowon, to step down from his position so that someone else could fill it. At the end of the visit, Ojukwu called his guests aside and showed them a room full of Biafran flags. "They will shoot me if I were to go back on the declaration of the State of Biafra."

Thus snapped the last straw of hope extended to Colonel Ojukwu, the Military Governor of Eastern Nigeria, by the most sincere of his friends who had genuinely believed in the innermost recesses of their robust hearts that Nigeria could be saved from falling over the precipice and that he, Ojukwu, was destined for a special role in the process. Alas! Ojukwu lost his moment in history on the Nigerian side although he did make history of sorts on the Biafran side. Could it be that the untold suffering visited on Nigerians by the civil war became inevitable only because Ojukwu would not suffer Gowon as Head of State? Was the war fought on a personality conflict between these two contestants, one of whom, Ojukwu, saw the other, Gowon, as an adversary?

The inexorable path to war

Even before the Ayida/Asiodu initiative reported here, several personal attempts had been made to persuade Ojukwu to return to the negotiating table as a platform for pressing his case for an amicable resolution by a consensus of all the parties in attendance. At the meetings of the Supreme Military Council held in Aburi, Ghana, on January 4 and 5, 1967, it had been agreed, among others, that the measures which tended to over-centralize the governance of Nigeria would be repealed not later than January 21, 1967. This date, however, became an impractical deadline in view of all the necessary legal inputs involved as well as the diverse, incompatible interpretations put on the Aburi agreements by both sides to the conflict. The East viewed this development as vacillation and a change-of-heart on the part of the federalists and insisted on the implementation of the Aburi protocols as agreed, or else.... Consequently, "On Aburi we stand" became Ojukwu's shibboleth, the excuse for leading the East into a disastrous civil war.

On February 25, 1967, the East made its first move: Ojukwu announced in a radio broadcast that if the Federal Government did not implement the Aburi agreements, the East would be forced to 'unilaterally' act on its own and implement them. To give teeth to this threat, Ojukwu gave the Federal Government up till March 31 to implement the agreements. On March 17, the Aburi Decree was promulgated by the Federal Government. This decree, Decree No. 8, which took its moral legitimacy from the Aburi meetings of January 4 and 5, 1967, raised several difficulties and was rejected outright by Ojukwu. However, since it granted the maximum possible autonomy to the Regions and ensured the non-interference of the Federal

Government in regional matters, it was thought that Ojukwu might be persuaded into accepting it, especially as the office of the Supreme Military Commander and Head of the Federal Military Government had been abolished. In its place was the office of the Commander-in-Chief and Head of the Federal Military Government. On March 27, a peace delegation made up of the Head of the Navy, Commodore Wey, the Deputy Inspector-General of Police, Chief Omo-Bare and the Military Governor of the West went to Enugu to meet with Ojukwu to persuade him to accept the provisions of the *Decree*. But the Military Governor of the East would not relent and responded with a number of conditions that would have to be met for him to accede to their request, namely:

- the North should express a public apology to the East;
- the Federal Government should 'repay' the sum of 11.8 million pounds 'owed' to the East; and
- the Aburi Decree, or parts of the decree not acceptable to the East, should be repealed.

One wonders whether Ojukwu was, in fact, acting in good faith since he must have known that, in the circumstances, his three conditions stood no chance of being met. Could it be that they were not, in fact, *conditions* but rather, a calculated subterfuge in an attempt to provide justification for putting into effect the threat that had already been made? If so, the conditions were no more than a *fait accompli* to validate the claim which Ojukwu could now make of "I had no choice but to..." in the face of alleged federal intransigence.

Events were moving at breathtaking speed. On March 30, the penultimate deadline of his ultimatum, Ojukwu issued three edicts: the Revenue Collection Edict; the Legal Education Edict; and the Court of Appeal Edict, all of which were meant to unilaterally put into effect the Aburi agreements as seen in the eyes of the East. As Billy Dudley puts it: "The East thus became, not only *de facto*, but also, *de jure*, an independent state" (Dudley, 1973).

Things were deteriorating fast and it seemed the East would soon declare itself a sovereign nation. Still, the East was not being left to go its own way. Other eminent personalities worked hard for a peaceful resolution of the contentious issues. Led by the Chief Justice of the Federation, Sir Adetokunbo Ademola, a National Conciliation Committee which had as some its members, Chief Obafemi Awolowo and Chief Sam Mariere, Adviser to the Military Governor of the Mid-West, went to Enugu on May 5 with the active encouragement of the Federal Government. Their objective was to determine the conditions under which Ojukwu could be persuaded to abrogate the March edicts and to pave the way for further negotiations. The Military Governor met with the delegation individually and collectively and it was suggested that the East might be willing to re-examine the edicts if the embargo placed on the East by the Federal Government on communications and foreign exchange transactions were lifted. And they were so lifted; but Ojukwu did not live up to his side of the bargain.

These were the prevailing conditions which compelled yet one more final attempt to persuade the East to relent. And so came the historic Ayida/Asiodu letter to Ojukwu written barely three weeks to the proclamation of the 'Republic of Biafra' on May 30, 1967! It would be difficult to argue that the letter came too late to have any effect for it is precisely at such times as the Nigerian crisis that the mettle of greatness is manifest and the course of history dramatically altered. Asiodu and Ayida counted on their firm friendship with Ojukwu to have made the move they made, believing that in the final analysis the ties of true friendship would prevail and the precipitous trend of events halted. They must have trusted that amongst friends even the apparently impossible becomes possible. After all, at Aburi, the

Military Governors and the Head of the Federal Military Government had all addressed one another by their first names - Emeka (Ojukwu), Jack (Gowon), Hassan (Usman), David (Ejoor), Bolaji (Johnson) and Robert (Adebayo) - all in an honest attempt to facilitate communication and engender conviviality and trust. The incipient success of the Aburi Meetings is owed, in large measure, to this environment of open and frank expression of one's ideas, fears, interests, etc. General Ankrah himself, the host of the Aburi Meetings and the Chairman of the National Liberation Council of Ghana, had given that impression in his welcome address in the following words:

> It is a saying that if Generals were to meet and discuss frontiers and wars or even go into the details to forestall war, there will never be any disagreements and there will be unity and no war because the two old boys will meet at the frontier and tell each other 'boy, we are not going to let our boys die, come on, let us get the politicians out and that is the end.'

The Ayida/Asiodu letter conveyed the awesome power and influence of its authors, as the following excerpt illustrates:

> The only answer therefore is the *immediate* resumption of discussions and negotiations by *all* including your representatives. Decree No. 8 which in many ways has de-centralised Nigeria much further than the 1963 Constitution need be no obstacle; it would be on the law books, so to speak, with or without amendments only as long as it takes to conclude the discussions envisaged. We earnestly plead with you to send trustworthy representatives to such discussions. The conclusions of the discussions will only become valid when they have

> been confirmed and accepted by you and members of the Supreme Military Council (emphasis added)

In other words, these two could be trusted to persuade the Federal Military Government to ensure that Decree No. 8 would not be a stumbling block to further discussions; that it could remain in the law books while negotiations were in progress and could be amended following discussions; and that the outcome of the discussions would need to be confirmed by Ojukwu *and* members of the Supreme Military Council. Surely, with this anticipated breakthrough, a resolution of all issues of disagreement would ensue? Whatever may have been the misgivings on both sides at the time of the letter, it certainly provided necessary and sufficient hope for the East to engage the Federal Government in everything and anything related to the future of the East and Nigeria.

It is striking that the duo had so much confidence in Ojukwu that they believed that he was the Nigerian equivalent of Nasser who would bring forth the Nigerian revolution and the one person destined to save not only Eastern Nigeria, but the Federation as a whole! The letter was confidential, but could Gowon have known anything of it, and if he did, did he regard Ojukwu in similarly glowing terms? If, indeed, Asiodu and Ayida believed that their letter would have the desired effect, then they must have been reasonably assured of the desirable outcomes their letter sought. This should be borne in mind when, later, the duo were referred to, more disparagingly than enthusiastically, as 'super perm-secs.' It is also remarkable that the two senior civil servants were prepared to give up their posts to make way for others: "People like us will only be too happy to make way for others in furthering a just quota system of official appointments to the highest positions," they had written. Yes, Ayida was, at such a critical point in Nigeria's history, prepared to make the supreme career sacrifice if it was considered necessary; today, Nigeria can continue to count on him to do whatever is necessary for the resolution of any national conflict in which his genius and fidelity can be put to best use.

The creation of states on 27 May, 1967 by the Gowon-led Federal Military Government, followed by the promulgation of the 'Aburi' Decree, Decree No. 8, the following day, May 28, may be described as the final straw that forced the hands of Lt. Colonel Ojukwu to declare the 'Republic of Biafra.' This assessment, however, bears qualification for it can be reasonably argued that Ojukwu was already resolutely committed to secession and, therefore, no power on earth could have persuaded him to the contrary. A number of questions would logically follow, such as: Did Ayida and Asiodu sincerely believe that their audacious, last-minute effort held much hope for success? Did they think that Ojukwu would dance to Gowon's tune on the sensitive issue of states-creation? Did they not realize that, according to the thinking in the East, the Cross River and Rivers States (which would surely find autonomous expression if states were created) were vital for the economic well-being and survival of Eastern Nigeria as a sovereign state? If, therefore, Rivers and Cross River States were carved out of the former Eastern Region, would Ojukwu not see this as further evidence of federal intervention in the affairs of the East at a time when the East strongly contended that the Federal Government, or any other central authority by whatever name, should not be seen to be exercising authority in the East?

The states-creation and other related questions were of great import since Ayida was the Chairman of the Committee of Federal Permanent Secretaries, the committee charged with the responsibility of submitting to General Gowon the list of criteria for creating states. To Ayida, however, the answer to all of this was quite simple and he himself had succinctly stated frequently that he would have worked strenuously for whatever, in his mind, promoted the interests of Nigeria as a united, strong, vibrant and indivisible nation. If states-creation was good for maintaining the integrity of Nigeria, then Ayida was all for it. If, on account of this, his enviable position in the public service was to be sacrificed, then he would all too willingly lay his career on the chopping block.

In every field of human endeavour, there are the weak and there are the strong. There are the faint of heart and there are the relentless. There are the sheep and there are the tigers. Ayida is not weak, he is not faint-hearted and he is not one of the sheep. So what is he, a tiger? Can someone so calm and peaceable be thought of as a tiger, what sort of tiger? When the federal forces invaded 'Biafra', it was thought the 'rebellion' would be put down quickly. As Ayida recalls the occasion, Ojukwu would call Gowon on the phone and the two would talk and talk, in bouts of banter all around. Gowon's apparent indecisiveness revealed the tiger in Ayida as he and other senior civil servants prevailed on Gowon to fight a full-scale war and stop the dilly-dallying, with the sole purpose of putting a quick end to the suffering in 'Biafra'. Even now in retirement, elements of 'the tiger in Ayida' surface whenever the occasion demands it, as members of the team that interviewed him for this book would testify.

Three days after the civil war ended, Ayida hurried to the East. From Port Harcourt he went to Aba and then Owerri. "What I saw I cannot forget: a woman had three children. She was in tatters and was in search of her husband." Though steeled in character and bearing, he wept uncontrollably. He helped as best he could under the circumstances, but the woman was inconsolable without her husband, and would not abandon her search. Ayida used his position as the Chairman of the Committee charged with the task of rehabilitation and reconstruction to maximize resources in the interests of the war-ravaged areas of Eastern Nigeria. Unbelievably, though, the administration of the East Central State, instead of cooperating with the federal efforts at alleviating the pervasive suffering in the area, indulged in acts of commission or omission to exacerbate it. For example, Ayida cited the frustration and pain of federal authorities in trying to get the East Central State to accept and instal 54 generators to provide electricity for a number of cities in the area. It took all of three months for the East Central State government to agree on where the generators would be installed. In the end, generators were not installed at all and they had to be sent to other towns in Nigeria!

5

Stirring the hornet's nest

Truth is often bitter and more so, it would seem, to African governments. Unfortunately for them, Ayida in his characteristic pristine candour revels in ideas and philosophies of development, the genre that African governments should espouse and uphold, but don't. In not embracing this line of reasoning, many African governments give the lie to their much-avowed commitment to progress and people-centred development strategies. In Ayida's own words, "'The Poverty of African Economies' is one of the most significant speeches I ever delivered, both for its immediate impact and the long-term effects on the UN Economic Commission for Africa."

The context was Ayida's opening address as the out-going Chairman of the Ninth Session of the UN Economic Commission for Africa (ECA) in 1969. In the address, Ayida challenged the Commission to position itself as the dynamic institution for fostering the rapid development of African countries and, therefore, to take their economic destiny in their own hands. What had brought Ayida unprovoked and unexpected trouble was his frankly painful observation that Africa occupied the lowest position in the world development order. He cited official statistics showing that 22 of the 31 countries with GDP lower than US $100 were from Africa. For example, he had observed that Ethiopia, the host country of the ECA and the oldest independent country in sub-Saharan Africa, ranked 91st out of 92 countries on the scale of level of development and Nigeria came a poor 79th! But, Ayida was sufficiently analytical to acknowledge that it would have been misleading to assess relative economic positions without taking into consideration the structural changes that were taking place in individual countries and their capacity to transform African economies as a whole. He pointed to India as an example of a country where the change in *per capita* income did not show the extent of industrialization and modernization - a structural change that was critical for sustaining India's future growth capability. His next remarks were directed at the very heart of the mission of the ECA in the following words:

> Looking over the past ten years, what I think is necessary for the future is *for the Economic Commission for Africa to give us an African Plan for Development.* We need a perspective plan which would provide the model framework, the priorities and the policy perspectives for the national development plans of member States. The focus of attention of such an indicative plan should be ***on the development objectives appropriate in the African context*** and the necessity for mutual co-operation among member States. The Commission would thus be helping the world to have a better appreciation of the development process in Africa. We need a better articulation of the real obstacles to economic and social development in our continent (emphasis added)

Ayida's unequivocal position on such a fundamentally significant subject was really stirring the hornet's nest. The ECA was being castigated for not portraying Africa's development and economic objectives in the best light. After all, the ECA was supposed to have the intellectual sophistication to enunciate African dreams for development in the language of an integrated, popular and participatory initiative for economic growth - what Ayida may have referred to as 'the new political economy.' As it turned out, however, the ECA received the truth of Ayida's address with scholarly candour, judging from the following observation by Ayida himself: "I am told the staff of the Commission responded to the challenge of the speech magnificently and the ECA would probably have played a more active role in African development if it had more convincing support from African governments and their agencies."

Sometimes the mere allusion to facts - supposedly well-known - may stir disaffection among segments of the populace who view such facts with great disfavour and discontent for 'advertising' certain unwholesome aspects of their life which, they had thought, were not all that bad. This is the 'all-is-well', or 'things-are-not-that-bad' illusion that, in a psychological perspective, makes an otherwise exasperating life somehow more livable. This appeared to be the case with students of Haile Sellassie University, Addis Ababa who, aware that their country was abjectly poor, suddenly organized a public protest to demand an explanation from the Ethiopian authorities why their country, the oldest independent country in Africa, had been ranked No. 91 out of 92 least developed countries in Ayida's address. Ayida observed that:

> The Nigerian Ambassador in Addis Ababa was summoned by the Ethiopian authorities and told that he [Mr. Ayida] had stirred up the populace and they were concerned about the unfriendly speech of the chairman of the ECA from a friendly country. It was not the beginning of the Ethiopian Revolution, but the seeds had been unwittingly sown.

This was 1969. Nigeria had already witnessed two military coups and going through major changes. Were the events the beginnings of another public address (to be considered shortly), the precursors of a 'Nigerian Revolution' whose content was actively agitating his mind at the time? We may never know how long it took him to make up his mind on the title and content of his Presidential Address to the Nigerian Economic Society, but we may be certain that he gave both a very serious thought. Perhaps the following words of a famous writer would whet our appetite for a critical analysis of that Address:

> All the stuff they write about me I read
> Casually, hardly seeing,
> As if they were not really meant for me,
> The appropriate words and the vicious ones.
> And not just because I refuse to accept
> the truth, good or bad,
> the polished apple as a present,
> or, on the other hand, the poisoned turd...
> Why, why, I asked myself, and others asked me
> Does someone else, loveless and ready with words
> prise me open and, hammering away
> with a nail
> pierce my wood, my sweat,
> my stone, my shadow
> the elements that are me?
> Why me? I live far away,
> I don't exist for them, I don't go out,
> I don't come home.
> Why do the birds of the alphabet
> Attack my nails and my eyes? (Neruda, 1964)

Perhaps no other public discourse of his life has received such mixed reactions and generated such controversy as his Presidential Address at the 1973 Annual Conference of the Nigerian Economic Society Enugu, entitled: *The Nigerian Revolution, 1966–1976.* The Nigerian press did full justice to the address by serializing it in four parts in the *Daily Times*, a government-owned daily newspaper. To some, the lecture was indicative of the politicization of the civil service and an errant expression of power by a civil servant who should be seen and not heard. To others, it was bold and imaginative. To most, however, it was a *magnum opus* of courage, sincerity and genius. First, we present examples of reactions to the Address before discussing its content and probable impact.

The reaction of G.C. Enukora of the Federal Ministry of Internal affairs (Administrative Division) was conveyed in his letter to Ayida, dated 30th April, 1973, in the following words: "I have read with considerable pleasure some extracts of your most incisive, objective address to the Economics [sic] Society. I feel greatly impressed. My ideas on the various issues coincide remarkably with yours...." Dr. A.A. Nwafor-Orizu, one time President of the Nigerian Senate, wrote from his country home in Nnewi, also on 30th April, 1973 to say,

> I have read the extracts from your presidential address to the 1973 meeting of the Nigerian Economic Society.
>
> Very few writings on contemporary political and economic issues have impressed me [as much] with its force and impact. It is full of practical knowledge, genuine prophecy, courageous diagnosis, detached observations and patriotic admonitions. Thank you my dear Mr. Ayida....

The ebullient Dr. K.O. Mbadiwe added his own encomiums. Writing from his Ikoyi address on 8th May, 1973, he congratulated Ayida thus:

> This new knowledge from you is a contribution to the area of new ideas and will serve as an indispensable factor to those who believe that only stability and permanent peace will bring untold happiness to this country.

> I have read your four instalments in the press with the greatest interest and I sincerely appreciate the effort, time and energy that you put into this work to make it available to your people and for it to serve as your own contribution in bringing happiness to this great country.
>
> Nobody will like to have the high cost of the civil war both in human and material resources repeated and it is only by having people with constructive and imperishable ideas that we can build a society where justice and fair play can prevail.
>
> I had wished that my late friend Atta had left a lasting record of what he thought we could do to achieve real unity in this country.
>
> Your contribution will go a long way.
>
> Once more, accept my congratulations.

Although Ayida had, rightly, not mentioned in his Presidential Address any names of those who had been retired in the state public services, two former state commissioners, nonetheless, saw it fit to write him requesting that he state categorically that he did not have them in mind when his Address referred to state commissioners who had been removed from office in the Federal Government's drive to combat corruption in public service. In a four-paragraph letter, dated 30th May 1973, a former state commissioner, who later became a federal minister, wrote Ayida to complain as follows:

> You said in a passage [in your Address that] at least 12 State Commissioners have been removed because of corruption and abuse of office. I was removed as Commissioner by the then Military Governor of the [state]. It was certainly not for corruption or abuse of office. Since the publication of your speech, many well-wishers have been asking if it was true that I am one of the people you referred to. As you are a friend, I thought there is no need to deal with the matter as a lawyer would. I

> should be grateful if you would take immediate steps to correct the impression you have given about me. Delay won't be wise.

The threat of possible legal action was hardly disguised!

A somewhat animated response came from another former commissioner who took all of two pages in seven paragraphs to tell Ayida, among other things, that:

> Since the inception of the administration of the state..., only five Civil Commissioners could be said to have resigned their public offices and they did so on their own. But the rest, over 25 were sacked or dropped. None was asked or forced to resign for any reason whatsoever. It is a civilized act to ask a person one has been working with for some-time [sic] to resign if one no longer requires the services of that person. But this can never be the case with the happy-go-lucky rulers who dread more than anything else, resignations of any individual from their cabinets, but who raven [sic] catchy newspaper headlines of "Me sack you first" just to bolster, in the eyes of their mentors, their ageing and tottering image.
>
> Hence your allegation published in the *Sunday Times* of 15th April, 1973 to the effect that at least 12 Civil commissioners have been forced to resign their public offices, in accordance with the attempt of the Federal Government to reduce corrupt practices, is baseless, misleading and embarrassing; embarrassing particularly to the Civil Commissioners who have left or dropped from office without blemish, but who, unfortunately, your allegation has lumped. You need to name the 12 commissioners concerned and their States to clear the air of suspicion which the allegation has engendered...

Within two weeks, on 4th May, 1973, Ayida had replied his

critics with genuine warmth and understanding, stating clearly that his strongest plea in the Presidential Address was that the Federal Public Service be not politicized. Concerning the circumstances in which one particular commissioner had been removed from office, Ayida tried to calm apparently ruffled feathers with the following words:

> As for Commissioners "forced to quit office", I had in mind cases where I was privileged to know the reasons for their "being sacked or forced to resign" as a result of public and private enquiries and otherwise. I am not aware of the reason why you were "dropped out or not given the opportunity to resign", but if you feel strongly about the matter, I am prepared to send a copy of your letter to His Excellency, the Military Governor... requesting him to let us know why you were left out! You and I can jointly agree on the next line of action on receipt of His Excellency's reply.

A copy of the Presidential Address was enclosed with Ayida's letter.

Three weeks later, and without taking up Ayida's offer to pursue his case further... the same former commissioner wrote Ayida again in a far more combative mood as follows:

> Many thanks for the copy of your Enugu speech sent. It makes an interesting reading, and, in fact, it is a politico-academic exercise written and delivered, *first of its kind, by a Civil servant.* Your newfangled and exultant political power must be discouraged by all Nigerians of goodwill. Governments come and go. But the Civil service which is the only insurance for continuity of administration, should not also come and go. *This, unfortunately, is going to be the case unless the Civil Servants stop politicising,* in any circumstances (emphasis added).

Evidently, nothing Ayida did had succeeded in shifting the former commissioner's entrenched position on the 'proper' role of the Nigerian civil service and its civil servants. But Ayida's vision and mission in delivering the address would not be vitiated, as the lecturer himself explains in the following words:

> It is interesting to note that when I delivered the Presidential Address to the Nigerian Economic Society and touched on the events which led to the disintegration of the Nigerian Federation around July 29 1966, especially the incident of the Rising Grass narrative in the first paper on "The Nigerian Revolution 1966 -76", some of my colleagues protested that it was too early for us to publish our insider knowledge of how and why Nigeria survived to date and on the governance of the country, especially since the attainment of independence.
>
> I remember I promised Alhaji Ibrahim Damcida that I would not write on the Nigerian situation again until ten years after my exit from the public service. I have scrupulously observed this promise to a very good friend and a highly respected colleague, even in the midst of an orchestrated provocation. For example, the *New Nigerian* newspaper which did not publish a word of the Enugu lecture, wrote three editorial comments on the substance and only stopped the series of personal attacks in the 'interest of peace and harmony and intervention of men of goodwill.'
>
> As explained to some of my colleagues, the declaration was a valedictory speech from an outgoing President of the Nigerian Economic Society. It was also meant to be my valedictory speech from the public service although there was an obvious need to 'set the records straight.' *What is significant in the Nigerian Revolution lecture is that in 1966, some of us believed that a revolution was in the making. We sincerely believed that the Nigerian society could be changed beyond*

> *recognition, for the better. We had faith. We hoped for a bright future.* The civil war with all its pains was treated as a tragic and temporary interruption. As late as 1973 when the lecture was delivered, I could still end on a peroration [by] proclaiming 'I am proud to be a Nigerian.' But over ten years later, I know better and I am not so sure (Ayida, 1987 emphasis added).

Ayida's 1973 Presidential Address to the Nigerian Economic Society must be clearly understood as a scholarly, academic exercise sustained by a thorough analysis of the national problems and aspirations of the time, in line with the Society's declared objective, cited at the very beginning of his Address which is as follows:

> The general aim of the Nigerian Economic Society shall be the general advancement of economic and social knowledge and in particular, to encourage the study of the economic and social problems of Nigeria.

Furthermore, the Society's constitution states that "the Presidential Address shall not be subject to debate," after the tradition of university inaugural lectures (at least at the University of Ibadan). Ayida had taken full advantage of the situation by copiously researching his subject, spending considerable time thinking through the dynamics of the Nigerian society of the day, and had, with robust courage and abiding faith, presented a creative treatise on the future of Nigeria never before attempted by a public servant. His approach had been innovative and destined to rattle some nerves Ayida had fully anticipated opposition to his speech because, as he himself admitted at the opening stages of the Address, "Needless to say, the subject-matter of this address would have been different [if] the experts and professional revolutionaries in our midst [were] in a position to disagree with me violently within or outside this Conference Hall."

Nigeria owes a debt of gratitude to this address, though she may not yet fully realize it, because for the first time, we heard a civil servant tell us 'like it is' and 'like it should be' and what we needed to do to move the country forward at a time when it was simply not clear what sort of Nigeria the people wanted. Ayida assayed to provide the guiding signposts along the way, as well as the benchmarks for measuring any success achieved.

It must be fully appreciated that Ayida adhered faithfully to the aims and objectives of the Nigerian Economic Society, and if any complaints should be made, they should be laid squarely at the door of the Society of which he was President. He fulfilled his obligation, and ably too. He saw a unique opportunity and made maximum use of it, knowing that the chance might not come his way again - a sure mark of a practical man, even of a genius.

Before we delve further into the content of the address, let us first hear Ayida pay tribute to the Nigerian Economic Society in the following words:

> We have been careful in the past in ensuring that this Society does not constitute itself into a pressure group for promoting sectional interests, not even of economists; that would be the end of the Nigerian Economic Society as we know it...
>
> It is my hope that *this Society and its members will continue to stand for truth and the search for truth, no matter the vicissitudes which face us in the task of nation-building.* I have always recalled with pride that we were one of the few national societies, if not the only one, which did not function in the three years of the civil war since our President and secretary were fenced in on "the other side" (Ayida, 1987:1-2) (emphasis added)

Whatever this elegant, refined and illustrious man had to say in his address was indicative of his keeping faith with his calling, with his duty, with his responsibilities. The pertinent questions we need to ask are: Has this man been truthful? Has he demonstrated the courage to live a life of truth? These are weighty questions in respect of any human, and we shall endeavour, in the following paragraphs, to provide evidence that would further illuminate the questions.

At least one critic of the Presidential Address had described it as "politicizing" the Nigerian civil service. There will be cause to return to this allegation later; for now, it is necessary to prepare our minds for a detailed analysis of the address by citing an early part of it as follows:

> One cannot analyse meaningfully economic and social determinants in such a complex situation [that is, the social and economic forces which had determined the course of events in Nigeria since 1966] *without making explicit one's assumptions about the future pattern of politics in the country. These underlying political assumptions are predictive rather than prescriptive. In other words, we are more interested in what is likely to happen than what we would like to see happen.* (Ayida,c1987:2) (emphasis added)

Making "explicit... assumptions" is one of the cardinal steps of a serious discourse, indeed, of the formal research process itself. Thus, from the outset, Ayida leaves his audience in no doubt about his "underlying political assumptions."

Ayida would seem to be anxious to share with Nigerians, through the medium of his Address, some of his inner thoughts on the past, the present and future of Nigeria as he had asked, "has there been, or will there be a Nigerian Revolution in the 1966-76 period?" And, as a corollary, he had wondered aloud, "when is a revolution a revolution"? Bearing in mind that the

Address was given in 1973, if the Nigerian Revolution had not occurred by then, what were the chances that the remaining three years, 1973-76, covered in the title of the Address would bring about the avowed Revolution?

One would have to imagine that, either Ayida was convinced, at the time of his Address, that the Revolution was already taking place and would continue into 1976, or that it had not taken off at all. He would have had to demonstrate which was which. Fortunately, he did not keep his audience in suspense for long as he proceeded to describe what a true revolution was all about, ideologically. He resolved the problem thus, "Only a left wing or progressive revolution in which the masses are involved or fully mobilized, can be a true Revolution. Where the masses, the peasantry and the proletariat are not ready or suffer from inertia, the intelligentsia or the vanguard of the revolution will speak up for them."

One might then be justified in asking, 'Did Ayida see himself and his fellow higher civil servants as providing this "vanguard" and, therefore, speaking for the people, or standing in for them with the powers that be since, under the prevailing military rule of the time, the intelligentsia represented by academia, had been rendered effete and moribund, except, perhaps, for those like Aboyade who were consultants to, or ministers/commissioners in, government?

Ayida himself provided the answer to our question in the following words:

> ...there have been many complex factors at play in Nigeria since the attainment of independence, and that since 1966, the method and organisation of the Nigerian society has undergone some fundamental changes which if not arrested, could qualify as the beginnings of a national revolution. *Unfortunately, the Nigerian Revolution is a Revolution without a vanguard.* The prediction is that unless a vanguard

> can be evolved to provide the leadership and the impetus for the revolutionary forces at work, the Nigerian revolution was bound to prove abortive (Ayida, 1987:3) (emphasis added).

In other words, Ayida was asserting before members of the Nigerian Economic Society that the apparent Nigerian Revolution was not a revolution at all. It lacked a core ingredient - a vanguard comprising the intelligentsia - to lead it and give it motion, not just movement.

Nevertheless, he believed that the country was experiencing a revolution - a military revolution - because, according to him, the entry of the military into government had provided a unique opportunity for fundamental changes that could not have been thought of at independence. And what were the changes? Ayida did not expatiate until later in his Address. Rather, he appeared more concerned with an analysis of the revolutionary impact of military intervention in Nigeria. As he saw it, two possible approaches were discernible:

> (i) to give a full and objective account of what happened to the body politic between 1966 and 1973 and leave it to others to draw the appropriate conclusions and lessons of experience, (ii) or to give an outline of the main events to date and attempt to predict the probable course of events up to 1976 and thereafter (Ayida, 1987:3-4).

Ayida opted for the second alternative and tried to predict the likely course of events on the basis of the knowledge at his disposal, just as any other Nigerian would. But Ayida put himself in some difficulty here: his knowledge of the workings of government and the military was far superior to that available to the average Nigerian. He thus opened up himself to possible criticism since he was widely regarded as a 'superman in Government' and he might be perceived, mindlessly or not, as speaking for the military establishment. But, this was a risk he was prepared to take since, convinced of the high erudition of his audience, he could safely presume a large measure of a balanced evaluation of his ideas. That is to say, he believed that his audience, which did not have the right of reply, would grant him the indulgence of speaking his mind sincereiy and with courage. In this regard, we would do well to be reminded of what Udoji had said, and cited earlier in this book, that Nigerians should endeavour to grant the public servant the same quarter granted to any other strand of society.

Ayida then proceeded to treat his audience to the dynamics of the Nigerian Military Revolution, through the eyes of the "New Political Economy." Of great significance in the recent experience of Nigerians is "the distribution of economic power and the public patronage among individuals and ethnic and rural groups...," which he contrasted with the dominant role of expatriate business enterprises in the Nigerian economy with their corrupting influence and power, then and now. Ayida then argued, with considerable conviction, the application to the private sector of the same tenets of Nigerianization applied to the public sector at independence, asserting that "a similar historical necessity prompted the *Nigerian Enterprises Promotion Decree.*" Ayida's verdict was unequivocal, if somewhat controversial. He contended:

> The programme of indigenization of the economy may yet turn out to be one of the most important landmarks of the military regime...There is little doubt that there is an economic revolution in Nigeria. Its character is not certain. Its political content and social impetus cannot be easily ascertained because of the style of the revolution...

Ayida went further by observing that the creation of states

constituted the second landmark of the Revolution, a fundamental change introduced by the advent of the military, a change that, in Ayida's opinion, could not have easily occurred under the rivalry and rigidities of party politics.

So far, so good: there is, perhaps, not much that would grate the nerves of anyone so far in the Address. But this would soon come as Ayida moved into the arena of military power, how it had been operated and by whom, and the place of the military after 1976. He approached this issue from the standpoint of an adviser under the military and concentrated on two categories of personnel, "public officers, notably senior civil servants and university dons [and] political appointees, notably civil commissioners." Here, we would need to quote Ayida extensively because the main thrust of the criticisms levelled against his Address related to the relative roles he assigned to the military, the civil servants, and the civil commissioners in governance. Ayida's categorical statements on these contentious issues illustrate, once again, his enormous courage. Hear him as follows:

> Under military rule, there are two basic approaches to the organisation of government business. Senior military personnel can be assigned to head Ministries and Departments, as members of the Revolutionary Command or junta or they can invite civilians and leading politicians to serve as members of the Cabinet as in Nigeria. In the latter case, properly conceived, such civilian Advisers are to assist the military to govern by interpreting the wishes of the people to the military and vice versa. Unfortunately, there is abundant evidence that the basis of civilian participation in the military administration is not abundantly clear even to some Civil Commissioners.
>
> It is revealing that when civilians were first appointed to the Federal Executive Council in June 1968, one of their early misgivings was the use of

> the appellation "Commissioner". Some of them wished to see a return to the "Minister" or "Secretary of State". They had to be content with Ministerial rank when on overseas tours. In spite of the appellation, "Civil Commissioners as political heads of their ministries" have full ministerial powers *but it is the military that is in power and not a political party.* The political power and prestige derived from the party caucus is not there. In the day to day conduct of business under military rule, *it is the barrel of the gun that determines the outcome of any political controversy or personality conflict.* The ultimate distribution of power in future civil governments may not be significantly different. The political reality in Africa today is that the fact of the elective basis of a government will not *ipso facto*, remove the ultimate sanction in the hands of the military. Can the military in Nigeria ever return to the barracks to play their traditional role in our life time? That is the million Naira question.
>
> If Civil Commissioners appear to exercise less power than the former Ministers, it is not because their functions have been usurped by Permanent Secretaries and other Senior [Civil] Servants. It is because *authority now resides in the military.* Commissioners and senior civil servants are fellow Advisers with different roles, to the powers-that-be who sometimes receive their advice from outside the two groups, to their mutual frustration and suspicion. *Commissioners were not appointed to run the government as political masters but as servants of the military, the new political masters* (Ayida, 1987:11) (emphasis added)

This is where Ayida's ship of sound reasoning, which up till this point appeared to have had a smooth sailing, apparently struck the rock of some sticky journalese: sections of the Nigerian press were distinctly hostile to any situation which ennobled the civil servant to speak out on national issues, particularly if what was being said had a political flavour. Thus, we might rightly ask: what is really wrong with civil servants speaking out on *any* issue?

Udoji had maintained, quite forcefully, that the job of a civil servant was to serve his political master, not the military-appointed Commissioners by whatever name they might be called. Udoji expatiated further by explaining that how the civil servant carried out his functions depended on whether executive power was vested in an individual, as in the Supreme Commander in a military regime in which Ayida had served. In such a situation, as Udoji had observed, the civil servant might not be expected to show the true mettle of which he was made. He might not be expected to be innovative or bold. And he might not be required to be original. All that mattered was that he fulfil his master's wishes. If such were, indeed, the mentality expected of Nigeria's top civil servants, nobody should really be surprised that the nation might remain, for a long time, in the doldrums of insipid and mediocre bureaucracy, with little room for an invigorating expression of personality rich in ideas and originality, imbued with sound morals. We would, as a result, have cultivated a civil service bureaucracy of listless morons, all doing what they were told, reminiscent of Fela's 'zombies', an expression which was actually used derogatively to describe soldiers!

Still, Ayida would not expect an easy escape, not even under the protective shield of the Nigerian Economic Society, when he stated, *inter alia,* that:

> the political reality in Africa today is that the fact of the elective basis of a government will not ipso facto, remove the ultimate sanction in the hands of the military. Can the military in Nigeria ever return to the barracks to play their traditional role in our life time? That is the million dollar question (Ayida, 1987: 11).

Surely, his was an academic exercise and one can rightly argue that all is fair comment in academics by asking, for example, why he did not raise the question of whether or not the military would be capable of continuing to play their traditional defence role? Having exercised full political powers for so long and having fought a ferocious three-year civil war and demonstrated marked prowess in diligence and diplomacy - 'no victor, no vanquished' - would it not be proper to begin to think aloud about the proper future role of the military? Would it not be right to suggest that Ayida was, in fact, flying a kite to provoke public discourse and comment on these important issues?

No, he was not testing the waters; he clearly used his esteemed position of one with an uncommon knowledge of the workings of the military in government to ask cogent and pressing questions of the time - questions on which the Nigerian public required clear leadership if not answers. For this, Ayida made and makes no apologies: he spoke his mind boldly, loudly and eloquently.

Professor Ladipo Adamolekun in his book entitled, *Politics and Administration in Nigeria* joined issues with Ayida's position in all of Chapter 5 of his book, captioned "Soldiers, Civilian Politicians and Administrators, 1966-79." During the preparation of this book, Ayida was taken to task on the issues raised in Adamolekun's book. He was asked whether he had seen he book and whether he had read it. He replied that he may have heard of it, but that he had not read it. One would have thought that some of Ayida's friends or loyalists might have called his attention to the book. But he did not recall that this ever happened. Considering the acerbic tone of Adamolekun's writing, he was asked if he had had any personal disagreements with Prof. Adamolekun that would have made the latter so bitter and raspy in his writing on him. All Ayida could recall was that he was a member of the panel that had interviewed him for a job at the University of Ife. Although the Panel had recommended that he be appointed, he (Ayida) had not scored him very highly; he thought that it was quite possible that Prof. Adamolekun might have found this out over the years.

We would need to examine Adamolekun's book in some detail. Chapter 5 starts with two quotations one, as stated above by Ayida, to the effect that "Commissioners were not appointed to run the government as political masters but as servants of the military who are the political masters", and another credited to Major General Shehu Yar'dua in 1978, "It is no longer a secret that civil servants have influenced major decisions in the last twelve years of military rule. They have enjoyed virtually unchallenged the exercise of power all these years."

Adamolekun is irked that Ayida, on one hand, makes political statements and on the other, states quite categorically that under no conditions should the civil service be politicized. It seems fundamental to make a clear distinction between 'political' and 'politicize'. This brings to mind the distinction that Professor Peter Ekeh makes between 'tribes' and 'tribalism' in his Inaugural Lecture at the University of Ibadan entitled, *Colonialism and Social Structure.* Ekeh would like us to know that,

> In spite of their affinities, there is only a negative relationship between the terms 'tribes' and 'tribalism'. Tribalism is a construct that defines a model of behaviour that is unacceptable in our new poly-ethnic relationships. Tribalism does have a linkage with tribes, not because tribes exist any more but because the acts that constitute tribalism have the atavistic aura of behaviour which is considered appropriate for a past form of existence in the tribal setting, but which is regarded as destructive in poly-ethnic systems of social life. A tribalist is a non-tribesman who exhibits anti-social

> behaviour in a non-tribal setting in such a way as to threaten the new forms of existence with reversion to a past form of restricted tribal social organization (Ekeh, 1980).

Although 'political' is an adjective and 'politicize' a verb, still the latter derives from the former, as *tribalism* has affinity with *tribe*. Just as there is nothing wrong with tribes, or politics, because the one is a fact of existence of a group of people, and the other an activity of a people, there is something wrong with 'tribalism' or 'politicize': they are both inappropriate in a system of relationships of different peoples in a government, or in a system, such as the public service, that serves all the different political groups in a society. Thus, that Ayida makes a statement construed as political does not *per se* mean that the type of work which he does - civil service - is now politicized. We remain ever so grateful to Udoji for giving us a quintessential characteristic of the Civil Service, a Service that lives under conditions that are not applicable to other walks of life, demanding of the highest degree of rectitude, accountability, and performance - all that is good to administer.

According to Adamolekun,

> To translate what was potential primacy into an actual primacy, the super permanent secretaries convinced the incumbent head of state, General Gowon to abandon the idea of a return to civil rule and instead to consider the alternative of proclaiming Nigeria a one-party state with himself as the party leader and president (Adamolekun, 1988).

Ayida was asked whether he had played any of the roles ascribed to "the super permanent secretaries" by Adamolekun in his book and had replied flatly in the negative: "*When the postponement was made I wasn't around. I was in Washington*

D.C. I found out only when I got back to Nigeria. It was as simple as that, I wasn't around." And prior to his departure, he had had nothing whatsoever to do with the postponement, he asserted. Why then would Adamolekun be so definitive about the alleged insidious role of the so-called super permanent secretaries in the postponement of Nigeria's political agenda at the time? Ayida does not give much credit to the book itself. He then added that, in fact, it was the military top brass themselves who wanted to perpetuate their power. People like the late General Murtala Muhammed, he observed, had wanted the military to take over power and perpetuate military rule. He, Ayida, had had absolutely nothing to do with the postponement, he repeated.

In the same book Adamolekun had also described how Ayida had humiliated Alhaji Shehu Shagari, his Commissioner of Finance, in the following words: "The story of the personal humiliation he suffered at the hands of the permanent secretary of the ministry of finance over which he was the commissioner lends credence to [his earlier] observation...." In support of that observation, Adamolekun cites from *Africa Now* (London) as follows:

> After a meeting of the commissioners of finance of all the governments of the federation over which Alhaji Shagari had presided, he expressed the desire to travel on from Bauchi [place of the meeting] to his home state, Sokoto, in the aeroplane made available to take the federal delegation back to Lagos. The federal permanent secretary of Shagari's ministry wanted to return to Lagos, without the detour through Sokoto that could have delayed his arrival in Lagos by about one hour. The permanent secretary's word was the law and the aeroplane flew back direct to Lagos from Bauchi (Adamolekun, 1988).

Again, Ayida had been asked for his reaction to this

seemingly damaging allegation. He simply laughed and answered as follows:

> It is just ignorance [on the part of the writer]... all gossip which is expanded into an article because there is no basis for all he wrote. When I read about the incident of the plane I laughed. That event never happened. It didn't exist at all. It was an imagination; it is as simple as that. Many of these things didn't happen. It did not relate to anything, and in terms of power and all that... it's pure fiction.

Commenting on government's white paper on the *Udoji Report*, Adamolekun accuses the super permanent secretaries in his book of "a desire to prevent the public enterprises and the universities from enjoying an autonomy that could enhance their status as elite institutions." The words "and the universities" seem rather strange as the *Udoji Report* contains nothing about universities! Adamolekun also accuses the higher civil servants as follows:

> While most Nigerians supported the economic nationalism that motivated the Nigerian Enterprises Promotion Decree (commonly referred to as the Indigenization Decree), there is strong evidence that the higher civil servants who developed the policy shared some of the most attractive benefits with their allies, the military politicians. Other groups within the society who were interested in taking advantage of the decree succeeded only to the extent that the higher civil servants allowed (Adamolekun, 1988)

This serious matter was put to Ayida for his reaction and had replied as follows:

> I chaired it [the Board implementing the provisions of the Decree] and because of that I didn't have one share in any company, one kobo [of shares] I didn't buy. They came to me to offer shares free, but I said, 'No'. You're doing a job, you better do the job and then the records are there. I didn't participate in the indigenization. My colleagues didn't either, but there was a problem. [One top military leader in government] had bought some shares so when a government-appointed investigation reported the shares bought by the military leader who had ordered that serving civilian and military leaders who had bought shares be disciplined, he was unaware that the number of shares he had bought was written in volume 3 of the investigation's report which was not part of the White Paper. So, I went up to him and said, 'I'm sorry that if what you ordered is done, you will be called upon to resign.' He replied that his mind was already made up and that he was going to do it. I told him that volume 3 of the report [which the military leader had not seen] contained the information concerning the shares he had bought. So, volume 3 of that Report never saw the light of day. But the chairman of the investigation panel paid dearly for daring to compile volume 3 of his report: he was retired from his job in the private sector.

More details of the incident may be found in Ayida's reaction to Gen. Obasanjo's book *Not My Will* as published in *The Guardian* of 1 April 1990 and reprinted in *The News* of 12 January 2004 as follows:

> My dear General, it is not my will to comment on your latest book. I am compelled, however, to send you this memo as a footnote on some episodes in the text for three reasons:
>
> - media claim that Allison Ayida will be one of those to take you and the publishers to court

when the book is published (I will do nothing of the kind);

- the continued denigration of the Civil Service and the unwarranted attacks on serving public servants who cannot answer back; and
- the need to set the records straight in a publication by a former Head of State on such vital matters as the Justice Elias case and the relationship between Allison Ayida and the late General Murtala Muhammed.

General Yakubu Gowon is still around and can speak for himself but let me remind you that during the hysteria of the media campaign for the British Government to extradite General Gowon for trial, you personally authorised me to inform the British High Commission in strict confidence that the Federal Government did not want the British Government to hand over General Gowon because you were not sure of his involvement and you could not guarantee his personal safety. If the High Commissioner doubted my authority as secretary to the Federal Government, SFMG, he could cross-check with a designated senior member of the Supreme Military Council, SMC. It was clearly understood that if the message was leaked to the press, you would deny it and castigate me publicly. I accepted the assignment in my line of duty knowing full well that I would be sacrificed if the mission misfired!

When we read Samuel Pepys' Diary in form one at the King's College, I started keeping a diary. When I was in the sixth form, I sat down one day to read my past records and discovered that every day was punctuated with "I" did this, "I" did that, I was "first" in this subject or "second" in that race. Where I was "last", I blamed the starter or forgot to record such aberrations. It read as if I was the only student in the College. It sounded like an ego trip and I realised that I could not be a Samuel Pepys but

I did not lose my penchant for record keeping. Somehow, *Not My Will* reminds me of my school boy diaries at King's. We also learnt early at Kings, the Latin expression *Quos dues vult perdere, prius dementat.* 'Those gods wish to destroy, they first make mad'. That was the way of the Romans. It is not the Christian approach where we are taught to forgive and forget. I am thus commenting without malice or bitterness on your "recollections of your time in government".

As far as one can see, the book is about the character of the author and the man behind the mask. In the days, when we had a proper system of confidential reporting and assessment in the Civil Service, when a superior officer prepared confidential reports on his subordinates, he was indirectly reporting on himself and his own character. I therefore, have no cause to take you to court.

As your former chief adviser, I feel like suing your publishers for such a shoddy job; however, such a step will involve too much self-seeking publicity for my taste. In spite of the court injunction, for which the publishers have alleged losses, my copy of the book was bought by a colleague along the Marina for N85.50. I nevertheless thank you for the complimentary copy sent me on your instructions.

Justice Elias' case is subjudice, therefore, I cannot comment beyond expressing my amazement that you mentioned General Muhammed and Justice Dan Ibekwe as the witnesses to what happened. They are no longer with us but Allison Ayida as SFMG was also involved and I am still around. The late Attorney-General on ethical ground, refused to participate in the proceedings. You and I strongly opposed the proposal to remove Justice Elias from office. At one time, you stormed out of General Murtala's office and offered to resign rather than be party to the removal of the Chief Justice, CJ, on the grounds that:

- Dr. Elias was reported by the BBC to have declared his loyalty and support for the new military government while in the West Indies thereby "compromising" the non-political status of CJ;
- Dr. Elias on return to Lagos, recommended two "Northerners" for appointment to the Supreme Court (General Murtala felt that he was doing so because he, Murtala, was a `Northerner) in spite of the fact that Dr. Elias showed clearly that the proposal had been agreed by all concerned before the change of government; and
- General Murtala felt Dr. Elias had stayed in public office for too long as Attorney-General under the late Prime Minister Balewa for many years, and as Attorney-General and then CJ under General Gowon for nine years, and now Murtala - "Haba!"

The last factor was the most important. It was a novel ideal in those days although it is common practice these days - longevity in public office as a basis for compulsory retirement with immediate effect.

After you angrily left the meeting, General Murtala revealed that you had been retiring other people for lesser reasons with alacrity and felt you were only trying to save the Yorubas who dominated the judiciary.

I defended you and emphasised the issue of principle involved; the independence of the Judiciary. The late Head of State was persuaded that Dr. Elias should be allowed to relinquish the post of CJ on grounds of ill-health. When the official announcement was made, Mrs. Elias even countered on the NTA 7 o'clock news that day that her husband was "hale and hearty". This rejoinder was deleted from later editions of the news on my intervention as Dr. Elias's next door neighbour and because of my anxiety that General Murtala might over-react and change his mind again.

If you cannot remember your opposition to Dr. Elias' removal, kindly contact Alhaji Ibrahim Damcida and some members of the public whom you approached to plead with General Murtala not to remove him. I have gone into these details, General, to persuade *you* to apologise to Dr. Elias and the nation and make amends.

There is however, a fundamental issue at stake. When Dr. Elias has risen to the highest judicial office in the world as the president of the World Court, would it not have been more appropriate to let sleeping dogs lie? Would it be dignifying for any senior colleague or former Head of State to write in derogatory terms about you if you rose to the post of Secretary-General of the United Nations? How could your government have supported the candidature of Dr. Elias for the World Court if what you wrote is correct?

For once, you were on the side of the angels in opposing the removal of Dr. Elias as CJ, but your admitting it publicly would have dented your macho image? If the case were not in court, I would have written more and drawn an analogy with the Permanent Secretary whom General Murtala "redeployed" for reasons you and I did not support but as soon as the General was killed, you tried to reinstate the Permanent Secretary to his former ministry but I refused because of the damage such a move would have done to the image and memory of the late General. For other reasons, I insisted on the Permanent Secretary, withdrawing from the service by resigning. I am not sure why you have been *so* anxious to take the lid off the Pandora's box. It is often a mine-field of surprises.

You are entitled to write about your experiences in government and I personally welcome it but you can do *so* without the abrasive and unwarranted attacks on personalities - the young, the middle aged and the elderly, and the gratuitous insults heaped on colleagues, friends and foes, alike.

I worked closely with the late Chief Obafemi Awolowo as the vice-chairman of the Federal Executive Council and Federal Commissioner for Finance and even more so, as the Permanent Secretary of the Ministries of Economic Development and Reconstruction and then Finance. I am sorry, General, you do not know the man you are writing about. What intrigues me as an insider in the corridors of power then, is that you did not reveal enough about the period you were prepared to back Awo for president. Apparently, you only made passing reference to the fact that you appointed him chancellor of ABU to give him the opportunity to mend fences with the Northern establishment and he blew it! Perhaps, you may recall that a member of SMC, General Akinrinade, once spearheaded an attack on the government for using the *Nigerian Tribune* for kite-flying and discussing SMC agenda in advance. He revealed that he used to read the *Tribune* for substantial issues and "progressive ideas" to be considered by SMC instead of the agenda notice. On behalf of council secretariat, I gleefully pleaded not guilty, but you assured council it would never happen henceforth and it did not.

My dear C-in-C, the Civil Service helped your administration and you personally more than any other Head of State or government. I have had the privilege to serve under from President Nnamdi Azikiwe and Prime Minister Tafawa Balewa to Generals Aguiyi-Ironsi, Yakubu Gowon and Murtala Muhammed, and indirectly President Shehu Shagari as my commissioner, and of course, Major-General Shehu Yar'Adua as *defacto* head of government: but you have done more than any other Head of State, to destroy the *espirit de corp* in the service, attack defenceless *civil* servants and destroy the institution. This is inevitable from your buccaneering approach to government business.

I will take a few examples by way of illustration on it. You mentioned S. B. Agodo and U. K. Bello as having "hatched" a plan to investigate the assets of all members of the Supreme Military Council and prepare a "dossier" on them, with Bukar Usman of the Cabinet Officer as chief executioner. If the investigations were "unauthorised", the officers concerned would have been summarily dismissed with immediate effect. What actually happened was that the investigations were duly authorised by the late Head of State with himself as the number one on the hit list, you were number two, not top of the list. The SFMG was on the list as well. U.K. Bello was responsible for compiling the list of shares and assets acquired particularly under the indigenisation exercise. He came to me and explained that your name featured prominently as shareholder in several companies and we agreed as a subtle move, that he should alert the ADC to the Head of State to whisper the findings to him. That the two officers, Agodo and Usman, were arraigned in front of you, was a smoke screen for calling off the exercise and reassuring you of the "confidence and trust" the late Head of State had in you. Both the late Head of State and I had no need to see our "dossiers" because we did not participate in the indigenisation exercise. You should indeed be grateful to U.K. Bello and S.B. Agodo instead of castigating them in your memoirs.

Let me explain that there was nothing wrong according to the rules in those days in public officers acquiring shares under the indigenisation exercise especially if they were not directly involved. I was the chairman of the Economic and Finance Committee of Permsecs, which worked out the detailed proposals for the consideration of council and I felt I was stopped from participating in the scheme. You were not yet involved in the government. Unfortunately, the Murtala Administration was committed to righting all the "wrongs" of the past and punishing the "lapses" of the past with retrospective effect.

However, when the mass retirement exercise was carried out on the military, the committee of officers who compiled the list, put your name and that of Col. Ochefu, then Military Governor, Enugu, on top of the retirement list. When I was told of the list through the usual Cabinet Office sources, because of its destabilising implication, I rushed to General Murtala who was furious that I was trying to interfere in military matters. I pointed out that his administration had just removed the military governor at Ibadan and to retire the Chief of Staff Supreme Headquarters and another military governor would tarnish the image of the new military administration. Believe it or not, my dear General, because of *you* I offered to resign from being secretary to the ensuring unstable administration Good listener as General Murtala was, he politely advised me to get back to my office and mind my business. Later in the day, he summoned me on the hotline to his office. He was a different man. He thanked me for my timely intervention which prepared his mind for the unexpected Army retirement list. I understand he had a stormy meeting with the young officers during which he offered to resign rather than retire you and Col. Ochefu. The young officers insisted that they applied the criteria laid down; divided loyalty, conflict of interest etc, and they would rather accept his resignation than apply double standard in the Army retirement exercise. I do not know why your name was put on the short list but I am sure you can ascertain the reason from any of your former colleagues who served on the committee to enable you lambast them in your next book.

However, the compromise reached was for either you or Col. Ochefu to go. General Murtala revealed to me that he preferred to retain you for two reasons; namely, that:

- Nigerians would believe that he got rid of you as his number two because you are Yorubaman; and
- as such, he had to appoint another senior Yoruba officer - the eligible officer to be "forced" on him was Brigadier James Oluleye. He said "if I had to work with James as Chief of Staff Supreme Headquarters, I will go on record as the first Head of State to have personally shot his number two and that will be a disgrace to Nigeria and Africa".

Hence he reluctantly agreed that Col. Ochefu, one of those who masterminded the coup, that brought you to power, should go for an alleged offence committed under General Gowon's regime, for which he had been pardoned by Gowon. You should therefore be grateful to James Oluleye about whom you made such disparaging remarks. I was doing my work as a good civil servant, committed to the success of the new administration.

The other occasion you were in trouble under General Murtala's administration was when your "estranged wife" wrote a damaging petition against you. I reluctantly mention this partly because the late Professor H. Thomas was compulsorily retired for a similar petition arising from family matters not connected in any way with his exemplary performance as the vice-chancellor of the University of Ibadan; but before the allegations could be investigated and found to be baseless and malicious, the man had died, heartbroken. In the circumstances, you had to seek urgent assistance. You went to the house of a permanent secretary for him to intercede with the late General Murtala on your behalf and he did successfully. But yet all you can see in the civil service is their "failures" in implementing your "dynamic" programmes.

As for my relations with the late General Murtala, you cannot provoke me to write about this yet. But at no time did you bring to my notice "things unbecoming" which I said about him. You must be mistaking me for the young military officer, who after the fateful SMC meeting on your appointment as Head of State, went back to his ministry and addressed his officers as a "young revolutionary", to the effect that General Murtala was dead but the revolution must go on and the revolution was greater than any individual. His permanent secretary reported on the meeting to the Chief of Staff Supreme Headquarters and the commissioner was redeployed. The permanent secretary, our common friend, was very upset about the removal of his commissioner.

Let me remind you of the circumstances of the death of General Muhammed and the high esteem in which he was held by all of us. I was shell-shocked at his death because my car was about 10 cars ahead of him when he was gunned down by Dimka's bullets. I heard the gun shots loud and clear and saw the confusion and the panic that followed.

The following day when the SMC met to elect a successor, I was the only civilian present. As the Secretary to the Council, I had to personally record the minutes but as I told council, I had come to that meeting to throw in the towel. I had had enough of bloodshed. But because of the mature way the council appointed you as the next in line of succession in spite of your protestation that you did not want to be gunned down like a fowl. I told council I was prepared to continue.

Immediately after the council meeting, you summoned me to your office and thanked me for being the first to congratulate you and accept you as the new Commander-In-Chief. As a matter of fact, I was the one to summarise the consensus of the deliberations which was not unanimous as some members pressed for a vote since they argued that such had no support in the military and could not therefore, be an effective Head of State. At the intervention of a prominent member of the council, it was the consensus that Col. Shehu Yar'Adua, who was out of the country, should be promoted and appointed Chief of Staff Supreme Headquarters to "link" the regime with, and preserve General Murtala's charisma, and General T.Y. Danjuma to head the Army. In this delicate balance of power, my job as SFMG and Head of Service was most challenging. Within the first six months at the end of which you promised SMC you would resign as Head of State, I had no problem because you had accepted your role as a *titular* Head of State and, Shehu was the *de facto* Head of Government. Thereafter, you started to assert your authority; I will give an innocuous example by way of illustration. The Restricted Telephone Directory of SMC members and ministers and top government functionaries, by convention, does not list the telephone numbers of the Head of Government.

Brigadier Shehu Yar'Adua told me not to list his number in subsequent editions, I mentioned this to you and you reacted angrily that "Shehu really feels he is Head of Government and successor to General Murtala's power". You instructed me to list his number. As an experienced administrator, I ordered the government printer to produce three editions of the directory, one with Shehu's numbers missing, the other with his old numbers, and a third with his new numbers, I then confronted the two of you with the three editions to select one. I did not have too much difficulty in persuading the two of you to agree on the directory with Shehu's old numbers!

General Murtala and I worked together very closely out of mutual respect for each other's guts and because of our experience from earlier encounters. He also had a human touch. When he went to the OAU summit in Addis Ababa, he returned with a Grundig Satellite Radio as a personal gift for me. I still use it in my bedroom for world news every morning. When he visited the late Sultan in Sokoto, he returned with three pouch bags with

"Allison Ayida" inscribed on tnem. They still adorn my main sitting room. I read in your book that you made similar trips as well but as your SFMG for nearly two years, I have no mementoes, not even a parting souvenir! How on earth can I say things "unbecoming" of Murtala? In any case, in my part of the country, we never speak ill of the dead! In this case, I had no cause to.

It would not strictly be correct that you have never said "thank you" to me. When the white paper on the Adeosun Indigenisation Panel report was drafted by one of the permsecs, Chief John Oyegun, whom you instructed in vain never to discuss the contents with me, you gave me the draft white paper and report for my comment within 24 hours.

You never understood or appreciated the loyalty and *esprit de corps* within the Civil Service hierarchy. John had kept me fully briefed.

There were no-go areas on some of the panel's recommendations which on your specific instructions included, "where a Nigerian had acquired the bulk of the shares in any enterprises outside Schedule I, the shares should be "confiscated" and forfeited to the Federal Government and the names of the 'money-bags' publicised. Apparently, you had not studied volume III of the report where names of such shareholders were listed. When I drew your attention to the pages where your name appeared, you readily agreed that the panel's recommendation should be rejected. And *you* then directed that I should take another week to redraft the white paper. When eventually the council memorandum was circulated, we agreed that Volume III should not be circulated or published but that *you* should mention in council that any member interested in the particulars of those who "cornered" the indigenisation shares, should see the SFMG. Several members contacted me for the list but no member saw the list of names! The permsec and I received a "big thank you" from you at the end of the exercise.

By an irony of fate, when I was returning by Swissair from Paris after the president's recent visit, I sat next to our Zairean friend, Victor Mpoyo, who was the prime mover in our dramatic change of policy direction in Angola and support for MPLA. I was trying to read your book. He was surprised you decided to publish the book against his advice that it should be severely edited. It is not too late. We both agreed that the story on Angola is not complete. For example, why did the Angola Government threaten to sue the Nigerian Government over the $20 million gift?

I should by the way demolish the myth of a Murtala Muhammed/Olusegun Obasanjo regime as a continuum. No, Sir. The late General Murtala ruled the nation and gave dynamic and purposeful leadership for six months. He was seen to be in charge. He was a man of action and was thus prone to make mistakes. He was man enough to admit his mistakes publicly and make amends. For the period I was SFMG under your reign, nobody was in charge. It was a triumvirate of Generals Obasanjo, Shehu Yar'Adua and T.Y. Danjuma, In fairness to General Danjuma, whom we all respected, he never interfered in the day-to-day affairs of government. But whenever he was involved in policy intervention, it was decisive. You were so preoccupied with personal survival that every other consideration was secondary. As a man of action, *a la* late Murtala, whenever you made mistakes, you were more concerned with cover-ups and scapegoats.

The style of administration under General Murtala was so different from yours that I am really surprised you made no reference to this in your book. For example, when the Supreme Military Council had to vote on a controversial proposal that there should be an appeal to the Supreme Court from Armed Robbery Tribunals on points of law, there was a tie, and General Murtala as the president of council had argued passionately against such appeals and voted openly against. He said there was no way he would use his casting vote to have his way.

There was a second poll which again ended in deadlock. General Murtala then proposed that the SFMG should use the chairman's casting vote. We thought it was a joke but he was dead serious. I could not cast a valid vote. I pleaded that the attorney-general should be the one to vote but the late General countered that the attorney-general's views were well-known. I voted for the Armed Robbery Tribunal Decree to be amended to allow for appeals to the Supreme Court.

General Murtala then concluded, "gentlemen, the SMC has through the SFMG decided by democratic vote, next item, please."

A similar situation arose when the Supreme Military Council was confirming the sentences on the coup plotters after General Murtala's assassination. The council was divided over the death sentence passed on an officer and when the poll was taken, the vote ended in a tie. You had voted openly in favour of the death sentence. Without any hesitation, you used your casting vote to hang the officer whom half of the member officer had given the benefit of the doubt. You were correct in law. But the Christian conscience in me felt sick for days that the casting vote of a fellow Christian could be used this way, especially as I did not speak up, not for want of courage, that it is morally wrong to use a casting vote in such circumstances. The late attorney-general felt the same and that night, as neighbours, we met to pray for the departed soul and forgiveness for your soul. It was one of the saddest days of my life, although I never met or knew the officer in his lifetime.

When a similar division of opinion arose when council was considering the findings over Brigadier

S. Ogbemudia, and the majority of members were likely to uphold the Tribunal verdict of not guilty, you ordered a retrial. The rest of the story should be left to the verdict of history which you accuse others of being anxious to rewrite.

I spoke on the phone with General Shehu Yar'Adua while in Lagos last week and told him that we are awaiting his true version of how he masterminded and manipulated the government while you were Head of State. He replied that we have to wait for a long time for his book.

He gave me the impression that the nation has to witness his second coming first! A thousand pity.

One minor observation on the book is that there are too many unanswered questions and too much fiction. I am certainly waiting for the revised edition or the final volume which in my humble opinion should be titled "The True Confession of General Obasanjo".

Incidentally, a family friend from Ibadan visited us at dinner the other evening and asked *oga,* have you read the *Satanic Verses?* Before I could answer, my daughter quipped "Rushdie's or General Obasanjo's". I replied, "I have read both, otherwise, I have no comment."

Meanwhile, permit me to join others in congratulating you on your new publication. After 10 years, you are free to speak out. I hope we can now follow your example in due course although we are constrained by the Official Secrets Act and a sense of decency.

With kind affection
I remain as always.
Your obedient servant
Allison Ayida.
Former Secretary to the Federal Military Government and Head of Service.

When asked about *The News* reprint of the above article, Mr

Ayida replied:

> No comment, I was confronted at the "Selfridges" in faraway London by a young man that he had been reading my article in *The News* before he left his flat and ran into me at the shop. What a coincidence. The reproduction of the article was without my knowledge. I have learnt to forget the whole episode on the intervention of columnists like Prof Akinyemi and Mr E. K. Clarke.

One wonders, then, what constituted the basis of Adamolekun's so-called "strong evidence" in making the serious charges levelled against Nigeria's top civil servants during Ayida's tenure in office. Mere gossip or hearsay?

Adamolekun makes other claims in the same chapter, all of which Ayida says were false. Take the case of membership of boards of federal parastatals. According to Adamolekun,

> Considerable mismanagement was also occasioned by a practice in which senior civil servants -- notably the permanent secretaries - served both as chairmen and key board members of public enterprises placed under 'their' supervision. This dubious practice of transferring civil service attitudes and practices to industrial and commercial undertakings was exacerbated by the fact that some permanent secretaries served on four boards at the same time - with the permanent secretary of the federal ministry of finance holding the record by serving on more than fifty boards at the same time in 1973 (Adamolekun, 1988).

When Ayida was asked to comment on this apparently serious abuse of bureaucratic power, he simply smiled, as is his wont when confronted with something he considers trite or silly. His reply was that though his name was there on paper, he had not, in fact, actually attended the board meetings of more than five such parastatals. Surely, he could not possibly have served on 50 boards; it would have been a logistical nightmare just to try to juggle the meetings, he had observed with a wry smile.

One would have expected that aspects of the presidential address would provoke contrary views, but certainly not the venom poured on it by sections of the Nigerian press. Given the total dominance of Nigeria's political life by the military, and the lecturer being popularly perceived as an 'insider' in the military government, or even as an 'architect' of the governmental style in force, Ayida could easily have been perceived as presenting the case of the military government, or even acting as its mouthpiece. But nothing in the lecture provided any reasonable grounds for levelling such charges against Ayida. It was hard-hitting and analytical, such as the following excerpt:

> But for the self-imposed low profile and style of government of the military administration, as soon as it decided to undertake major reform measures before organizing the return to full civilian and representative government, *it qualifies as a revolutionary regime*. The original aim of returning the country to civilian rule without pre-conditions, automatically becomes a subsidiary objective and the regime has to be judged in terms of its performance relative to the tasks to be accomplished. Sometimes unconsciously, the military leadership has been driven to take part in the politics of the country. Even the decision in 1966 to take charge of the government is a major political move since government is the art of politics (Ayida, 1987:16) (emphasis added).

It could be argued that Ayida displayed egregious political

insensitivity in relegating to a subsidiary position the transfer of power to civilians by the military when, in fact, this issue would be the most important matter affecting civilians who had eagerly waited to take control of their lives through a representative government. Whatever the military may have achieved, the people would, probably with justification, have felt that this should be left to history to judge. Surely, someone like Ayida who was right in the thick of the battle - the military domination of political space - would have hardly been the right person to present an analysis of the encounter? The public just would not have taken it, for good or ill. But they had not reckoned with the brilliance and forthrightness of a civil servant like Ayida who, in their view, should not have been pontificating on political questions in the first place. If only the criticisms levelled against him had been fair and in good faith, all would have been well. All in all, no matter from whatever perspective the Address is judged - such as: 'Ayida should have known Nigerians much better than his address displayed' - it should always be borne in mind that Ayida was addressing an academic audience, the Nigerian Economic Society, and not the general Nigerian public.

Ayida had earlier asked the question, 'When is a Revolution a Revolution?' and had provided an answer by suggesting that a revolution involved certain minimum requirements of socio-economic transformation of society before it could truly qualify as a revolution. As far as he was concerned, the military had, in fact, initiated a number of such transformation that had significantly altered the structure of society. He argued quite successfully that in the context of the prevailing national political economy a revolution had, indeed, occurred.

However, he had gone further by predicting, but not prescribing, the way he expected things to unfold in 1976 and beyond, bearing in mind that Ayida was speaking in 1973 and looking ahead to 1976 in his address. It is instructive to examine his exact words in this context as follows:

> The crucial question relates to the organization of political parties...
>
> There are two models here from the lessons of experience. The first approach is for the military administration to declare party politics open and leave it to 'democratic forces' to settle the issue of national leadership. In this connection, the causes of the failure of the Ad Hoc Constitutional Conference of 1966 have to be carefully analysed although the ground rules now are hopefully different. If the ground rules are different, this presumes that the authorities will insist that no party can operate outside such rules which have to be spelt out, for example, no group will be allowed to advocate secession or engage in activities likely to threaten the territorial integrity of the nation. Where does Big Nation or Small Tribe chauvinism come in?
>
> The second approach is for the military to sponsor a National Movement outside which no serious opposition will be allowed. This alternative has very serious implications and should not be lightly embarked upon without a full appreciation of the repercussions. There cannot be such a national movement without a revolutionary vanguard made up of a body of highly dedicated men and women with a clearly defined national purpose and sense of mission. It is difficult to see how such a group can be formed without the military hierarchy politicising itself.
>
> This raises the issue of the future role of the political process. I am more than convinced that military rule without the total mobilisation and involvement of the people is an aberration and is basically unstable. On the other hand, in the light of our recent history, there is equally convincing evidence to demonstrate that a national leadership acceptable to the country as a whole, will not

> emerge in 1976 through an autonomous election like *deux ex machina*. (Ayida, 1987:19).

Adamolekun quarrels with Ayida's position thus,

> Mr. Ayida advocated the continuation of the 'revolution' (the term was not defined either in the decree or in the address) through a 'National Movement outside which no serious opposition will be allowed.' He favoured this option because of his conviction that 'Military rule without the total mobilization and involvement of the people is an aberration and is basically unstable.' He predicted that: 'The vanguard which will ensure the survival of the military revolution will have to be drawn from...probably the military, the universities and the former ruling class' (Adamolekun, 1988).

Surely, Ayida deserves better treatment than this! Where, in the address, did Ayida advocate the continuation of the 'revolution' "through a National Movement outside which no serious opposition will be allowed"? Certainly, if Adamolekun had read Ayida closely enough he would not have quoted him out of context. Unfortunately, he had simply stitched together pieces from different parts of the address to level his unfounded allegation against Ayida. No, the lecturer had not advocated anything: he had simply presented two points of view and, like the sagacious administrator he is, pointed out the demerits of each option. On the question of the military revolution, he did tell us what he meant by this and gave us the conditions under which the revolution would survive, that is, if it was sustained by a national vanguard of the intelligentsia, as we saw above. Later, he repeated this position in concluding his address.

Indeed, Ayida had categorically stated as follows: "I do not advocate a political role for the Armed Forces as such." The phrase, "as such" needs some expatiation. In this context it means the Armed Forces as they were, as we understood them to be, in the prevailing conditions of the time in Nigeria. Ayida, in fact, did not quite know what role to assign the military, come 1976 and thereafter. He tried hard to cover all the possibilities he could envisage, based on the accumulated experience at the time. On this issue he went further to assert that:

> The truth is that the military administration can only hand over to a national leadership with a viable power base. Such a leadership has to emerge by popular election or otherwise. It cannot hand over power in vacuo. But far more important is the fact that Nigeria no longer has a ceremonial Army. We are building a large modern Army, of well-trained, self-conscious and intelligent young men who will not be content to be relegated to the barracks for keeps (Ayida, 1987:19-20).

One may ask, how did Ayida know the Army would not be content with going back to the barracks for keeps? Did they ask him to speak for them to try and find some role for them in post-1976 Nigeria? Did they confide their plans to him?

Ayida had spoken entirely from the evidence available to him, from what he had seen, and from what he knew. He could, therefore, look into the future and play stargazing. It should not be forgotten in this regard that the great Zik had advocated a 'diarchy', a military-political system of governance for Nigeria using similar reasons argued by Ayida. Zik could get away with it, being a politician who could subject his views to the populace in an election and win or lose, based on the extent to which he could sell his manifesto to the electorate. But Ayida would not be forgiven: he did not have a political constituency, or mandate, nor could he contest elections as a public servant. But it must never be forgotten: he was speaking his mind to his own 'constituency' of economists and they could readily accommodate his views, based on how soundly he presented those views. It would seem unfair, therefore, to judge the address by using other criteria or other contexts.

Ayida had ended his presidential address with the following words:

> It follows, in conclusion, that the vanguard which will ensure the survival of the military revolution will have to be drawn from outside the Civil Service, probably the military, the universities and the former ruling class. Thanks to the petroleum boom and the indigenisation programme, those engaged in the further acquisition of wealth and new businesses under the new dispensation in the private sector, will probably be too pre-occupied to opt to join the new revolutionary leadership likely to emerge by 1976 or some time after (Ayida, 1987:21).

Is this so awfully disagreeable? Most fair-minded people would probably agree that it isn't.

6

The 'super perm-sec' in retirement

Allison Akene Ayida is deep, yet simple and sincere. A man of courage, he submits to his conscience which fastidiously guides his actions. His mind is well nurtured and sagacious, perceptive and resolute. He is explosive when confronted with silly and unfounded gossip. Above all, he is clear in his mind on what to do at any given time: the choices he makes set him apart from the pack. Nigeria may not see his like again. In service and commitment to all that is good and worthy, Ayida had few peers. In retirement, his best qualities - inner strength, charity, immeasurable tolerance and forbearance - shine forth for all to see.

As part of preparations for producing this book, a group of four gentlemen had an appointment with him at 10.00a.m. on Wednesday, 21 May 2003, but did not get to his home till 10.17a.m. They were ushered into his tastefully appointed home with elegant seats that receive kings and lords and comely annexes, and little rooms for quiet conversation and heart-to-heart reflection in splendid friendship. There are other spaces and corners for a quick disposal of affairs brought to his attention by the inquisitive or overbearing herd. Ayida is a man who knows how to receive both friend and foe; to each he gives the best for the occasion - a smile, or a snare. He was upstairs, the group had been told, and would soon come downstairs to receive it. Taking in the delicately magnificent living room, you bask in the warm sensation of beauty and order. You are bathed with the fragrance of tropical frangipanis and the alluring essence of queen-of-the-night. This home is living poetry, a song to lively mirth....

In a few moments, Allison was with his visitors. You should see him - impeccably attired, as must be his wont, in a white lace *kaftan* and *sokoto,* as white as Asaba *akwa ocha.* He received his guests with ease and took them to one of those little cozy rooms with seats snuggling up to each other, four in all, with a chair brought in to make five, a table in the centre. He sat facing the group, with his back to the glass window, the light golden curtains drawn. His hair was lowly cut, no strand out of line and his nails well manicured. He was remarkably elegant, freshly intoning the music of his splendid and inviting home. Yes, here the group was face-to-face with one of the living legends of the modern Nigerian state, in retirement from the commanding heights of public service, at peace with himself and his God. One wonders, shouldn't Nigeria have thrown all of her considerable weight behind this man as her candidate for the office of the Secretary-General of the United Nations when the office was reportedly 'zoned' to Africa? He is, perhaps, the best Secretary the UN never had! It is, oh! so difficult to think of another Nigerian like him in whom virtue and brilliance sit so comfortably well.

Retirement is many things to many people. To some, it is a time to do what you like, or to relax and take things easy, or become a consultant and get paid much more for less work by the same people who had paid you less for more work while in active service. To others, it is a time to write one's memoirs or change jobs and continue working, by putting one's experiences of life to best use in new challenges, or live new dreams and try to do what one had never done before. But, let us listen to

Ayida and take in what he has to say on the subject:

> Some of us are often asked what life is like in retirement. When, during the Murtala/Obasanjo administration, Perm Secs and other senior officers were invited to declare their assets, some of the returns were revealing. There was a Perm Sec who had been building his only house in his village for over seven years and the half-completed bungalow had been financed from his personal savings. The authorities thought the Perm Sec was a joker, but there were many others in a similar predicament. There are many retired Perm Secs and Brigadiers-General and other former senior public officers who, in Nigeria of today, are losing the battle for survival. Some are living in abject poverty because their pension and retirement benefits cannot sustain their families. Unfortunately, the public is frequently misled by the successes or affluence of the few among them.
>
> In the past, the expectations were different. The senior public officer would, before retirement, probably have been allocated a plot of land in Victoria Island or Ikoyi or the GRA in his home state. The spectrum of beneficiaries in the days of Brigadier Johnson as Military Governor of Lagos State, included Perm Secs and top military officers and civil servants and leading university professors and professionals. On retirement, such officers were appointed to the boards of parastatals by successive governments...
>
> Premature retirement sometimes means premature death and misery for those who cannot adjust to the emotional aspects and psychological impact of retirement from public office or positions of influence and power. Suddenly, you wake up one morning, your free official [living] quarters is gone, your chauffeur-driven car gone, your "friends" and "admirers" disappear and you are left with your family and a few trusted friends who had no access

> to you when the "palace-seekers" were around...No more invitations to state banquets. You are likely to be late for your meetings, if any – driving yourself and finding a parking space.
>
> These are the trappings and paraphernalia of power which many a retired officer cannot forgo. Hence, some functionaries cling to public office at all costs. Those of us who found the ceremonial aspect of public office oppressive will find relief in retirement. You suddenly find you have time for your sporting activities, for developing your hobbies, and for social activities although the invitations no longer come in the same large number. You feel nearer to God and find time for religious activities....
>
> My advice to those who are about to retire from public office is that they are being given a chance to start life a second time. This time you have a choice. The quality of your new life should be more important than the material considerations. You may not be a naira-millionaire but you have a million experiences to sustain your new life which you can live in your own way...My hope is that the nation will continue to recognize and accord due respect to those who served in the past and deserve the honour to live and die in decent retirement (Ayida, 1988).

Ayida expressed these thoughts in a 1988 lecture, "Power without Corruption", given to the Bendel State Public Service Forum on the occasion of the 25th anniversary of the State. He would, thus, qualify as one of those for whom retirement, as he puts it, is a time to put one's life experiences to best use in new challenges; a time to live new dreams and do those things one had always wanted to do but could not find the time to do them. There is, however, a rider to all this: one should also have the financial muscle to do what one wants to do. This should not be too difficult if one lives a life in consonance with one's circumstances, and if one appreciates and seeks joy in the grandeur of the ordinary things of everyday living. Let us then find out how Ayida shares his experiences with fellow Nigerians, how he is doing the sort of things he has always wanted to do but could not, and how the pinnacle of his life is simply finding joy in ordinary, everyday living. Yes, Ayida is not just a book, he is a library and we are just about ready to open the front door, gain entry to the first floor, and open the first book. What does he tell us?

Before we seek an answer, let us first deal with a troubling question that has an immediate bearing on retirement and life-after-retirement. Let us ask, why did Ayida retire from the public service so early? Had he had enough? Could he no longer 'perform'? What manner of problems confronted him at this time, and how did he deal with them? Or, in fact, could he have given more of his best in the service of his dear country?

We might step back somewhat and take a cursory look, as it were from a distance, at the account of another public service giant, Chief Jerome Udoji, who had retired in August 1966 from the Eastern Nigerian public service when Colonel Odumegwu Ojukwu was Governor. According to Udoji's published record:

> The last eight months of my twenty years in the Civil Service were under Col. Ojukwu, Military Governor of Eastern Nigeria. It was a trying and painful period...Trouble started right from our first meeting. He was unnecessarily abrupt, aggressive and dictatorial. In vain did I try to put him at ease with the assurance of my loyalty thinking he was behaving under the weight and stress of his new responsibility...I was not aware that I was dealing with an ambitious political animal...He was ill at ease with me and did not waste time to indicate that I was not wanted...
>
> The Ironsi government, in its attempt at unification, [had] ruled that the Estimates of the

> Federal and Regional Governments should be considered in Lagos by a joint meeting of Federal and Regional representatives...After the preparation of the Eastern Region estimates, the Governor, myself and Sam Oti, the Permanent Secretary of the Ministry of Finance, left to represent the Eastern Region at the Lagos meeting...After considering the Northern budget, Ironsi called on Ojukwu to present the Eastern Region budget. Before he did so Ali Akilu, the Secretary to the North Regional Government whispered something to Lieutenant Colonel Hassan Katsina, the Governor of Northern Nigeria. Governor Hassan as a result of the whisper enquired what had happened to the post of Chief Secretary to the East Regional Government.
>
> To my surprise and that of every member [present at the meeting] my post had been deleted from the estimates. Immediately, Ironsi bellowed, looking at Ojukwu, "What has happened to the post...?" I felt so small and humiliated in the presence of my colleagues and compeers...
>
> But that was not the end of my harassment. The following day, three senior policemen led by Superintendent Mike Ibekwe came and took me from the budget meeting to Alagbon Close...I was released but I was so angry that I decided not to continue the budget meeting. Rather, I went to Ironsi and offered to resign since I was not prepared for further humiliation... He offered me the chairmanship of a commission to enquire into the unification of the educational services of the country. I accepted on...condition that I would leave the service at the end of the enquiry... I physically left the service on the 13th of August, 1966 (Udoji, 1999).

There you have it: Ojukwu had cudgelled Udoji into retirement, spilling the blood of spirited service and honour, leaving in its wake a dilapidated soul! But Udoji had ridden the storm with fortitude and had drawn fresh vigour and energy from his inner reserve of strength and courage: "I dusted my wig and gown and set up legal practice in Port-Harcourt - the then 'oil boom city' of Nigeria," he recorded triumphantly.

We can now quietly return to Ayida. He had meant to retire from the public service on three occasions predating his actual retirement on April 1, 1977 when Lt. General Olusegun Obasanjo was the Head of State. The first hint of this is in the 'Introduction' to his book, *Reflections on Nigerian Development,* where he tells us that his 1973 lecture entitled, "The Nigerian Revolution, 1966-76" to the Nigerian Economic Society was meant to be his valedictory 'speech' from the public service. Later, in another 'Introduction' to his book entitled, *The Rise and Fall of Nigeria* he again tells us that during the 1975 retirement exercise, he had twice threatened to resign his post as the Secretary to the Federal Military Government and Head of Service as a matter of principle. But on both occasions, the former Head of State, late General Murtala Muhammed had "saved the situation."

What were the prevailing circumstances of his experience that set into play his final disillusionment with the public service? For an answer, Ayida himself may have given us a clue from his second book cited above in the following words:

> When one occupies a position of power and responsibility, one can no longer afford the luxury of the one mistake to be pardoned because there is no forgiveness at the top. The competition is too intense, the prize too high. The same rule applies in the public and private sectors.
>
> Three turning points come uppermost in my mind and I am not sure which of them is the 'mistake' of my career. Only the course of history will tell. The first is that, with the benefit of hindsight, I may have sacrificed too much to shore up and protect the Public Service as an institution during the 1975

> mass retirement. If we had allowed the floodgates to open, the succeeding leaders, especially the military, would have learnt more about the follies of mass retirement. I threatened to resign my post as the then Secretary of the Federal Military Government and Head of Service twice during the exercise as a matter of principle; on both occasions, the Head of State, late General Murtala Muhammed, saved the situation (Ayida: 1987e).

The words: "there is no forgiveness at the top" ring uncomfortably loud in the ear! It is a penetrating observation that suggests how one occupying a position of power and responsibility should treat matters. In essence, Ayida was quite clear in his mind that he would not be pardoned if he committed any serious error. Perhaps, the greater pain would come from within Ayida's soul: he would not forgive himself for any gross error. Thus, he would be expected to strenuously strive to avoid the temptations and evil that are usually associated with power - arrogance, nepotism, corruption, etc. Which of these ills would we say Ayida was guilty of?

To those who may not quite know how to contend with his fortitude, transparent bearing and incorruptible mien, the man, Ayida, exudes naked arrogance. Similar subjective views had been expressed by some of those who had taken great exceptions to his 1973 *Nigerian Revolution* lecture. That he was clearly aware of the grave consequences of failure at the top meant that Ayida would scrupulously endeavour to do the right thing at all times and that he would rather resign from office than do what he considered improper. Little wonder, then, that many years after he had left the Service, the General Abdulsalami Abubakar-led Military Government awarded him the most distinguished honour a Nigerian civilian can receive, the Grand Commander of the Order of the Niger (GCON).

Meanwhile, President Obasanjo is yet to decorate him with

the award. Although he did cancel many awards made by General Abubakar in the twilight of his administration, the President did not cancel the honour bestowed on Ayida. Asked why he had not yet received the award, Ayida had replied that he did not know. Only under strong pressure by his interviewers did Ayida finally agree to try and find out why he had not been decorated with the award. It is not unlikely, however, that he had not considered it necessary to do anything about it and, perhaps, would rather let sleeping dogs lie.

In response to a related question, Ayida had reflected in the following words:

> The third lecture entitled, "The Federal Civil Service and Nation Building" was my valedictory message to the Service before my imminent exit from the Public Service. Because of the critical comments on the mass retirement of public servants in 1975/76 and related developments, and the fact that the message was meant as a testament to future military leadership at Jaji, the lecture was not released to the general public...I believed that by imploring the young officers at Jaji not to engage in the mass indiscriminate retirement of public officers, they would improve on the mistakes of 1975 when they subsequently came to power. I was mistaken. The same mistakes have been, and are being, repeated. *Wrong people are being removed from office without remedial measures and what is left of the public service is demoralised*. I cannot be and am not against removing corrupt and incompetent public officers from office, *but the way it is done* is bound to lead to grave miscarriage of justice nobody can do anything about... *The approach of the military leadership is that 'it is better for one innocent person to suffer than for ten guilty ones to escape'* (emphasis added).

It would appear that the Nigerian military leadership had not read Voltaire who cautions, "It is better to risk saving a guilty man than to condemn an innocent one." Ayida retired from the Service because he could not continue to serve the military government in a public service that had been humiliated, brought to its knees and rendered effete - all too whimsically by executive fiat and with scant regard for the rules of fair play or decency. A fair-minded, thorough gentleman of admirable mien, the shenanigans and idiosyncrasies of the abrupt and abrasive Head of State under whom he served rubbed him on the wrong side and he could not stomach it. One might ask, How was he able to survive two previous military Heads of State, Generals Gowon and Muhammed? It is not unlikely that Ayida would have offered to retire at some point during the Muhammed stint as Head of State (after all, he had twice threatened to do so), but we shall never know because General Muhammed was cut down not long after the coup that brought him to power. That he served in the Gowon era from 1966 to 1975 probably says something about Ayida's compatibility with the former Head of State.

Given the benefit of the recent exchange of correspondence between Nigeria's Nobel Laureate, Wole Soyinka and President Obasanjo (who was Head of State when Ayida retired in 1977), we might begin to appreciate the difficulties under which Ayida might have laboured during his last days in the Service. As carried in *The Guardian* of Sunday, August 3, 2003 Soyinka had written as follows, in response to the Head of State's earlier letters:

> *Dear OO!*
>
> ...That is how our late mutual friend, Ojetunji Aboyade and I generally evoked your presence in our discussions. OO stood for many things that reflected our reactions towards your latest act or conduct at

> that time – fondness, optimism, indulgence, exasperation, battlement, despair, anger, etc., etc. It also stood for OO as in 007, but minus the scripted finesse, more the Rambo type who shoots first and thinks later. My mind retains that last image of you at this moment: Rambo on the loose, so over-abundantly manifested in your intemperate, irrational and totally unwarranted letter of July 11, 2003. This must rank as the low-water mark of your correspondence career...To insinuate, as you did in your second letter – that of July 14th – that my attacks on your governance and style have become more 'virulent' because you failed to place 'nominees' in your list is unworthy of you. *This is the real abyss of perfidy, a cheap blackmail intended to inhibit my criticisms of you...Listen OO, you simply do not know me! You lack the depth to ever fathom who I am* (emphasis added).

Does the reader still want to know why Ayida retired from the Service under the General Obasanjo-led military government?

We might side-step this question for a moment and quickly consider Ayida's thinking in "The History and Philosophy of an Experiment in African Nation Building", a 1987 Convocation Lecture that he had given on January 27 at the University of Jos, ten years after his retirement. In it, he stoutly stated his belief in the capability of Nigeria to survive as a modern nation-state, despite overwhelming odds. True to the theme and spirit of the lecture, Ayida had asked Nigerian historians and intellectuals two pertinent questions as follows:

> Why do some nations decline and fall while other nations seem to sustain their prosperity? Every Nigerian student of my generation can tell you off the cuff why the sun set on the British Empire and the so-called Commonwealth died. Why then is

> Nigeria following the path to its decline and imminent fall? Having been associated with some of the landmarks in the recent history of Nigeria, we shall be concerned mainly with *the intimate experiences and the lessons of experience* (Ayida, 1987) (emphasis added).

As we ponder the questions, let us attempt to delve into Ayida's mind and see what he has in store for us by first looking at the Nigeria of 1987. Since the retirement of Ayida from the public service in 1977, Nigeria has had, in succession, as Heads of State, by 1987, General Obasanjo, President Shehu Shagari, Major-General Mohammed Buhari, and President Babaginda. At the time of the lecture, President Babaginda had been in office for about two years and the debate on the IMF loan was at its hottest point. But then, Ayida's concern was longer and deeper than his post-retirement period. As he saw it, there had been a period that could truly be described as 'the rise of Nigeria' from about 1954 to 1964. One could throw in a few more years after the civil war and extend 'the rise', this golden age, to, say, 1974, depending on one's perspective. It would appear, Ayida had observed, that the decline of Nigeria from about 1965 onwards could be laid squarely at the door of the military who had shot their way into power in January 1966 and had left a legacy of ruin, vice, greed and subterfuge in their path.

Before scrutinizing Ayida's position further on the questions, we shall examine the thoughts of another illustrious Nigerian at about the same time as Ayida's lecture.

In 1985, Professor Adegoke Olubummo (one of the first two Nigerian professors of mathematics appointed on the same date at the University of Ibadan), gave his Valedictory Lecture entitled, "What Does It All Add Up To?" In the lecture he had good reason to re-visit the past and had lamented thus:

> If I were to be asked the period that I regard as the most glorious in the history of the University of Ibadan to date, I think that I would say the decade 1955 to 1965. Some people will probably push this back by two or three years and say the decade 1953 to 1963 because, as from this last date among other things, the criteria for advancement became somewhat ill-defined and the university began to feel some of the stresses and strains that were later to rack and nearly ruin this country...My concern and my worry is this. Is it possible that there will grow up and indeed that there are already growing up generations of students and lecturers who do not know or care for what is called a liberal education and who do not understand that a university is meant to be a community of scholars, generations of students who leave the university just as they came in, generations of teachers who are indifferent not only to their teaching but also to their students? Are the young men and women in this audience this afternoon going to look back in twenty years' time and regard this period as part of the time we were in some sort of doldrums or are they going to look on these years with the same kind of nostalgia with which I look back on the 1955-65 decade? Does all our work in the Faculty and the University make us and our students better people?
>
> My answer is that it should, but does it? Are the students we present for graduation worthy in character and learning? For that matter, are we their teachers worthy in character and learning? *(Olubummo, 1985)*

Indeed, the present generation of Nigerian lecturers who are still active in teaching and research and who greatly value scholarship and intellectual pursuits will look on the 1980s as a period of comparative academic sophistication in comparison with what obtains at present at the dawn of the 21st century. We can, thus, learn from Olubummo that the University of Ibadan during the period 1953-65 or so, lived true to its purpose - academic excellence, a stringent and faithful adherence to standards and traditions, and a total dedication to knowledge. Here the makings of a university are clearly enunciated. A departure from these ideals would, therefore, not be too difficult to discern. When, however, we deal with nations and societies, the perceived ideals and norms may vary from one group to another, from one individual to another. Even worse, individual or group interests may override those of society and the nation, and then 'things fall apart' and the centre no longer holds. What then is of overarching importance, in Ayida's eyes, in his vision of a Nigeria on the rise?

The period under consideration, 1954-64 and 1970-1974 encompasses one critical and glorious part of Nigeria's colonial history, 1954-60. What was glorious about this period? For a plausible answer, we have reason to seek recourse in Professor Peter Ekeh's inaugural lecture, Colonialism and Social Structure. Professor Ekeh recognizes the supra-individual consequences that flow from colonialism and that transcend the time-space specifications of colonization and reactions to it. We are urged to absorb the totality of colonialism in its own right and search for the social formations and transformations, of epochal dimensions, that have occurred under colonialism and whose life span extends beyond the colonial experience. Of particular importance in this regard is what Ekeh refers to as "emergent social structures in colonialism." Interestingly enough, these structures were neither indigenous nor necessarily imported by the colonialists; they had their existence and logic in the peculiar circumstances of the time although they have some analogues in the West. As an example of these social structures, we need only recognize urbanization, the social formation of ethnic groups and ethnicity in both pre-colonial and colonial Nigeria.

We also need to recognize, as we saw earlier, that the

atavistic concept of tribalism grew out of our colonial experience – a tribalist being a non-tribesman exhibiting anti-social behaviour in a non-tribal setting in such a way as to threaten the new forms of supra-individual and supra-ethnic existence with a reversal to a pre-colonial system of restricted tribal organization. The nation, Nigeria, was born in colonialism by a welding of disparate ethnic and wildly adversarial groups into a modern nation-state. We must, therefore, seek glory in these same structures that have made Nigeria a nation and have sustained it for over 40 years after independence.

We have cause to return to Ekeh, once again, in our analysis of what was right in the period of 'the rise' in Nigerian politics:

> This concerns the development of the moral order in colonialism...The rule in the West is, behaviour can be classified as either moral or immoral. An important distinction of colonialism is that it has bred a duality of moral perspectives. In the colonized world of Africa there are two broad spheres of moral and amoral behaviour. That is, in addition to the broad sphere of moral and immoral behaviour on the one hand, there is another deep area of behaviour that is governed by amorality, in society *(Ekeh, 1980)*.

Admittedly, moral behaviour does operate in the systems Ekeh identifies as "transformed indigenous social structures" and of the "emergent social structures." It is in the conduct of those aspects of social life related to "migrated social structures" – those that were almost literally transported intact from the colonial home post – that the anomalous, amoral behaviour is most extant. To illustrate this, Ekeh relates the experience of a prominent Nigerian politician who had retorted, "politics is not church," when challenged about the 'morality' in his style of politics which had induced the destruction and burning of houses of political opponents outside his own ethnic group, but well within his domain of political control in pre-civil war Nigeria. The politician's reaction was simply his own way of saying, "politics is amoral." Herein lie the ingredients of greatness – a total commitment to the oneness of a nation, Nigeria, and the conduct of its affairs, particularly its politics, in a morally acceptable manner. It must, however, be quickly added that the prevailing conduct of Western countries in world affairs leaves one to conclude that amoral behaviour also rules their behaviour outside their home base, witness the American invasion of Iraq in 2003 and Guatemala much earlier!

What went wrong? Ayida is of considerable help here, as the following excerpt from his *The Rise and Fall of Nigeria* illustrates:

> I feel sad because of the sense of doom around and the shadow of doubt hanging over us. There is too much human misery around. The emmiseration [sic] of the rural poor and the pulverization of urban dwellers demonstrated in the apparent lack of collective will to survive has gone too far... There has been too much preoccupation with economic depression, especially the fall in petroleum production and pricing, which to the historian and philosopher is a blessing in disguise. It is a challenge for us to re-examine the great issues that face us as a nation. If the petro-naira were still flowing, many of us would have thought that the Nigerian nation was endowed with great statesmen and leaders at the helm of affairs (Ayida, 1987).

Poor management, then, he concludes, is the curse of the Nigerian economy. But why is the fall in petroleum pricing a blessing in disguise? His answer is simple and straightforward: "it provides valuable...time for us to pause and think of the basic issues in this Great Society of ours."

We must bear in mind that as Ayida, now in retirement, is exhorting us to "pause and think" of the basic issues in Nigeria, we are being invited to become historians or, at least, philosophers in the Nigerian cause. And what are the issues? Nigerian unity and sound morals in social and political conduct. As in marriage, when things are not going smoothly, couples need to engage in sober reflection of their giddy, romantic days of courtship; the irresistible and compelling attractions that had brought them together; and, finally, their marital vows, "for better, for worse." Such reflection does not, however, engender fortitude, endurance, or understanding, the necessary ingredients of a successful marriage. History may teach bravery, learning, and morals but it does not make us brave, learned or virtuous. It does, however, help to put issues in a clearer perspective, and once they are sufficiently clear, then, with patience and determination, one can move into the realm of philosophy and try to pick one's way through the challenges posed by the issues. It would seem as if Ayida is strenuously trying to inculcate this philosophy in the Nigerian body polity.

Were there great minds in government during Nigeria's decline, the period of its fall, who had devoted much of their energies to Ayida's "basic issues in this Great Society," or did we have only highly placed public servants who seemed content with seeking the 'fall guys', the persons to blame, while the basic issues got worse as they remained largely ignored? Ayida himself was there during the period of the fall, from about 1964 till 1977, including the post-civil war interregnum, 1970 to 1974, that could be included as part of the rise of Nigeria. His public service career has been x-rayed over and over again and we are now familiar with both the ecstasy and the pain he had endured. It need not be repeated here except to state that Ayida's brilliance, clarity of mind and thought had done much to stay the dreadful hand of the military in their ruthless pursuit of power. Are we wrong, then, in concluding that Nigeria had exceptional public servants, such as Ayida, who had given of their very best to ameliorate the suffering of starving and dishevelled Nigerians, and that things would have been much, much worse, without such public officers?

If they were like Ayida, we would be led to answer this question in the affirmative. But Ayida himself lets us into just how powerful public servants could be by their incompetence in his choice of the following memorable words:

> The state apparatus and the military establishment and the bureaucracy are powerful groups in Nigeria, the latter chiefly through inefficiencies and errors of omission. Its power to do evil and deprive the individual of 'life, liberty and the pursuit of happiness', is almost limitless (Ayida, 1988:9).

He gives an example of how things used to be in the early days of his career when, if your car was damaged by a government vehicle, you would receive compensation even when government was not legally bound to do so. In other words, government did what was morally right for its citizens without apportioning right or wrong. Ayida laments the situation during military rule, when, alas, the bureaucracy was so powerful and disorganized that when your vehicle was overrun by a military or police van, you were beaten up or charged to court for resisting the beating! Nobody compensated you for your damaged property. Thus, Ayida rhetorically asks, "How then do we blame the armed robber for not respecting the property rights of other members of society?" Government is to blame, he concludes. No nation can rise and develop beyond the level of its leaders who set the moral tone of society and its ideals. Where government is corrupt and amoral, society is doomed, as Nigeria's recent history clearly illustrates.

But, Ayida is not yet done with what went wrong and how the great Nigerian nation has been plunged into the quagmire of poverty and moral depravity. He saves his harshest and most scathing criticism for the military. One might find this rather surprising as Ayida's finest hour had been recorded in the military regimes he had served with exquisite brilliance and distinction. It was generally assumed that he had wielded vast powers and influence as, perhaps, the jewel amongst the 'super perm-secs'. Would it then not be morally improper for the same man to bite the hand that had fed him?

Let us first get what Ayida said and then analyse his thoughts. In his own words, now is the time for us to pause and think of "the basic issues at stake in this Great Society of ours."

Ayida gives us the following telling assessment, in his *The Rise and Fall of Nigeria*:

> The one mistake of practically all the military administrations in this country is their excessive preoccupation with the economic mismanagement of their predecessors without being able to improve on their performance. Admittedly, *economic disaster* is more often than not, *the product of political incompetence*. It is difficult to appreciate how succeeding military administrations in this country can supply the necessary political skill and social engineering which will result in the good management that can minimize or avoid economic disasters. *The military are neither by inclination nor by training equipped for the job* (Ayida, 1987f: 10) (emphasis added).

This assessment is not inconsistent with his earlier position that the entry of the military into Nigeria's national political consciousness had provided a unique opportunity for a revolution that could not have been anticipated at independence in 1960. Thus, Ayida had stated, among other things, that:

> ...there have been many complex factors at play in Nigeria since the attainment of independence, and

> that since 1966, the method and organization of the Nigerian society has undergone some fundamental changes which if not arrested, could qualify as the beginnings of a national revolution (Ayida, 1987b: 3).

Ayida insists that a historical necessity similar to the Nigerianization of the public service, in preparation for independence, had prompted the promulgation of the *Nigerian Enterprises Promotion Decree*. As he sees it, the programme of indigenizing the Nigerian economy may yet turn out to be one of the most important landmarks of the military regime. He further affirms that there is little doubt that there is an economic revolution in Nigeria, although its character is not certain and its political content and social impetus cannot be easily ascertained because of its style. In Ayida's opinion, the creation of states constitutes the second landmark of the Nigerian Revolution, a fundamental political change introduced by the military that could not have been easily accomplished in the context of the rivalry and rigidities of party politics. As the ever-patriotic, elder statesman in retirement confesses rather sadly:

> What is significant in the Nigerian Revolution lecture is that in 1966, some of us believed that a revolution was in the making. We sincerely believed that the Nigerian society could be changed beyond recognition, for the better. We had faith. We hoped for a bright future. The civil war with all its pains was treated as a tragic and temporary interruption. As late as 1973 when the lecture was delivered, I could still end on a peroration proclaiming, 'I am proud to be a Nigerian.' But over ten years later, I know better and I am not so sure (Ayida,1987e: viii).

"The Rise and Fall of Nigeria" lecture was given in 1987 when President Babaginda was at the helm of affairs. By then Nigeria had seen the latter years of the Murtala/Obasanjo regime played out by the Obasanjo/Yar'Adua era, which handed over power to the administration of President Shehu Shagari, the insipid and vacuous civilian government of 1979-83, only for the Army to shoot their way back into government, yet again, on the eve of 1984 with Major-General Buhari as Head of State. Understandably, Ayida's palpable discontent stems from the dismal failure of all these regimes, political and military. Even when, during the 1991 Gulf War, Nigeria had reportedly earned unprecedented revenue from oil - pejoratively referred to as the 'oil windfall' - Nigeria's economic fortunes had fared no better. Where all the money had gone remains a mystery, the findings of the Okigbo Commission of Enquiry into the matter notwithstanding. Yes, Ayida has good reason to lament the seeming demise of the Nigeria he had hoped would become strong and united, a land of equal opportunity for all, and where justice and fair play would reign supreme.

It would appear that what pains Ayida the most is this: Nigeria as a nation seems to be falling apart, right before his federally-adjusted eyes. He cannot bear the torment, and screams for anyone who cares to hear in the following excerpt from "The Rise and Fall of Nigeria" lecture:

> By way of illustration only, I should like to point out that when the heroes of the Nigerian civil war, who upheld the federal cause in those critical days of our national history, turn around to advocate confederation and the parting of ways as the final solution for Nigeria, we should all begin to search our hearts. Something has gone wrong. Take the case of Abuja, the federal capital. I know that Abuja was conceived by the Murtala Muhammed/Obasanjo

> administration as the new soul of the nation where all Nigerians will expect and receive equal and just treatment at all levels...It was to be a no man's land. [However,] The project is being implemented in a manner such that it may lose its status as the symbol of national unity...Unless there is a change of heart the fiat of the Federal Government will no longer be recognizable in some parts of the country, thereby resulting in further alienation of the Federal Government from some sections of the citizenry (Ayida, 1987f: 14).

This was 1987 and the June 12, 1993 presidential election had not yet happened. Bashorun Moshood Abiola, the *Are Onakakanfo* of Yorubaland, the widely acclaimed winner of that election that many regarded as the freest and fairest general election ever held in Nigeria, was still alive and full of vigour and vitality. The despotic and barbaric butcher of Abuja, who later became Head of State, was the Minister of Defence in Babangida's military government. 'Maradona' (as General Babangida is popularly called) was still playing his game of political cards.

Babangida evidently had a good hand and seemed to be winning as most Nigerians thought he was genuine and sincerely wanted to hand over power to an elected government. He must have been familiar with game theory and politics, as in Billy Dudley's masterpiece, *Instability and Political Power*. But he may have forgotten that every game has rules and that one plays a game by its rules, or it is no longer the game being played. One cannot, for example, play soccer with the rules of American football: in soccer you do not handle the ball, only the goalkeeper may do so. Either way, 'Maradona' appeared to have been a poor student of Nigerian politics and lost out in the end. And the butcher came wielding his sword. Fortunately for Nigeria, Almighty God in his infinite mercy sheathed the butcher's sword and put him to eternal sleep, there to dream dreams of vanquished injustice. Nigerians could thereafter sleep in relative peace.

The year 1987 was also before 1999 when that hard-working, hard-driving, but inexcusably vindictive farmer from Otta returned to State House, Abuja to dance one more time to the tunes of power and influence. If Ayida's dream of requited justice for Nigeria is not being fulfilled, we know whom to hold responsible; many of them are still with us....

Ayida has a truly large heart. His civil service career was not just a job, it was life itself, his life. If he exercised power, it was always to do good, to serve the nation, not merely to serve the Government of the day. In his life, the interests of the nation always came first.

The bright student that he is, Ayida learned very early in his career that a civil servant's career might critically depend on what was done with, and to, the person's letter to an arm of government, say, a ministry. He learned that a letter was not just a piece of paper, it had a life all its own and could, indeed, be a matter of life and death for the civil servant. The way a letter is disposed of is, therefore, a very important instrument in the conduct of government business. When a file is marked, "PA", that is, "put away", it means the matter is closed and all issues raised in the correspondence assumed to have been satisfactorily dealt with. That is, the issues are 'dead' and nothing further can be done to resurrect them. For Ayida, the nation is like a file, alive and well, worthy of fair treatment, eagerly awaiting a full resolution of all outstanding matters. For this reason, he goes to great lengths in search of appropriate answers to national problems, using all the force of good moral conduct and sound reasoning at his disposal. Nothing is really ever put away; everything is "kept in view."

In the public eye, the civil service is the life of the nation, the bureaucracy responsible for getting things done. The performance of government, military or civilian is, invariably, judged by the performance of the civil service. The idea was presented to Ayida, in retirement, some time in June 2003, that civil servants could be more dynamic, more proactive, and more expressive of their ideas so that their ingenuity may shine forth; that public officers need not be confined to just giving advice to government: they should also speak up on issues affecting the nation. Ayida would have none of this and underlines his position as follows:

> The civil servant is a record keeper. The ruling of the [Nigerian] Supreme Court that a civil servant has the right to be elected is a wrong decision, unless the [existing] rules are changed, and the government must put it aside... These records I will preserve. I want to hand over to another record keeper and to nobody else. If the civil service is to be a source of political power, I don't know how you manage the transition.

In response to the suggestion that a civil servant should speak up and make his own views known, Ayida tells the following story:

> A Permanent Secretary (PS) went to address a meeting and it was reported. The same Permanent Secretary gave the same material to his minister for another meeting. When he got it and discovered that it had already been reported, he put it to the Head of State that his PS was not serving him, that he should leave. The man was sacked.

The PS in question was the former Governor of former Bendel State, J.F.K. Oyegun.

It is somewhat ironic and, indeed, instructive that Oyegun had served on a committee of eight permanent secretaries (two of whom later went into politics, Oyegun himself and Dr.

Emeka Ezeife, who was elected Governor of Anambra State in 1991) that had submitted a report to The Political Bureau. In the report, the group addressed the challenge of leadership in Nigeria, of appropriate development strategies and stability, the divisive combination of 'tribalism, regionalism and statism,' the tripodal nature of power politics in Nigeria, the country's inability to organize and conduct free and fair elections, and the frequent changes between military and civilian forms of government. Evidently, Politics and the Civil Service, like fire and dynamite, do not mix.

Oyeleye Oyediran, writing on The Political Bureau, further illuminates these fundamental issues in the following words:

> Setting up a Political Bureau to do exactly what this powerful and influential group [of permanent secretaries] had addressed in their report was an affront to the bureaucracy. What was worse, and was seen as a way of rubbing it in, was that no civil servant was allowed to serve on the Bureau, not even as secretary. As the first three-month report of the activities of the Bureau pointed out, 'stringent bureaucratic procedures at the Cabinet Office have been making it difficult to draw even the funds available for quick execution of many urgent matters of the Bureau.' After about six months, the bureaucracy reluctantly accepted that the Bureau had come to stay and would not be deterred from completing its task simply because the federal bureaucratic elite was unhappy [about it] (Oyediran, 1997:67).

The "powerful and influential group" that had submitted position papers to The Political Bureau comprised the committee of eight federal permanent secretaries referred to above and the National Institute of Policy and Strategic Studies. Their papers had attempted to "define and chart the pathways to democratic consolidation in Nigeria." One might, therefore, wonder why the Cabinet Office had posed such a severe obstacle to the functions of the Bureau when, in fact, a committee comprising the Cabinet Office's fellow permanent secretaries had made contributions to the success of the Bureau. The whole truth may never be known, but one can guess at it by saying that the Nigerian Civil Service as an organized body – a body organized by what Ayida calls "record keepers who want to hand over to other record keepers like themselves" – wanted to be in control and dictate how events were to flow. They wanted to be in charge and to be seen to be in charge. But how did they want to be in charge?

We have reason to examine Adamolekun's article, "Transforming the Civil Service" found in *Transition Without End* for some illumination on the subject. According to Adamolekun,

> Until the advent of military rule in January 1966, the inherited British tradition of higher civil servants giving 'non-partisan' and 'impartial' advice to their political masters while accepting to implement settled policies faithfully was generally accepted as the norm. The complementary norm of 'anonymity' also required that civil servants were not to be named for praise or blame. The civil war period and the immediate post-war years witnessed an abandonment of these norms. My favourite illustration of this point is Mr. Allison Ayida's famous speech, 'The Nigerian Revolution, 1966-1976'. In this speech, Mr. Ayida who was a permanent secretary at the federal level at the time, took sides on controversial political issues such as the creation of more states and the role of the military in politics while asserting the need to preserve the anonymity ana non-partisanship of the civil service. According to General Obasanjo, the civil service in 1975 'was reasonably unchecked and

> felt uncheckable, entrenched, omnipotent, secure and a law unto themselves. What they ordained and what they wished would happen, in most cases, no matter the pronouncement or desire of government.' There is a real sense in which the progressive politicization that began with the 'purge' of 1975 was intended as a check on civil service power (Adamolekun, 1997).

Ayida had repeatedly asked this question during interviews as part of data collection for this book: How can the best brains in the Nigerian civil service better put their intellect at the service of the nation?' Ayida still insists on the traditional role of the civil servant as a record keeper and had narrated the following incident to illustrate the difficulty of a civil servant who wants to make his views known:

> I went to Calabar for a talk on government participation in banking. It was a speech we prepared for [Chief Obafemi] Awolowo. But Awolowo could not go [and] I had no Commissioner. I delivered the speech. They liked it. Two weeks later, they were debating the speech. That's how we took 40% control share in the three major banks which controlled 70% of the deposit system. I was praised but I could well have been hanged. It is up to an individual. It is up to the system. For a government that is groping for solutions, it does not matter from whom or where the solution comes. But a government trying to hide something will frown at anybody trying to expose it. *It is walking a tight rope.*

When it was put to him that the civil servant can still somehow get the truth out through a third party, Ayida responded, dejection and sorrow written all over his face: "How many Nigerians want to know the truth?" No more questions were put to him on this subject; for the final answer, the views of the Nigerian people would have to be ascertained.

Ayida in retirement continues working steadfastly in the cause of the nation. In his 1988 National Day Lecture, entitled: "Self-Sufficiency: The Path to a Virile Nationhood," Ayida observes wryly, "Self-sufficiency is an attitude of mind. Until there is a radical change of attitude on the part of the government and the governed, this nation cannot attain self-sufficiency." One could argue that Ayida was not telling us anything we did not already know or, if we chose a no-holds-barred criticism of his observation, we would say Ayida was being facetious. But we know he was, indeed, serious and sincere, and that the observation is worthy of our serious consideration even today. He develops his theme by quoting from the notes for a talk he had given in 1990 at the Lagos Island Club, as follows:

> In my perception of Nigeria in the 21st century, I have visions of a great nation. It is the reality of the African situation. We, however, need a leader of vision to get us to the promised land, because the question that worries some of us today is whether Nigeria can survive the crisis of confidence, if not one of national identity, arising from the recurring crisis of management and leadership by example.
>
> If Nigerians are to survive SAP [Structural Adjustment Programme] and whatever may be coined as a shibboleth in its place, the major issues to be resolved as part of the agenda for the 21st century include the following:
>
> i. One nation, one common citizenship, no first and second class citizens in any part of the Federation (a Nigerian should enjoy all the rights of common citizenship wherever he may go, the right to the land, and property; equal access to education and health services for his children on payment of taxes);

ii. Justice and fair play for all citizens is a *sine qua non* for the survival of the nation. The constitutional provision for reflecting the federal character in all public appointments should be given a new and wider interpretation. It is not enough to appoint one or two Ministers and Permanent Secretaries/Directors-General and Directors from each state. For Nigeria to come of age and survive into the 21st century, the economic and strategic ministries and parastatals should not be seen to be reserved for functionaries from certain parts of the country. 'All ministries are equal but some are more equal than others.

iii. With historical experience as a guide, it is difficult to perceive Nigeria operating a two-party system by the year 2000. The Nigerian political operators abhor the party in opposition. The system of party political structure is critical to the emergence of a national leader with vision and a sense of mission, to consolidate the nation-building effort...there has to be a minimum of three parties including the two officially sponsored parties. Without a properly organized party with credible ideological commitment, there can be no effective social mobilization which will capture the imagination and enthusiastic loyalty of the people.

iv. The professional and middle class should not be squeezed to death since they provide the vehicle for transmitting technology and modern management in public and private enterprises...The present level of graduate and general unemployment cannot be sustained in the long run when we are all dead. There must be an answer before the turn of the century. The increasing polarization between the 'haves' and the 'have-nots' will further weaken the fabric of society and the ability to maintain law and order.

v. ...It is difficult to imagine how the urban poor survives in our cities today. The survival of the rural poor has become a miracle. An agrarian revolution can only succeed through changes in technology and farming techniques...We have the manpower and the means to succeed. What is lacking is the will, the appropriate educational system and the absence of leadership by example at all levels.

Ayida is extremely dissatisfied with the way government is run today and illustrates his point by analyzing how the government budget has, progressively, ceased to be the powerful instrument of government policy it is meant to be. His words were pungent and urgent when interviewed on the subject:

> The essence of government is encompassed in the budget which guides what everybody does. But it is different now. It was bastardized during the military era. Awolowo took over. He prepared a statement in which he brought out full employment, free education, etc. When he was to read it, it was then the Government decided that the Head of State was the only one [entitled] to read the budget. That was a complete departure from normal practice. They wrote a new speech for the Head of State. What the Minister had to say can come in as comments on the budget [it was decided]. The budget became a different instrument. It was not guiding anybody. Now (today, in 2003) there is no budget. The Government doesn't know what the budget is. The Minister goes to the House and reads a statement. You can't make a story out of it. Now we have a market economy which says Government action is just part of a whole. That "whole" should be determined by the market [they say]; nobody protects it; nobody guides it ... nobody is in charge; nobody is trying to achieve anything. We hope in his

> second term the President will see the folly [of this *laissez-faire* approach] and return to a planned economy.

Ayida is not a very happy man in retirement. He suffers because the Nigerian revolution on which he had pinned so much hope and which he thought would truly transform Nigeria has not materialized. If at all it did, it had been in fits and starts, with no real, tangible benefits to the people. The inescapable conclusion from his post-retirement lectures and contributions to public discourse is that Ayida is an unhappy man. Being sophisticated and cerebral, he has relied on his intellect and conscience to see him through his onerous tasks in the civil service. He must have believed that all his efforts and those of his fellow compatriots in the higher civil service would not come to naught. But Ayida had apparently not fully reckoned with the whimsical and self-destructive character of military rule and, as he himself admits, each successive military government has been worse than the one preceding it; things just kept going from bad to worse, plunging Nigeria into abysmal darkness and despair.

In a revisit of his 1973 Nigerian Revolution lecture that had evoked such controversy, Ayida reminisces, in 2003, as follows:

> [A] re-consideration of the *Nigerian Revolution 1966–76* [perspective] is a Herculean task. With the benefit of hindsight, it is an uphill task. It can be accomplished. With my head bowed and subdued, I can say with little hesitation that the Nigerian Revolution never took place. Alternatively, it did take place in the wrong direction.

Does one, then, join all of those who had asked for Ayida's neck when he gave the lecture and, with the benefit of hindsight, conclude that Ayida had gone too far, had been too optimistic of the performance and revolutionary ideals of the Military Government of his day, and had not fully understood the military devil he was dealing with?

One has the feeling that Ayida had a lot of faith in Gowon, especially after the latter had displayed remarkable forthrightness and candour in prosecuting the civil war and post-civil war reconstruction efforts. Could he have foreseen the mass retrenchment of civil servants so ruthlessly pursued by General Murtala? Surely, such a gross travesty of justice could never pass for a people's revolution? Or, could Ayida have anticipated the likes of Buhari, Babangida and Abacha as Heads of State? Could any of these have put in place what, even with the longest stretch of the imagination, could have been construed as a 'revolution'? Of course, with the benefit of hindsight, as he himself concedes, these questions can now all be answered in the negative. And, perhaps, that is why Ayida concludes that the revolution may have been in the wrong direction. This point need not be flogged any longer; Ayida deserves to be allowed to enjoy his peace in retirement after he had so courageously made his point at a public lecture whose audience comprised essentially academic economists.

In a nation awash with miracle-seeking people and a surfeit of prophets who find ready ears in a largely gullible populace, there are always many who claim that their proclamations come from a vision of the supreme, all-knowing God, and that they are but mere transmitters of His voice. Ayida is not one of this tribe. He has always based his conclusions on the persuading, non-contradictory evidence of his own personal experience in private and public life and, above all, on history and philosophy. If we take the trouble to consider the full ramifications of his evaluation of our nation state in 1988, we should honestly ask the question: Have we fulfilled the promise of a virile, vibrant nation or, as Ayida fears, we are still frittering away our opportunities to attain greatness?

It would be difficult to do justice to this question without writing the history of modern Nigeria, a task that is clearly beyond the objective of this book. Nonetheless, some comment would still be in order. By all honest accounts, Nigeria is in dire straits. We do not yet have a system of sound political parties. Most of our so-called politicians appear to be little more than a conglomeration of money-grabbing, money-flouting opportunists, rather than policy- and ideas-driven compatriots. The people do not know what the parties stand for or what distinguishes one party from another. It seems all too easy for a politician to simply cross from one party to another within forty-eight hours of being elected and get elected on the platform of the new party. It seems to be politics of anything goes!

One of the continuing pains and disappointments of Nigeria is that its citizens do not yet have a national identity, such as is advocated by Ayida, that is, the feeling of being at home wherever they are in the country and enjoying the same rights and privileges as the 'sons-of-the-soil.' Not only are Nigerians still being segregated on the basis of ethnicity, invidious religious divides have also recently assumed deadly proportions. Religious riots cause mayhem and the death of innocent people as the cry for a national conference remains strong and unabating. All of this does not make Allison Ayida a happy man in retirement.

Ayida knows from what he has seen and continues to see of Nigeria, that it is a nation still in the making. As he quietly contemplates the sad and persistent pestilence in the Delta between the major ethnic groups, the Urhobo, the Ijaw, and the Itsekiri, trying every way he can to help find lasting solutions to the seemingly intractable problems of the area, he must continue to wonder, despite his extraordinary experience and negotiating skills in public service and in retirement, *Why are Nigerians not interested in the truth*?

Part II

Perspectives on development

7

Resource utilization and management

> God has invested so much in this nation. Nigeria is one of the most endowed nations on the face of the earth. Other countries can only envy the sort of resources God has deposited within our shores. Yet, we have not yielded the commensurate fruit. We have not shown gratitude and loyalty to God. Rather we have squandered our resources and opportunities (*ThisDay*, May 5, 2002).

Introduction

Economic development deals essentially with the transformation of resources into goods and services, over space and time. Consequently, resources are central to achieving sustainable development. Resources, which can be broadly classified into human, material, physical and financial, need to be mobilized and utilized for development to take place. However, the availability of resources does not automatically guarantee development. The ways and manner in which the resources are utilized and managed are of critical importance for meaningful development to occur. Additionally, the sustenance of the development process requires the efficient management of the mobilized resources. In fact, the most critical aspect of development management is how resources are utilized. As Kayode (2003:v) puts it, "...economic development is more about the uses to which resources are put than the mere availability of resources." Making the best use of available resources is the major driving force of progress and economic transformation.

Differences in the level of development between the developed and less developed countries have been logically and empirically linked to differences in the availability and, perhaps more importantly, the utilization of resources. Less developed countries are often characterized by unutilized or underutilized natural resources, low levels of human resources development, and low levels of capital accumulation. Such factors as the level of technology, existing institutional arrangements, socio-cultural patterns and policy affect the ability to mobilize resources and the efficiency with which resources are utilized. Consequently, increased emphasis is being laid on the role of these factors in explaining development outcomes. The emphasis on resource mobilization, utilization and management as opposed to resource availability *per se* is not unjustified, given the fact that several underdeveloped countries do possess large amounts of natural resources and labour. The major challenge of economic development in such countries is, thus, how to mobilize and allocate resources for growth and sustainable development.

The Nigerian situation provides a good illustration of the importance of resource mobilization, utilization and management in explaining development outcomes. Its low level of development occurs in the midst of an abundance of natural resources and a large population, earning it the unenviable description of a country experiencing "poverty in the midst of plenty." Despite Nigeria's wide array of natural resources, including various mineral ores and metals, however, crude oil remains its dominant source of income, with other mineral resources remaining largely untapped. Nigeria's over-dependence on oil has adversely affected the development of its other natural resources, including land. Its agricultural sector, which had been the mainstay of the economy, has suffered neglect as a result of the discovery and commercial exploitation of crude oil. The human resources situation is hardly any better. Massive unemployment and low levels of productivity characterize the Nigerian labour force. The economy is also characterized by low levels of capital accumulation. Although the 'oil boom' period witnessed massive government investment in physical infrastructure and social services, the subsequent reversal of economic fortunes, coupled with bad planning and mismanagement, soon resulted in Nigeria's inability to maintain neither the infrastructure nor the quality of social services provided.

An important tool of resource mobilization in Nigeria has been the production and implementation of *National Development Plans* since 1962, an activity in which Allison Ayida has made remarkable contributions. Ayida's doggedness in the resolve to bridge the development gap, through emphatic use of local rather than external resources, remains as solid as ever. To him, only resources mobilized from within can drive national value-added with no strings attached. Ayida maintains that a major problem of resource mobilization in Nigeria emanates from its utilization. In this respect, he concludes that, "the treatment and management of the enormous foreign exchange earnings from oil exports [is] one of the most critical and sensitive areas..." (Ayida, 1987:100).

When the existing resources are not judiciously utilized, it would be quite difficult to mobilize additional ones, Ayida contends. The central message from his position is that meaningful resources cannot be mobilized where transparency and accountability are pushed to the background. In Ayida's view, it is not only the financial resources that are badly mobilized and utilized in Nigeria, the human aspects are equally wrongly mobilized. For example, he argues that the way the "federal character" and "quota" systems are being used has promoted the mobilization of mediocres for the management of the national wealth; has encouraged the inefficient deployment and inequitable treatment of officers and citizens; and has hindered the effective mobilization and utilization of resources in the country. To him, the quality of human resources determines the magnitude and quality of other resources within society. The decadence in the country's human resources, as reflected in the public service and the educational system, has a significant bearing on the quality and effectiveness of other resources, Ayida observes. In his public lecture titled, "Before Tomorrow Comes," Ayida argues that poor management of the country's resources has been a major factor in her level of political instability. In his words, "...lack of competent management and rational allocation of our resources have often been the *raison d'être* for military intervention in the political process." (Ayida, 1990:5)

A consensus seems to have emerged that the Nigeria's problem is not basically that of lack of resources, but that of mis-management. This can be inferred from the simple fact that the country has had so little to show for the vast amount of oil wealth accruing to it over many years. There is, thus, an urgent need to ensure the effective and efficient mobilization, utilization and management of resources in the Nigerian economy to realize the objective of economic development. This concern constitutes the central focus of this chapter.

Resource management

Resource mobilization can be defined as a process of, or a series of activities geared towards generating, accumulating and directing resources in the right form and in sufficient quantity for optimal utilization. It is a process of drawing or steering resources to socially appropriate investments. It connotes the generation, accumulation and organization of productive factors for the purpose of satisfying human wants. Resource utilization, on the other hand, refers to the use, application or employment of resources in productive activities. From the perspective of economic development, the critical issue in resource utilization is the efficiency of resource use. Under-utilization and non-utilization of resources constitute some of the variants of sub-optimal use of resources. Under-utilization of resources occurs when an employed resource produces below its potential. Non-utilization of resources refers to the existence of idle or unemployed resources. The goal of resource management is the minimization of resource under-utilization and non-utilization.

Resource management encompasses both the mobilization and utilization of resources and involves a process of decision-making in which resources are allocated over space and time according to the needs, aspirations and desires of humankind within the framework of their technological inventiveness, as well as their political, social, legal, and administrative institutions. It is about exerting some measure of control on the amount, quality, timing, availability and general direction of resource development. Within the context of economic development, resource management seeks to ensure an efficient, effective and sustainable use of resources to satisfy human needs.

Types and dimensions of resources

Various classifications of developmental resources abound in the literature. Those commonly referred to are: natural or physical, human, material, and financial resources. Natural

Wedding photo with cousins, Mr & Mrs Frank Ogbemi

Graduation Day for his two sisters, Jolomi and Esimi, at the University of Ibadan, 1986

The Ayidas' wedding in London 27th September 1957

Lagos Lawn Tennis Club, 1970

Chairman, UN ECA Conference Press Conference in Lagos February 1967

Alhaji Shehu Shagari, Federal Minister of Finance and Mr Celestine Okobi, the Managing Director, Nigerian Bank for Commerce and Industry – 1973

Bendel State Civil Service Lecturer, 29th July 1988

With Andre Kamal, Managing Director, Dumez Nigeria Ltd

Berger Paints Nigeria Plc AGM 1981

The Review Panel on the Civil Service Reforms (10th Oct. 994 30th April 1997). From LR: (1) Alh Shehu G. Omar (2) Alh Abubakar Umar, OON (3) Alh A. Liman Ciroma, CFR (4) Mr Allison A. Ayida (Chairman) (5) Alh Ibrahim M. Damcida (6) Chief Innocent D. Nwoga, MNI (7) Chief Augustus Adebayo, OFR (8) Mr Paul N. Ibeku, MNI

With Ambassador Walter Carrington and Chief Anthony Enahoro at the Anniversary Lecture on late Chief Rewane, October Club

Dr D. Desalu, Chief A. Guobadia, Mr Seyin Ayida (Managing Director), Chief J. I. Obi and *Mr W. Oranika (Directors), Capital Bank International Ltd in Recess Birthday Break*

CBCLN Board meeting in London 8th July, 1995. From LR: Alh B. Ismaila (Director), Miss Adu (Company Secretary), Chief A. Guobadia (Director), Mr. G. Dufour (Director), Chief M. Okoya-Thomas (Director), Alh A. Joda (Director), Mr M. Frealle (Director), Mr R. Cessac (Managing Director),
Mr A. Ayida (Chairman), Mr B. Normard (Director), Chief P. Balogun (Director), Mr D. Choquart (Director), Mr D. Bordier (Credit Lyonnais Paris), Mr M. O. Fashola (Deputy Managing Director)

Launching of the book on Professor Aboyade, sitting next to Professor Wole Soyinka

Family cruise to Miami in August 1997

With some grand-children at home August 2001

Our Saviour's Church Fund Raising Committee-2000

With Mrs Ayida & Chief Michael Omolayole at the Odutola Family Remembrance, Ijebu-Ode, 2000

Family cruise–Miami–August 1997

With granddaughter, Miss Efena Otobo, after a Church service at Our Saviour's Church

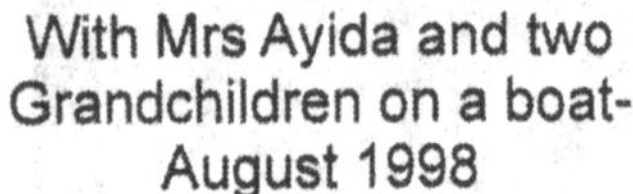

With Mrs Ayida and two Grandchildren on a boat- August 1998

With ten grandchildren on Christmas holidays in 2002

resources refer to non-human productive factors that are given by nature, or exist naturally. These can be further sub-divided into renewable (non-exhaustive) resources, such as timber, wildlife and fisheries, and non-renewable (exhaustive) resources, such as mineral resources. Human resources refer to a nation's population. Human resource productivity depends on the stock of knowledge and skills (human capital) possessed and applied by human beings in the productive process. By implication, knowledge possessed but not applied is not a productive resource.

Material resources are man-made inputs in the production process. They include machinery, equipment and infrastructure facilities. These resources are accumulated over time and are also subject to depreciation. Financial resources refer to funds that are available for investment. They relate to the monies mobilized or generated in the economy. A nation's financial resources comprise, among others, government revenue and investment in securities, stocks, etc, financial savings in the hands of financial institutions (both formal and informal), as well as loans made to other countries. Financial resources can be generated internally or externally. The former are referred to as domestic resources while the latter are foreign resources and could comprise loans and grants made to other countries, as well as private capital inflows and outflows.

Although all the forms of resource mentioned above are important in any development process, more emphasis is often placed on material resource, i.e., capital accumulation. This is because sustained increases in output often require capital accumulation. Even technological progress is usually embodied in new capital goods. This fact notwithstanding, capital accumulation cannot take place unless financial resources, or capital funds, are made available to finance it. Such funds may either be generated internally or externally. In most cases, however, the level of savings in developing countries usually falls short of what is required to engender the required growth rates. This low level of savings in turn arises from low levels of income. A vicious circle of the elements of under-development is thus perpetuated which may necessitate government action to induce involuntary savings through taxation, compulsory lending to government or credit expansion.

The ability of governments to generate additional savings through these means in most developing countries, especially in sub-Saharan Africa, is limited. The constraints arise from a variety of factors, such as low levels of per capita income, a low tax base, weak institutions, worsening terms of trade and the destabilizing effects of inflation. Consequently, such countries often have to complement domestically generated resources with external resources. External financing may be in the form of foreign aid from government to government, cross-border sovereign lending by commercial banks, private foreign investment (direct and portfolio investments), loans from the World Bank group, and access to the country's drawing rights in the International Monetary Fund (IMF).

External resources perform two main roles. In addition to filling the resource gap, they help developing countries to bridge the foreign exchange gap that often arises in the course of financing their development plans. The use of external financial resources in developing countries, however, raises several issues of concern. First, there is the difficulty associated with obtaining such resources. The experience of several countries in sub-Saharan Africa is replete with examples of inability or failure to obtain required external financing. This has often led to failures of plan implementation and other macroeconomic problems. Second, reliance on external financing usually carries a cost of servicing obligations that have to be met in foreign exchange. In several African countries, the worsening terms of trade, poor export performance, and continued dependence on imported capital (and sometimes consumer goods as well) have increased such reliance and culminated in a debt crisis. The poor growth prospects in such countries make it difficult to attract non-debt forms of external financing, such as foreign direct investment and portfolio investment, and these countries often have to resort to more borrowing, effectively putting them into a debt trap.

Significance of resources in the development process

Over the years, there has been changing emphasis in development thinking on the relative importance and relevance of the different categories of resource in the development process. Based on various growth models, development thinking from the 1950s to the 1970s emphasized capital accumulation. Several of these models in their practical application also suggested an important role for government and foreign capital. This was because developing countries were seen as being caught in a low-level equilibrium trap which tended to perpetuate a vicious circle of poverty. Thus, the countries remained poor because they were poor and were unable to generate the required level of savings that would set them on a path of sustained growth. Given a weak domestic private sector, the panacea for growth in such countries has often meant deliberate government intervention through massive doses of public investment and external financing. This approach to the development process provided the theoretical underpinnings for the massive public sector investments undertaken in Nigeria in the 1970s, which were financed from oil revenue as well as external borrowing. While the Nigerian economy and the economies of several other African countries that followed the same strategy grew substantially during this decade, growth did not translate into development.

The emphasis on physical capital accumulation has given way to the concept of investment in human capital. Investments in physical capital, if they are not to be rapidly subjected to diminishing returns, need to be complemented by improvements in the quality of the labour force, through education and skills and knowledge acquisition. The practical application of this approach in developing countries also involves government intervention, through the provision of basic education and human capacity building.

The role of natural resources in the development process has also been the subject of some debate. Although the possession of natural resources has not been emphasized as the key to development, development economics has long ascribed an important role to natural resources in the development process. The importance of natural resources derives from the fact that they provide food and raw materials for industry and foreign exchange through exports. Natural resources are thus viewed as being crucial, particularly in the early stages of development when a society may not yet possess the skills and technology to counteract basic resource deficiencies. Other things being equal, a resource-rich country may be expected to develop more rapidly than a relatively resource-poor one. The actual experience of several resource-rich developing countries has, however, called into question the validity of such an assumption.

The economic performance of several natural resource-rich developing countries has been worse than that of their relatively resource-poor counterparts. This observation has provided the basis for the "resource-curse thesis" in relation to mineral resources. Evidence from such countries experiencing a poor growth outlook, irrespective of their rich resource base, reflects a number of features. First, mineral production, unlike most primary product exports, is strongly capital- intensive and employs a small fraction of a country's workforce, with large inputs of capital from foreign sources. It typically displays marked enclave tendencies and little linkages with the rest of the economy. Second, mineral-rich countries display low revenue retention, since a large fraction of export earnings flows to service foreign capital investment. In such a situation, fiscal leakage (i.e., low taxation) dominates the mining sector's contribution to the economy. Third, the existence of substantial rents, when captured by the government through taxation, can be destabilizing to the economy. The imprudent domestic absorption of mining sector rents may render manufacturing and agriculture internationally uncompetitive. This occurs through the 'Dutch-disease' syndrome as the exchange rate appreciates as a result of the rapid inflow of mineral rents. The competitive activity lost during the boom period of the economy may not easily be restored during down swings.

The Nigerian experience has closely followed this pattern. The oil wealth which accrued to the nation was not used to positively address the problems of the country. Unlike Indonesia, Nigeria neither emerged from the oil windfall era with strengthened agricultural and manufacturing sectors, nor with potentials for generating appreciable non-oil exports and employment. Its tradable sector weakened as overvalued exchange rates encouraged importation rather than local production. Consequently, the economy was worse off after the oil boom than before. This clearly shows that it is the management and utilization of national resources that matters for a nation's development experience. Nevertheless, it is quite possible that natural resource abundance may induce specialization in primary production, as opposed to manufacturing/industrial production that generally promotes better scale economies and promotes technological inventiveness. Under such conditions, long-run growth may be higher in natural resource-poor countries than in the resource-rich ones.

More recently, attention has shifted in development discourse to issues of non-renewable resource management. Non-renewable resources constitute a stock of natural capital, many of which are crucial for life sustenance. Long-run growth and welfare depend on the preservation of these crucial resources. One of the central issues that arise in this regard is that of pricing of natural resources. Although increased attention has been devoted to these issues in Nigeria, the management of both natural and environmental resources remains weak. Consequently, environmental problems - oil spillage, deforestation and soil erosion, desertification, water pollution, urban industrial pollution, and gas flaring - remain serious issues of concern.

Framework for resource mobilization, utilization and management

The effectiveness or efficiency with which a society's resources are mobilized, utilized and managed depends on the prevailing economic, socio-political and legal arrangements, as well as the level of skills, knowledge and ideas governing the 'what's' and 'how's' of its production activities. The overriding framework for mobilizing and utilizing Nigeria's resources was, for a long time, a series of national development plans. Indeed, prior to the resurgence of the neo-classical approach to development management in the 1980s, the designs of national development plans provided a good basis for foreign financial assistance. The quest for mobilizing foreign resources for the country's development informed the drawing up of the Welfare Development Plan in 1946, the medium-fixed development plans between 1962 and 1985, and the three-year rolling plans since 1990. The development of The *Vision 2010* document has also been premised on the need to mobilize and utilize resources for growth and development. Another instrument for mobilizing and managing resources is the annual budget which provides the basis for harnessing resources for managing development. Resources cannot be effectively mobilized, utilized and managed without an adequate legal, institutional and macro-economic framework.

The provision of an appropriate legal framework for resource mobilization, utilization and management in Nigeria, however, continues to remain a challenge. Some of the challenges facing the country in this regard include poor enforceability of laws, the failure to carry along various stakeholders in society in the design of such laws and, most importantly, the inadequacies/non-comprehensiveness of the laws that often hinder their ability to achieve stated objectives. The laws are also beset with other inadequacies, such as the non-existence of other complementary laws and institutions.

The experience of many developing countries over the years has underscored the need for "getting institutions right." Broadly speaking, the institutional framework for resource mobilization, utilization and management in Nigeria comprises the myriad of organizations and arrangements, formal and informal, public and private, that are engaged in the production of goods and services. Of particular relevance for the effective and efficient utilization of resources are those institutions that deal specifically with capacity building aimed at resource development. The lack of requisite human and institutional capacity has been identified as a critical factor militating against developmental efforts in Nigeria. The problem cuts across the public and private sectors and is further aggravated and perpetuated by the collapse of educational systems and training capacity. Various capacity building institutions exist in Nigeria, cutting across a wide range of resource types - natural, human, financial, and material resource mobilization and management institutions - as well as broad-based agencies.

The macroeconomic framework for resource mobilization and management consists of sets of aggregate economic variables and the interrelationships among them that constitute the yardstick for assessing both the performance of an economy and for predicting it. This framework provides an analytical basis for national economic planning, management and analysis. The basic building block for the various models is the framework or system of national accounts that provides a comprehensive and systematic presentation of the various economic transactions among significant groups of operators during successive periods in an economy. The transactions can be broadly grouped into those relating to production, exchange and use of goods and services by kind of economic activity and/or institutional sector, as well as by distributional transactions and financial transactions which refer to changes in the financial assets and liabilities of the different sectors of the national economy.

Extensions of the system of national accounts are sectoral balance sheets, input-output tables, as well as flow of funds and social accounting matrixes. These national accounting identities or relations are also brought together in the form of behavioural equations that provide tools for making projections, analysis, policy formulation and planning. Such systems and models have been used at one time or the other and to varying degrees in Nigeria's economic planning experience. The successful use of models in policy analysis and formulation has not, however, been achieved as models have often been characterized by substantial deviations between projected and realized outcomes.

Several reasons can be adduced for the unsuccessful use of macroeconomic frameworks in Nigeria. Firstly, and perhaps most importantly, are the problems of data generation and compilation. The data collection system in the country remains weak and characterized by inadequacies, inconsistencies, unreliability and datedness. These weaknesses, in turn, make it difficult to apply the results in any sufficiently meaningful or realistic manner. Other problems associated with the use of the frameworks include the economy's susceptibility to external shocks arising from its over-dependence on oil, inadequate human capacity for the proper design and utilization of models at the various levels of government, and the inappropriateness of some of the models arising from unrealistic assumptions about the behaviour of economic agents and market structures.

The challenge of resource management in Nigeria

There is a fair amount of consensus that Nigeria's development problems have more to do with resource management rather than resource availability *per se*. Nigeria is frequently used as a worse case study on issues bordering on best practices in development management. In fact, it is commonly mentioned that the country's resource endowment is a *curse* rather than a *blessing*. The Nigerian experience has, to a large extent, shown that availability of resources does not drive progress. Rather, development is driven by how best the available resources are put into use. Most of the economic and political problems in the country have been linked to the abundance of resources on one hand, and the extent to which they have been squandered by the country's elites and the political class on the other. This situation has induced a culture of undue dependence on government resources, even at individual level. The inability to convert immense resources into genuine development has made economic development a mirage to most Nigerians.

The country's resource abundance rather than translate into economic self-reliance has not only led to a source of conflict, but also to heavy dependence on external resources. While her contemporaries are using their exports to capture the whole world, Nigeria is using her economy as a dumping ground for the world's exports. Despite the country's huge resource base, Nigeria still carries one of the world's worst external debt burdens. Nigeria's external dependence is not only on financial and man-made resources, but also on foreign experts, even when local expertise is readily available. This is a significant part of the irony of the country's wasteful and under-utilization of scarce resources in the face of chronic shortages.

With a poverty incidence involving over half the population, the challenge for the nation is how to efficiently harness and utilize her resources to achieve sustained growth, raise living standards, eradicate poverty, and promote sustainable development. In this regard, there are several critical areas of challenge that must be addressed, some of which are briefly considered below:

Human resources

Arguably, the most crucial challenge for Nigeria is how to address the problem of unemployment. Furthermore, there is a need to appropriately match the labour market's demand for labour with the educational system's supply of labour. Related to this is the issue of funding of education, particularly at the tertiary level. There is also a need to build and develop human capacity in both the public and private sectors through training and other human resource development strategies. The professionalization of the civil service and the development of entrepreneurial ability in the private sector are crucial for improved economic performance. Undue reliance on foreign experts, even when there are local ones, is a source of serious concern. Local experts must be encouraged by being optimally utilized in the development process. It is also important to make maximum use of the potentials of all stakeholders of development, including the local communities.

Natural resources

With an abundance of natural resources, especially petroleum, there is a need to harness and develop Nigeria's other mineral resources as a means of diversifying the nation's export and productive base and generating more revenue and foreign exchange. To ensure self-sufficiency in food production as well as provide raw materials for industry, agricultural sector development remains a critical challenge for Nigeria. There is a need to create appropriate incentives and adopt appropriate modern technologies to boost agricultural output and productivity. The pricing of exhaustible natural resources, such as petroleum products, in an environment characterized by poverty, remains a highly contentious issue in Nigeria. Similarly, there is a need to promote the sustainable utilization of resources that minimize the negative environmental impact associated with their use.

Capital accumulation

While the savings rate in Nigeria is still low when compared to the average rate for middle income oil exporters, the challenge of capital accumulation in Nigeria goes beyond increasing the level of resources available for investment. Capital accumulation in Nigeria requires, first and foremost, the creation of a conducive and enabling environment (including appropriate political, legal and institutional arrangements) that will promote long-term domestic and foreign investments, rather than rent-seeking activities. Closely related to this are the provision of an adequate social infrastructure and the design of an appropriate industrial policy that not only encourages increased industrial output, but also promotes the development of a capital goods sub-sector. Another crucial issue is the development and use of appropriate technologies in the manufacturing sector.

Financial resources

Nigeria's use and management of external financial resources in the past has resulted in a debt crisis that now threatens the nation's development. There is an urgent need to improve export performance in order to generate foreign exchange, while at the same time seeking debt-relief. Encouraging savings, enhancing the tax base, and improving tax administration are the measures required for better domestic resource generation and simultaneous reduction of dependence on external financial resources. Continued financial sector reform and development, through an improved regulatory framework, and money and capital market improvements are also required to enhance domestic resource mobilization.

Institutional, legal, and other issues

The effective and efficient mobilization, utilization and management of resources will require a complementary set of legal, political, socio-cultural, and institutional arrangements. While building institutions is definitely more difficult than changing policies, there is an urgent need to strengthen the existing laws and institutions as instruments for accelerating the nation's economic development. At the same time, there is a need to streamline such institutions and laws to avoid unnecessary duplication of functions and consequent waste of resources. Another crucial issue is the need to define public and private sector roles in economic development. Emphasis is currently being laid on promoting private sector participation in the economy while cutting down on government's direct involvement in economic activities. Questions of privatization and deregulation still form the subject of an unsettled debate in Nigeria. Achieving an optimal public-private sector mix is a challenge that needs to be addressed quickly in the coming years. The question of resource control will also, invariably, have to be addressed in a manner that will ensure the continued existence of a stable democratic polity. Most importantly, the nation needs to confront and address the issue of corruption. It is generally agreed that corruption constitutes a major factor in Nigeria's dismal economic performance. Failure to successfully address this problem may continue to make Nigeria's development hopes and aspirations a mirage.

Ayida on resource management

As a veteran of the Nigerian Civil Service who has been actively involved in national economic planning and management, Allison Ayida has had an influential voice in the debate on various issues associated with resource mobilization, utilization and management. As a professional planner, he views national development planning as an important tool for mobilizing and allocating resources for development. Particularly in the 1960s and 1970s, he observed that it would be very difficult for many developing countries to mobilize enough resources for development without development plans. His view on this can be summed up thus: "Most lenders nowadays insist on lending substantial capital only to countries with National Development Programmes and sometimes to projects within such programmes." (Ayida, 1987:63)

He has, however, warned that developing countries should be very careful in accepting aid from many developed countries because of the tendency of tying components of aid to the import of machinery and equipment from the lending countries, and also because such imports may not be consistent with the development aspirations of most developing countries.

In his lecture titled, "Before Tomorrow Comes" Ayida argues that the poor management of the country's resources has been a major factor in her level of political instability. He posits that lack of competent management and a rational allocation of

Nigeria's resources have often precipitated military intervention in the country's political process.

He strongly believes that, given its abundant resources (money, men and materials), Nigeria has no excuse for not running and sustaining a self-sufficient economy. The poor state of the economy is as a result of the poor management of the country's resources, he contends. To him, resources have been diverted from the national treasury to individual pockets to such an extent that in Nigeria "many individuals can own and operate private jets" whereas the indebtedness of the nation continues to mount as her per capita income continues to nose-dive. For Nigeria, finance is not a problem but the management of the resources and he concludes thus:

> ...Nigeria is potentially a rich country and...the availability of development finance for a properly selected investment programme is not the problem. The critical question is our curious scale of priorities and the quality of investment decisions, notably in the public sector, and the proper management of our resources. Financial discipline and integrity have been in limited supply through successive Nigerian governments (Ayida, 1988:7).

Ayida sees the mobilization of existing resources as the most effective way of mobilizing new ones. He considers the treatment and management of the enormous foreign exchange earnings from oil exports as one of the most critical areas of resource leakages that have hindered effective mobilization of new ones, arguing with considerable conviction that when the existing resources are not judiciously utilized, it would be quite difficult to mobilize additional ones.

In addition to all this, Ayida observes a lack of effective communication between Nigeria's development stakeholders (public officials, the private sector, the beneficiaries, etc) on issues such as the delineation of national priorities, and the rational allocation and responsible use of available resources. This is clearly evident in one of his lectures titled, "Basic Issues in Financing Nigerian Agriculture in the Seventies" (Ayida 1987a:108).

To Ayida, the quality of human resources determines the magnitude and quality of other resources within society. The prevailing decadence in Nigeria's human resources, as reflected in the public service and the country's educational system, has had a significant bearing on the quality and effectiveness of other resources, he concludes. Ayida's views and actions have probably had the most impact in the areas of human and institutional capacity building, especially the Civil Service.

According to him, it would be difficult to mobilize and utilize resources effectively if the Civil Service were not professionalized and made more efficient and effective. But rather than making full use of the Civil Service and other Nigerian experts and learning from experience, Ayida observes that Nigerian leaders appear to derive an intriguing pleasure in engaging foreign consultants and experts. He expresses this view rather strongly in his National Day Lecture entitled, "Self-sufficiency: The Path to Virile Nationhood" in which he asserts that:

> ...Nigeria has the money, the men and the resources to establish a self-reliant and self-sufficient economy. We will discover that in the utilization and deployment of professional and trained manpower, the governments in the federation tend to rely more on international agencies and foreign consultants than Nigerians...but this in-built preference for foreign consultants has a deleterious effect on the programme of national survival and self-sufficiency (Ayida, 1988:5).

Consistent with this position, Ayida had objected to the choice of a foreign banking institution to verify and collate Nigeria's external debts when there were many Nigerian experts, both at home and abroad, who could have done it as well, if not better. The pursuit of this policy in the midst of mass national unemployment has led, in his opinion, to what he calls "Nigeria's vanishing professionals and middle class."

Ayida also advocates a corollary to the use of local expertise: that the development of the technological skills of the domestic human resource base is at the core of fruitful resource mobilization and utilization. He argues that over-dependence on the multinationals for transfer of necessary technologies cannot lead to progress. Because multinationals have vested and beneficial interests in the delayed transfer of such technologies to their local subsidiaries, there cannot be a genuine transfer, he contends. Rather, according to him, we should build the capacity of Nigerians to master and adapt the existing technologies, instead of reinventing the wheel.

Ayida also highlights other factors that have hindered Nigeria's effective mobilization and utilization of resources. One comprises the activities of smugglers and business fraudsters whom Ayida refers to as "the new international elite of business men and women." Another concerns the challenge of mobilizing appropriately qualified men and materials at the right time and deploying them for the implementation of national development plans. According to Ayida, the challenge has defied solution for so long due, in part, to geographical, ethnic or state balancing of personnel, through the inappropriate application of the "federal character" principle and a low executive capacity in the management of the national economy. Finally, it is the view of Ayida that the extravagant way of life of many Nigerian leaders sends the wrong signal to the populace and has had the effect of weakening citizens' confidence in the country's leadership and development goals.

8

Institutions and governance in Nigeria

> The market relies on a 'glove' of rules, norms, and institutions – and the demands that this glove be made transparent have reached a fevered pitch (Pleskovic and Stigliitz, 2000:7).

Introduction

At the core of any meaningful development are institutions and governance. Evidence from several rapidly developing countries clearly points to the important role of institutions and governance. Arising from the recognition given to both issues in the development process, some scholars have linked the gap between the Asian and African countries, in their development outcomes, to differences in the degree of importance attached to best institutional practices of which good governance is a component. Hence, institutions and governance are perceived as constituting critical elements in any attempt to reorganize, reconstruct, or transform a nation and its economy.

As Ayida points out in several of his public lectures and speeches, there has been the absence of a clear national goal and a set of norms for the conduct of public affairs in Nigeria. This conspicuous absence seems to have left the country at the mercy of the local ruling elites who, for the most part, have consistently promoted their personal interests in every sector of the economy to the detriment of the collective needs of the people. Consequently, it has been difficult to draw any sharp distinction between the personal interests of the ruling elites and those of the nation. Apparently, the most common strategy often used by the former is to evoke various emotive cleavages, such as religion, ethnicity and statism to create disharmony and distrust among a gullible citizenry, thereby distracting them from the collective resolve to understand and pursue common national goals, that is, necessary economic development and transformation. Ayida has argued, repeatedly, that in the absence of good governance, spearheaded by a dedicated and charismatic leadership, and built on the foundation of fear of God, truth, justice, fairness and the rule of law, the present state of decay and decadence may soon bring Nigeria to a chaotic halt. As the country derails rapidly from the institutional foundations of its existence, most infrastructure facilities seem to be disappearing and are being replaced by distrust and disunity in an environment in which 'nothing works'! And because bad institutions are replacing good ones, Ayida observes, "Successive governments have ruled the country and left office with government performing a little less than its predecessors" (Ayida, 2002:1). The consequence is all too predictable, as he suggests in his lecture, "The Rise and Fall of Nigeria," "...economic disaster is more often than not, the product of political incompetence" (Ayida, 1987:10).

Ayida strongly believes that the existing structure of government in Nigeria poses a serious challenge to the institutional setting for good governance in the country. He notes that the military establishment that had dominated the country's terrain of governance for so long lacked the necessary political and social engineering skills for good economic management, and lacked the secret weapon of modern power –

organizational ability to mobilize people. He warns that the entrenched practice of making the leadership of the country the exclusive preserve of a section of the federation portends danger. Similarly, he warns that the Presidential system of government, without proper checks and balances, concentrates too much power in the hands of one person. This arrangement, in the absence of a dedicated and strong leadership, is the fastest way to political annihilation, he fears.

The remainder of this chapter examines issues related to institutions and governance in the context of the evolution of Nigeria's social, economic and political systems. The theoretical framework for good governance is first examined, followed by a discussion of the evolution of the Nigerian eco-political system. Finally, we highlight Ayida's position statements on the continuing debate on governance, an appropriate institutional framework, and economic management in Nigeria.

Institutions and governance: concept and theory

One generic conceptualization of institutions defines them as: "large establishments or organizations that have a particular kind of work or purpose...established systems in the economy and society..." One implication of this definition is that large establishments or organizations within a given socio-economic framework would exhibit definitive legislative, judicial, educational, religious, traditional/cultural, and administrative constructs that may not be shared by similar organizations elsewhere. Nonetheless, all institutions of a kind would be expected to exhibit discernible basic similarities, irrespective of their location.

Governance may be defined as the task of running a government or any other human entity. A richer conceptual analysis of governance describes it as the conscious management of regime structures with a view to enhancing the legitimacy of the public realm. The ultimate concern of governance is to create the conditions for ordered rule and collective action. It refers to the creation of a structure or an order that cannot be externally imposed, but is the result of the interaction of a multiplicity of interest groups involved in governing and influencing actions. Within the macroeconomic context of state management, however, governance can be conceived as the mechanism through which institutions or organizations (the family, the nation-state or the elements of it) incorporate the participation of relevant interest groups in defining the scope and content of their work.

An elaboration of this conceptualization of governance shows that its scope and content may be defined by reference to a number of relevant interest groups (institutions). First, is the *capacity* to mediate among such interest groups, particularly during periods of socio-economic and political crises. Second, is the *means* for demonstrating accountability to the supporters within the process of the missions mandate. Third, is the *manner* in which a government or state governs the territory and people that it controls, in terms of the judicious, optimal and effective application of available resources in the pursuit of developmental goals. Simply put, governance is conceived as the exercise of political power to manage a nation's affairs.

The process of a state's socio-economic and political management shows that it encompasses institutional and structural arrangements, decision-making processes, an implementation capacity, and the relationship between government officials and the public. Broadly examined, these dimensions of governance cover all aspects of the complex and myriad relationships that exist between the leader (government) and the led (people). In order to make the relationship effective, two key elements seem critical: participation and accountability. If any of the two elements is missing from the linkage between the leader and the led, it could constitute a crisis situation and result in bad governance.

What, then, is good governance? Good governance involves normative judgement, indicating a preferred relation that should ideally govern the interactions between state and society and between a government and a people. Thus, good governance connotes the following four elements:

- Accountability, based on the notion of popular sovereignty and public choice;
- A legal framework that guarantees the rule of law and due process;
- Popular participation in decision-making processes, based on political and social pluralism, freedom of association and expression; and
- Bureaucratic accountability, based on impersonality of office, uniform application of rules, and rationality of organizational structure.

A closer examination of the foregoing suggests that good governance guides society along a course leading to the attainment of society's desired goal of economic development by means of established institutions. In particular, governance in the context of macro-economic management can be viewed as a means by which power is exercised in the management of a country's socio-economic and political resources for national socio-economic development. Therefore, the framework for good governance, from the macroeconomic perspective, can be seen as a set of institutions empowered to exercise legitimate economic, social, legal, legislative, administrative, etc., coercion over a defined territory and its population, usually referred to as society.

The concept of governance has evolved through several stages, over time, in terms of its practical application. Classical thought about governance was based on the assumption of an efficient and well-functioning market system in the context of which forces of demand and supply determined prices that, in turn, dictated an optimal allocation of societal resources. In this system, the private sector served as the engine of growth and the public sector assumed minimalist responsibilities, focusing largely on "law and order" issues. In practice, however, markets have not generally been perfect and well-functioning. The existence of market failures has provided justification for the forceful entry of government into the management of the socio-economic system, both to correct market imperfections and to adjust income distribution.

This ascendance of the public sector was itself eventually challenged. Instead of correcting market imperfections, "government failures" further complicated matters. Hence, the thinking about governance and economic management has, increasingly, moved away from both of these extreme positions. Current thinking emphasizes the defects of minimalist public sector involvement in economic management, as well as the inefficiencies of an interventionist government. Consequently, the need to shift to a middle ground where a more pragmatic mix of public and private sector cooperation obtains has been vigorously canvassed. In this mix, the private sector would retain the primary responsibility for the allocation of resources in the economy, but the public sector would provide an "enabling environment" of institutional support and regulatory powers for counteracting the defects of the market system.

Economic management in Nigeria

The framework for economic management in Nigeria appears to have evolved over time. During the period immediately preceding the nationalist struggle for independence, as well as during the struggle itself, the country's economic management framework was essentially one of *laissez faire* with the associated feature of minimalist government. During this period, the various governments were foreign-controlled, the private sector was also foreign-dominated as its indigenous component was in an infant stage.

Interestingly, however, the emergency of conscious national development planning as a tool through which the public sector controlled, or at least guided, the nation's development process had its roots in this period. The Colonial Development and Welfare Act of 1945 provided the legal and economic framework for the ten-year plan of development and welfare, 1946-1956. While the plan provided for the allocation of public funds to certain key sectors, it did not include properly articulated national socio-economic policies or national goals. Within the post-independence period, however, four national development plans and a series of rolling plans have been implemented as a framework for managing the Nigerian economy.

Each of these plans has had to address, in varying ways, the changing views regarding the roles of the public and private sectors in the process of economic development. In other words, choices were made implicitly or explicitly with respect to:

- The degree of mix between public and private sectors in the allocation of national resources;
- The extent of government interference with private decision-making processes; and
- The degree to which the private sector could be integrated into the national development planning framework.

More specifically, the 1962-68 and 1970-74 *National Development Plans* had their approaches and policies built around the development of an economy in which the private sector would be dominant, although planned expenditures were solely those of the public sector. Thus, even though the Plans assigned a dominant role to the private sector, they were not comprehensive in the sense of including fully articulated private sector project expenditure estimates and projections. Mid-way through the 1970-74 *National Development Plan*, however, the emergence of large windfall gains from crude oil exports appears to have changed the pressured relationship between the public and private sector, as well as their respective roles in the development process. In effect, the oil-revenue-inspired *National Development Plans* of 1975-80 and 1981-85 assigned the leading role in Nigeria's economic development process to the public sector, through the so-called doctrine of making Nigerians attain the "commanding heights" of the economy.

The envisioned shift in the framework of Nigeria's economic management did not endure for a full decade. By the early 1980s, the bottom had fallen out of the economy; the oil sector had collapsed and the huge investments in public enterprises made in the 1970s had become largely unviable. The design of many of the public enterprises, or parastatals, was being increasingly questioned; some appeared, in retrospect, to be beyond the executive capacity of the parastatals. In addition, many of them performed rather poorly and were yielding net returns that were generally considered unsatisfactory. As a result of government's sharply curtailed revenues, the accumulation of external debt which required expensive servicing, and the serious balance-of-payments and foreign exchange constraints that had emerged, the 1981-85 *National Development Plan* could not, in fact, be implemented as originally designed. The "commanding heights" doctrine had, apparently, collapsed under its own weight.

Eventually, the national development planning framework was dramatically altered. With active financial assistance of the World Bank and the International Monetary Fund, Nigeria adopted a structural adjustment programme (SAP), with effect from 1986. This new approach had three basic components as follows: a sharp contraction of public sector investment, particularly in the production and distribution of goods and services in the economy; a more dominant private sector role in national development; and the return of economic management based largely on market forces and deregulation. This approach led to the abrogation of the existing indigenization decrees and the promulgation of privatization and commercialization decrees. The new framework provided for a reduction in the size of the public sector, the restructuring of government expenditure policies in accordance with the transfer of economic activities to private sector institutions, and the fostering of financial and market discipline in the economy through the adoption economic efficiency principles.

Although the basic elements of the SAP approach have continued to drive economic management in Nigeria since the second half of the 1980s, the approach has experienced significant problems. During the 1993-97 period, in particular, governance worsened and along with it some of the basic policies associated with SAP were stalled or even reversed under the so-called "guided deregulation" doctrine. During the late 1990s and early 2000s, however, many of these policies were restored, even though institutional constraints continued to bedevil the full implementation of some of them, including privatization. In addition, the improving environment of governance increasingly revealed the crippling economic and socio-political consequences of rampant corruption. Some of these clearly existed before SAP, but the appetite for corruption had apparently increased quite sharply since the advent of SAP, even though it remains difficult to view the two phenomena in a 'cause and effect' relationship.

Ayida on Nigerian governance, institutional framework and economic management

Ayida believes that the institutional arrangements in a federal structure can serve as a double-edged sword capable of making or marring the development process. During the First Republic, from 1960 to 1966, federalism served as a centripetal force in advancing the cause of development in Nigeria (Ayida, 1987). Thereafter, the opposite has been the case, according to Ayida (1990:4).

Ayida observes that the existing structure seems to pose a serious challenge to the institutional setting of governance in the country. In particular, he warns that the practice whereby the leadership of the country is seen as the exclusive preserve of a section of the federation portends grave danger to the country as a nation state and capable of fomenting social disorder. Instead he strongly supports a rotating Presidency (without a Prime Minister) and multiple Vice-Presidents as a means of fostering national unity. Furthermore, he warns that the Presidential system without proper checks and balances, concentrates too much power in the hands of one person as an institution. Such over-concentration of power elevates ethnic sentiments and religious bigotry to a dangerous dimension in Nigeria's development process, he concludes. To Ayida, the over-concentration of political power in an individual or very few individuals is a manifestation of poor governance.

In his book, *Reflections on Nigerian Development* (1987) Ayida makes it clear that the level of competence and effectiveness of a federal apparatus, to a large extent, depends on the quality and professional skills of the staff operating it. Continuing his analysis, Ayida argues that with the adoption of the quota and federal character systems, the Nigerian nation has become a relic of its old glory where mediocrity promotes mistrust and anti-patriotic tendencies which, in turn, have engendered a culture of treasury looting. Furthermore, the practice of federalism in Nigeria and the widespread results of applying a system of 'patronage and corruption' have had disastrous consequences on national development, he laments. His view suggests that the driving forces of institutional decadence in Nigeria are the continuing politics of patronage, the maintenance of a large bureaucracy, and a diverse and often fractious polity. Specifically, Ayida (1987) points out that the disastrous effects of corruption on the Nigerian economy emanate from:

- Obvious moral problems and an inequitable income distribution;
- Inflation of contracts resulting in a serious financial burden on budgets and plans;
- Substantial distortion of national development priorities arising from the selfish motives of operators;
- Bad foreign private investment that often drives away genuinely honest and efficient ones; and
- Inefficient and incompetent administrators and officials occupying strategic positions at the expense of efficient and competent ones.

Ayida (2001:10) estimates that corruption in Nigeria, as at the end of the 20th century, had led to the abandonment of 4,800 projects with no hope of recovering the funds committed to them or rehabilitating them. In order to tame the monster called corruption, Ayida urges the present administration to do away with rhetorics and adopt the path of pragmatism. To him, the failure or success of Obasanjo's government will be determined by the extent to which corruption is reduced or eradicated in Nigeria's public life. For now, however, Ayida appears unconvinced that government is serious about taming corruption in the country. To him, the current fight against corruption is more of a slogan than a call to action. Consequently, Ayida's avowed position on the subject in 1996 remains unchanged today:

> There is no convincing evidence to suggest that there is firm control over the distortions arising from misuse of resources and misplaced priorities and widespread abuse of office and corruption (Ayida, 1996:24).

Ayida's perception of the role of institutions in national development is unequivocally affirmative. In his opinion, the military as an institution and individuals, are anathema to development, a clog in the wheel of any national administrative machinery geared towards sustainable development, particularly during their second coming from 1983 to 1999. Their incursion into governance has not only made it difficult for politicians to learn from their past mistakes and difficulties, it has also shaken the country to its foundations to the point of threatened disintegration (Ayida, 1987).

Ayida's verdict on military rule has been mixed in terms of plan management. While in their first phase of assuming political power (1966-1979), Nigeria's military rulers appeared to have strengthened the planning process with a culture of discipline and a unified command structure, an "anything goes" approach seemed to have dominated their second stint of power. His view is summarized as follows (Ayida, 1996:24):

> Planning and plan administration appeared to have been strengthened with the advent of military discipline and its chain of command...In the second phase of the military administration, indiscipline and the breakdown of law and order became the order of the day. The financial crisis which followed the petroleum oil boom resulted in the abandonment of planning, followed by the presidential interregnum

when the system of plan administration ground to a halt.

The culture of discipline and orderliness, both central to development management and, consequently, good development outcomes has, in Ayida's view, been totally destroyed by the military. Consequently, he concludes, at the beginning of the Third Millennium, practically all institutions in Nigeria are at a state of disrepair, with social and physical infrastructure nearing total collapse. The effects of this decay, coupled with a significant dose of mismanagement and indiscipline in the private sector, too, have crippled the operations of the private sector, in particular, and the whole economy in general. To him, Nigeria is facing a crisis of lack of professionalism and of ethical standards today more than ever before. In his Public Service Lecture, titled "Professionalism and Ethics in the Civil Service," Ayida (1999:1) bares his mind on the fundamental issue of professionalism in institution building in the following words:

> Not many seem to recognize that professionalism and ethics would seem to be at the bottom of this: if policy makers were professional enough, a good deal of adversity might have been averted or minimized; if the soldiers were professional and kept to the ethics of their profession, they would have stayed in their barracks, nor would they have damaged many institutions in civil society in the manner in which they have; if managers were professional and upheld a decent level of ethics, a great many finance houses, banks, trading and manufacturing companies might not have gone under; and if teachers and lecturers were more professional, the educational system might have survived in a better shape.

Ayida strongly believes that the solution to Nigeria's institutional decadence lies in inculcating professionalism in all aspects of national life. He observes that in both private and public sector institutions, many unwritten rules and conventions guide operational conduct almost as strongly as the written ones. To make and sustain progress, he concludes, all such rules, written and unwritten, must be strictly followed. Professionalism and ethical standards must be nurtured to the point of evolving an enforceable national code of conduct where 'sacred cows' do not exist and punishment is meted out swiftly and impartially against all transgressors, he insists. In the absence of this, the transparent " 'glove' of rules, norms, and institutions" that make both governments and markets to work effectively would be lacking and good development outcomes would continue to be elusive, he finally submits.

9

Planning and directional focus

Introduction

The growth experiences of a wide variety of developing countries suggest that the process of development is facilitated by a systematic framework which gives it a sound directional focus. Planning constitutes an important and, perhaps, inevitable mechanism in this context.

Planning may also be regarded as the area where Allison Ayida has had, arguably, the most remarkable and lasting impact in shaping the course of Nigeria's development process. As an apostle of government's control of the "commanding heights" of the economy, he has consistently viewed government intervention in economic activity primarily as a way of promoting and protecting the public interest, a role which tends to be of paramount importance in developing countries where "public goods" are typically underfunded and the private sector is often dominated by foreign interests. In this context, Ayida would argue that government intervention in economic matters is necessary to provide the leadership and honest administration required for the attainment of a national sense of purpose which is, in turn, the prerequisite for achieving purposeful national development. Without necessarily doubting the efficacy of markets in principle, Ayida would also argue that the private sector in Nigeria should not be left on its own to determine the direction and content of economic growth and development, given that doing so could be fraught with social and political danger. Accordingly, Ayida (2001; 15) maintains that:

> There has to be a historically-influenced national political direction and socio-economic priorities that constitute the framework within which all operate, and it is only the state that can determine such - not private companies seeking private profit.

In other words, a developing country should articulate its vision for development under the direction of government and through the mechanism of planning.

Perspectives on development planning

The evolution of both the theories and application of development planning has been influenced by several key factors, including learning, changes in ideology, changes in the international environment and changes in country-specific constraints and aspirations. Learning through new insights and evidence of outstanding real world successes or dismal failures, garnered from empirical and theoretical research, provide springboards for new thinking. Similarly, as political ideologies go through changes and transformations, they provide new prisms through which old theories and policy prescriptions are viewed. Perceived inconsistencies between old and new ideas necessitate a re-formulation aimed at achieving or re-establishing congruence. At the level of the international environment, significant technological innovations (such as the information and communications revolution) and major global institutional transformations (such as the creation of the World

Trade Organization) can raise new issues, open new opportunities and lead to new development challenges. Finally, it is an inherent nature of the dynamics of development to significantly restructure domestic institutions, relax some constraints, tighten others and bring new aspirations to the fore. These forces of change interact together to generate new thinking about various areas of economic management and policy-making which impinge upon the concept, purpose, scope and methodology of development planning.

In the context of these changes, thinking about development planning has evolved through several stages. In its earliest stage, the focus was on a single-cause and, hence, single-remedy, theory of development. The basis was the presumption that under-development was largely due to a particular constraint or missing factor and that the elimination of this constraint, or the existence of this missing factor, would automatically bring about development.

The first "missing factor" identified was physical capital. The proposition that deficiency in physical capital was the fundamental cause of underdevelopment served as the rationale for the establishment of the World Bank, regional development banks and a series of bilateral and multilateral foreign assistance programmes. These institutional developments concentrated on supplementing, on concessionary terms, the meagre domestic savings available for domestic investment. Correspondingly, development planning focussed on determining the amount of capital required for an economy to grow at a specified rate and on how to mobilize this capital by raising the domestic savings rate, attracting foreign direct investment and filling the remaining savings investment gap with bilateral and multilateral aid.

Following the observed diminishing returns on injected additional foreign assistance capital, it was suggested that the typical developing country capacity for absorbing and productively using physical capital was constrained by the absence of domestic entrepreneurs. The limited pool of potential industrialists was thought to be responsible for low economic growth. One policy response to the deficiency-in-entrepreneurship diagnosis was that government would have to perform the entrepreneurial function at the outset while, at the same time, fostering the development of a cadre of private entrepreneurs that would eventually take over. Consistent with this response, development planning shifted its focus to the establishment of state-owned enterprises which were increasingly used to capture the "commanding heights" of the economy, not only with respect to the provision of infrastructure services, but also in direct production of core industrial, mineral and agricultural goods. The development planning paradigm of this vintage justified pervasive government intervention in the economy on the basis of associated deficiencies in physical capital and domestic entrepreneurship as well as malfunctioning and/or inadequately developed market systems.

However, the typical developing country whose development process was being orchestrated by an interventionist and hyperactive government was not entirely free of constraints either. Thus, by the mid-1980s, low human capital endowment was generally identified as the primary obstacle to the realization of the cconomies of scale inherent in the industrialization of developing countries. This follows from the idea that the productivity of raw labour and physical capital is magnified by the levels of human capital, technology and knowledge. The corresponding development planning objective would be to substantially increase investment in human capital, technology development and knowledge acquisition as a means of elevating the economy from a low-growth to a high-growth trajectory.

It is not difficult to see why "single-cause" paradigms of

development planning are basically deficient. Economic growth is a dynamic process which involves the systematic reallocation of resources from low-productivity to high-productivity activities. This allocation is driven by a system of incentives and sanctions whose efficiency and effectiveness play a major role in determining both the speed and magnitude of resource flows. The correct alignment of relative forces (in a well functioning market system) should dictate an optimal allocation of resources to the activities in which they earn the highest returns. In other words, "getting prices right" may basically be all that is needed to ensure that resources are reallocated from low-productivity to high-productivity activities.

There are, at least, two caveats to this broad view of the development process. One is that there may still be need for government action to propel an economy from a low-growth equilibrium trap to a high-growth and dynamic equilibrium path by *improving* the functioning of markets and by eliminating coordination failures which could prevent the full realization of the economy's capacity for increasing returns to scale. The other is that market failure (which is often used to justify government intervention) may be compounded by government failure. Policy-induced distortion associated with discretionary interventions in markets, through various types of regulatory controls, may give rise to rent-seeking activities by private entrepreneurs and lead to significant economic inefficiencies. The development planning paradigm which reflects these considerations would incorporate a dynamically changing mix of state-market interactions in which a development-friendly government plays a significant role in investment mobilization, human capital formation, acquisition of technology, institution building, and the promotion of policy and institutional reforms. Its instruments and mechanisms would focus on improving and using markets and market institutions, rather than replacing them. Hence, it would reflect an economic management framework in which the private sector plays the leading role in economic decision-making while the government provides an enabling environment.

The Nigeria planning experience

Nigeria's experience with development planning has been shaped by the general evolution of the concept and scope of planning, changes in the political structure of the country and the corresponding changes in the planning machinery.

Development planning in Nigeria is generally traced to 1944 when the British Secretary of State for the colonies initiated an effort in this direction which resulted in the launching, in 1946, of the *Ten-year Plan of Development and Welfare*. The formulation and implementation of this *Plan*, up to 1954, were the responsibility of a small Central Development Board which consisted exclusive of senior colonial government officials.

The *Plan* suffered from two major defects: it was highly centralized and it failed to satisfy, perhaps, the most important requirement of good planning, i.e., the involvement of the people whose welfare it was meant to promote. Subsequent development planning efforts continued to confront these two problem areas, with varying degrees of success.

The introduction of the federal system of government in October 1954 put a pre-mature end to the *Plan of Development and Welfare*. As Nigeria became a federation with three regions (East, North and West) as well as Southern Cameroons and the Federal Territory of Lagos, each of the Regional Governments and the Federal Government formulated and launched their own *Plans* covering the 1955-62 period. Prior to this, the report of a World Bank Mission to Nigeria led to the establishment of a National Economic Council which, in turn, created the Joint Planning Committee as the primary organs for ensuring that the development programmes of the different governments which, naturally, had varying goals could, nevertheless, be built around a common frame of reference. The *1962-68 National Development Plan* was the first post-independence effort at development planning in Nigeria. This may explain why it is commonly referred to as the *First National Development Plan*. Preparations for this Plan were initiated by the decision of the National Economic Council, early in 1959, that:

> a National Development Plan be prepared for Nigeria with the objective of the achievement and maintenance of the highest possible rate of increase in the standard of living and the creation of the necessary conditions to this end, including public support and awareness of both the potentials that exist and the sacrifices that will be required.

In its design, this *Plan* made conscious efforts to set and quantify national objectives as well as ensure a common national planning framework. But its structure was similar to that of the *1955-62 Plan* in the sense that it embodied separate programmes with projects in different Regions. However, the recognition and acceptance of common objectives and targets by the various governments gave the *1962-68 Plan* an apparently national character.

In spite of its careful design, this *Plan* faced severe implementation problems arising, primarily, from the political sphere. For instance, the creation of the Mid-West Region in 1963 meant that its own component of the *Plan* had to be incorporated. But more importantly, a series of political crises was initiated by the military take-over of government, including the restructuring of the Federation into twelve states in 1967 and the civil war of 1967-70. These events not only led to the virtual abortion of the *1962-68 Development Plan*, after its first four years of implementation, but also made it impossible to prepare its successor before its scheduled completion in 1968.

The *Second National Development Plan (1970-74)* specified the policy framework for, and the programme of, the reconstruction of the war-damaged areas as well as the construction and development of the rest of the country. In its articulation, the *1970-74 Plan* explicitly confronted several of the key issues in development planning. It stated, for instance, that the *Plan* had to be "implemented by the governments as well as the people of this country; all public sector institutions and private sector and individual initiatives will be involved in the execution of the Plan in one way or the other."

In reality, however, this *Plan* was not fundamentally different from its predecessors in the sense that its formulation was based on a top-down approach and the private sector was not directly or actively involved in either deciding *Plan* objectives or setting *Plan* priorities and targets. In fact, the designers of this *Plan* were apparently so deeply convinced of the futility of "partial planning" which is restricted to public sector programmes and of the ineffectiveness of planning what government did not control, that they incorporated two important decisions into the *Plan*. First, it was decreed that resources such as land, mineral deposits and other natural endowments must be owned and their use effectively controlled by nationals of Nigeria. Second, it was asserted that government would play a dominant role in the public sector by having both access to and control of all the major national resources and, in particular, by controlling the "essential and growth-sensitive sectors" of the country in the fields of commerce, industry, fuel and energy, construction, transport, finance and education. These two decisions reflect the underlying philosophy of the *1970-74 Plan* that was designed for government to take over the "commanding heights" of the economy.

There were two other important components of this philosophy. Arguing that what Nigeria lacked most in the past was a national sense of purpose, especially in economic matters, the designers of the *1970-74 Plan* had decided that the Federal Government would occupy the "commanding heights" in the quest for purposeful national development and provide the leadership and honest administration necessary for the attainment of a national sense of purpose. It was, perhaps, relatively easy to endow the *1970-74 Plan* with a philosophy based on public sector, and especially, federal government control of the "commanding heights" of the economy. The unified command and control structure of the military regime at the time provided the political muscle necessary for imposing this view of development planning.

The third component of the "commanding heights" philosophy was concerned with Nigeria's development strategy in relation to development in the global economy. Arguing for an economic nationalism directed at the progressive elimination of foreign dominance in the national economy, the designers of the *1970-74 Plan* decided that Nigeria would quicken its pace of development through the use of her own resources, instead of relying unduly on external aid.

This philosophy continued to guide the *Third National Development Plan, 1975-80*, with renewed emphasis on diversification of the economy and indigenization of economic activity. Recognizing that an undiversified economy is especially vulnerable to changing economic situations, the *Plan* sought to achieve greater diversification through a rapid expansion and broadening of industrial activity by a wide range of public sector projects covering building materials, agro-allied, petrochemical and other industrial products. The objective of increased participation of Nigerians in domestic trade, industry and other economic activities, which was first articulated in the *Second Plan*, was to be pursued with greater vigour during the *Third Plan,* through policy directed at ensuring that Nigerian entrepreneurship was present and dominant in all sectors of the economy.

The major long-term objectives and priorities of Nigeria's development planning efforts remained stable through the *Second* and *Third Plans* to the *Fourth National Development Plan, 1981-85*. In the *1981-85 Plan*, the areas of particular emphasis were to include not only diversification of the economy and increased participation by Nigerian citizens in the ownership and management of productive enterprises, but also greater self-reliance, i.e., increased dependence on domestic resources in seeking to achieve the various *Plan* objectives.

Compared to the focus of the *Second* and *Third Plans*, however, the *Fourth Plan* sought to internalize three areas with respect to which lessons of experience could be learned. First, a conscious effort would be made to ensure optimal utilization of scarce financial resources by inculcating in all government functionaries a high degree of cost-consciousness in the conception, design and execution of projects, and by leaving little or no room for grandiose or prestige projects. Second, the *Fourth Plan* would be focused on the consolidation and maintenance of existing facilities so as to prevent the gains from previous development efforts from being lost through rapid deterioration of productive assets. Finally, sustained effort would be made to diversify the economy away from the over-dependence on the petroleum sector by widening the base of public revenue and export earnings.

The basic philosophy, i.e., public sector control of the "commanding heights" of the economy, which drove the *Second, Third* and *Fourth Plans* was fuelled by what was, apparently, perceived as a permanent (rather than transitory) oil wealth. The *First Plan* of 1962-68 involved a capital expenditure of ₦2.2 billon over six years or about ₦0.37 billion per annum. The *Second Plan* of 1970-74 had a capital expenditure of ₦3 billion over four years, or approximately ₦0.75 billion per annum. For the *Third Plan* during 1975-80, the planned capital expenditure of ₦30 billion was eventually increased to ₦43.3 billion, or an average of ₦7.22 billion per year. Finally, the *Fourth Plan* of 1981-85 had a projected total capital expenditure of about ₦82 billion or roughly ₦16.4 billion per annum! The dramatic increases in capital expenditure projections reflected continuing access to increasing oil revenue.

The overall financing strategy for the *Plans* was thus quite simple. Due to developments in the oil sector from the early 1970s, substantial resources were becoming available to the country by way of government revenue, private income and foreign exchange. The strategy was for government to utilize these oil resources to develop the non-oil productive capacity of the economy by creating the economic and social infrastructure necessary for self-sustaining growth in the longer run when the oil wealth might have been dissipated. To give effect to this strategy, the revenue allocation formula was designed to ensure that all governments in the Federation would have adequate financial resources to fully implement their *Plan* programmes.

The *Third Plan* was launched against the background of buoyant financial resources, following sharp increases in both the price of crude oil and Nigeria's level of production. Availability of financial resources was, therefore, not expected to pose any serious problem for implementing the *Plan*. But, due to the volatile nature of the oil sector, the rosy picture soon turned gloomy. Nigeria's crude oil production dropped sharply by as much as 35%, and the price of crude oil declined by 12%. These unexpected developments greatly distorted the expected flow of financial resources. However, rather than scale down the capital expenditure projections in the *Plan*, government decided to decumulate its foreign exchange resources and engage in massive borrowing from the Eurodollar market and from bilateral and multilateral institutions. By the end of the *Plan* period, actual aggregate public sector capital expenditure amounted to ₦29.43 billion or only 68% of the projected total capital expenditure of ₦43.3 billion. In addition, loans which were not accorded any major role in the *Plan* accounted for almost 17% of the financial resources disbursed during the actual implementation of the *Plan*.

The appropriate lesson from this experience was, apparently, not drawn and applied in the design of the *Fourth Plan*. The oil sector was booming again, of course, and this probably explains why the new *Plan* was even more ambitious than any before it. But history repeated itself rather quickly; within nine months of launching the massive *Fourth Plan*, the world oil market had crashed and Nigeria's access to external loans had virtually dried up. Hence, the *Fourth Plan* was essentially aborted as the country scrambled to put in place one short-term economic crisis management measure after another during the 1928-85 period.

Nigeria's experience with traditional development planning formally came to a halt in 1986 with the adoption of the Structural Adjustment Programme (SAP). The SAP explicitly jettisoned the "commanding heights" philosophy in favour of a private sector-led, more open and more outward-oriented development strategy in which the primary role of government is to provide an enabling environment, including ensuring the maintenance of macro-economic stability and an efficient delivery of public services. In pursuit of this new strategy, the economy has undergone various liberalization, deregulation and privatization programmes, all of which have had the effect of sharply curtailing public sector involvement in the production and distribution of a wide range of goods and services, as well as discontinuation of the indigenization of privately-owned foreign enterprises. In other words, the policy and institutional reforms implemented since 1986 have been directed at dismantling the key components of the "commanding heights" philosophy around which Nigeria's development planning efforts had been largely built.

The end of a series of fixed-term national development plans was not, of course, the end of planning in Nigeria. Planning, in fact, resurfaced in a different form in 1990 when it was decided to institutionalize a three-tier system of planning, comprising a 15 to 20-year *Perspective Plan* that encapsulates the long-term vision of the economy; a series of 3-year *Rolling Plans* that constitute specific operational phases of the *Perspective Plan*, and *Annual Budgets* being used to implement the *Rolling Plans*. This new planning format dovetailed into the *Vision 2010* document which attempted to map out the country's longer-term development aspirations, strategy and growth trajectory.

Several advantages are being claimed for this new planning arrangement. It is thought to be better adapted to take account of projects with long gestation periods, while articulating a vision for the economy and society that would be clear enough to stimulate an appropriate private investment response, despite unavoidable short-term fluctuations in the economy.

Meanwhile, the extensive machinery and structures for development planning that have been painstakingly built up during the 1970s, have virtually disappeared. Hence, the new planning format lacks an effective design culture and an efficient operational base. Whether these are worth re-creating in the context of the prevailing democratic and federal structure of government remains to be seen. It is clear, however, that under the current constitutional arrangement of a more open economic management system, only a bottom-up approach to planning can ensure that the resulting plans would broadly reflect the aspirations of the people and are effectively "owned" by them.

Ayida's contribution to development planning in Nigeria

Between 1957 and 1977, Allison Ayida was synonymous with development planning in Nigeria. Even after his retirement from public service, he continued to play a prominent role in this project. His experience with practical planning started with his membership of the committee charged with the establishment of the Central Bank of Nigeria in 1958. Apart from being the Chief Executive of the Ministry of Economic Development for several years, Ayida's sojourn in the Ministry of Finance gave him an oversight responsibility over many planning issues, as well as being an important member of many planning bodies. In addition to serving as a prestigious member of the Committee that had designed the *Second* and *Third National Development Plans,* he was also a member of the Vision 2010 project that developed the first long-term development plan for the country.

In addition to his extensive professional contributions as a planner, Ayida's academic and intellectual writings speak volumes about his contributions to the theory and practice of development planning in Nigeria. In his efforts to justify the need for national planning, Ayida points out the centrality of a collective wish for central planning and the coordination of economic activities for meaningful use of scarce resources to achieve meaningful development. In one of his lectures titled, "The Contribution of Politicians and Administrators to Nigeria's National Development" as published in *Reflections on Nigeria's Development*, Ayida (1987:30) unequivocally defends the need for development plans thus:

> It is now generally recognized that market forces alone and the existing market price structure in developing countries cannot generate a satisfactory

> rate of growth. There must therefore exist the will to plan and manage the economy at the national level, however decentralized the system is.

He has consistently taken the position that the activities of the private sector, if not well managed, are sometimes antithetical to national development aspirations. His belief in the moderation of market forces, through government intervention in economic activities, is summarized as follows:

> Sanity should be restored to the banking and financial system through concerted rationalization of the interest rate structure, abolition of stabilization securities, etc. Industry cannot survive in the long run with annual interest rates at about 40% and above (Ayida, 1992:9).

As observed earlier in this chapter, an important means of mobilizing funds for national development in the 1960s and 1970s was to have development plans. Since the profitability of projects matter for private creditors, a wise way of benefiting maximally from the supplemental nature of foreign capital is to institutionalize development planning. From his paper titled, "Contractor Finance/From and Supplier Credit in Economic Growth", Ayida (1965) points out that "Most lenders nowadays insist on lending substantial capital only to countries with National Development Programmes and sometimes to projects within such programmes." Thus, planning is an important way of mobilizing foreign resources for development, Ayida maintains.

Ayida unequivocally supports the participatory approach to planning as against the erstwhile elitist style. His conviction about the bottom-up approach in preference to the top-down approach has always been strongly canvassed. In his view, a planner must be cautious so as not to supplant the community's preference function by invoking his own subjective conception of social will. While this is a necessary condition for a plan to succeed, there must also be a political system characterized by positive, dynamic and charismatic leadership. Besides, he points out that traditional conflicts between national and group interests constitute a major problem in the country's planning process. He maintains that national plan priorities have been distorted because of the inordinate ambition of the major ethnic groups in the country. For instance, while planners had proposed only one Iron and Steel Project for the country on purely economic grounds, ethnic and political colourization had led to the duplication of the project in several parts of the country. His reaction to this unfortunate development is clearly reflected in the following observations:

> In such moments of national survival, through the art of compromise, economic considerations did not seem to matter. Nigerians were assured that they would soon have three Iron and Steel Projects, though on financial and economic grounds the Nigerian market was barely large enough to sustain one modest plant (Ayida, 1987:27).

The administrative, political and institutional aspects of planning where practical problems of plan implementation are the overriding consideration, constituted Ayida's major preoccupation while in service. Plan implementation during the military era was considered unrealistic in many respects, such as poor financing possibilities, a weak executive capacity, lack of effective coordination, and inadequate and untimely mobilization of resources. While all of these were considered central to plan failure in the country, issues of financing possibilities and a weak executive capacity were even more appalling at the state level. In most cases, there was a total violation of the existing rules and procedures, particularly where military and political leaders approved unplanned projects whenever they were involved in meet-the-people tours of their 'constituencies.' Ayida expressed his fears as follows: "The only danger comes when you begin to add projects at random and without any kind of adequate preparation or meaningful reconciliation with what is already there" (Ayida, 1987:103).

A recurring issue that features very prominently in Ayida's writings is the 'intellectual capacity' of the political and administrative system. The determination and maintenance of plan priorities is a technical exercise requiring specialized skills. Such specialized skills and talents are to be used to marshal evidence and collate data to assist the political heads of plan administration in Nigeria. The political heads, in turn, derive their authority from the legislature which provides the legislative basis for planning (Ayida, 1996:9-11). It is important to quote one of his favourite expressions in this respect as follows: "In national economic planning, there can be no substitute for inadequate political leadership. Administrative leadership, however competent, cannot rise above the quality of its political leadership" (Ayida, 1987:29).

In development planning, charismatic leadership is ineluctable. On this issue, Ayida shares the view that in the absence of political commitment, the most advanced form of planning will not make a significant contribution to development. But, given stable, strong, and devoted leaders, he agrees that the inadequacies of any type of plan would not seriously impede development. To him, all problems of plan implementation derive mostly from leadership problems, as the following clearly suggests: "The planning machinery may appear *prima facie* inchoate, diffused and inconsistent and on the whole totally ineffective because it lacks determined political support" (Ayida, 1996:8).

Ayida takes every opportunity to point out the efficacy of the national planning machinery, always emphasizing leadership attributes and administrative capacity. He demonstrates that the absence of these two factors in particular make the realization of plan objectives impracticable, even at the federal level.

Ayida's intellectual contribution to the practice of development planning revolves around some essential attributes. As far as he is concerned, good plan administration involves much more than the art of balancing and making compromises that have been a major feature of the Nigerian planning process. He insists that it requires the ability to establish a set of priorities and the will to maintain and execute the laid down priorities. His position is corroborated by the best practices on development planning - all of which emphasize plan discipline and technical competence. The salient features of Ayida's writings on development planning are the following ten guiding principles or, the "checklist" of successful development planning:

- The collective will of the people to plan and coordinate their resources;
- Competent technical planning apparatus;
- Collation and systematic analysis of statistical data on the economy;
- Effective system of budgetary controls and sanctions that would not only relate expenditure to available resources, but also keep within plan allocations, targets and priorities;
- Effective machinery for rational allocation of foreign exchange resources;
- Management and coordination of external aid to reflect development priorities;
- Tailoring research to meet planning requirements;
- Continuous application by adaptation, transplantation or innovation of modern science and technology to economic development;

- Provision of adequate manpower budgeting and continuous training of planners; and
- Accessibility to political power.

In Ayida's view, any country that downplays one or more of these attributes is not likely to benefit optimally from development planning.

Part III

Impressions of the man

10

Allison Akene Ayida

– *Izoma* P. C. Asiodu, CON

My first meeting with Allison Akene Ayida was in January 1947. He had just entered King's College, Lagos in Class I. I was in Class II having entered in January 1946. However, having performed brilliantly in the June examinations, Allison Ayida was given double promotion and started Class III with our group of 1946 in September 1947 and we have remained friends since then.

Fate arranged it that Allison Ayida should be placed in the same House in King's College, Hyde-Johnson's House, as myself, that we should go to the same college in Oxford, The Queen's College, and that we should read the same subjects – Philosophy, Politics, Economics (PPE). Thus we spent our important formative years together. Friendships made during school days are normally the most enduring ones. Growing up closely together, interacting day in day out for years on end should enable two individuals to know each other very well. But it also means that it requires great care and effort to remain objective on the part of one describing or commenting on the attributes and character of the other.

In appraising our impressions of one another at King's College, Lagos, three domains of activities were considered important, namely academic, sports and cultural – that is, extra curricular pursuits.

I have already referred to Allison Ayida's rare distinction of earning double promotion to join us in Class IV. He performed very well in our class and in overall scores was always among the best three. He had a good career in Oxford and went on in Autumn 1956 to the London School of Economics for post-graduate studies.

Although we were fully engaged in the Civil Service, we both cultivated close relations with professors and lecturers in our leading universities, particularly, Ibadan. We would deliver lectures in the universities occasionally. Allison Ayida, indeed, as the Permanent Secretary of the Ministry of Economic Development and Reconstruction over a period of eight years, (1963-71) had to maintain the closest liaison with the Faculties/Departments of Economics in the universities. He was a member of the Board of the Nigerian Institute of Social and Economic Research - NISER - and his Ministry, the Ministry of Economic Development and Reconstruction, was the principal source of subventions for the Institute.

Moreover, being a founding and very active member of the Nigerian Economic Society and one time President of the Society gave Ayida more opportunity for academic pursuits. He co-edited with Professor Bola Onitiri *National Development and Growth,* which collated the proceedings of the 1969 Conference 'Post-Civil War Reconstruction and Development' in which various stakeholders from academia, business, the civil service, the Armed Forces, multi-national companies, the Bretton Woods Institutions, etc. all participated under the Chairmanship of Chief S. O. Adebo. The Conference was very much his initiative. There are, of course, the numerous scholarly publications to Mr Ayida's credit.

We spent many weekends in university campuses, particularly Ibadan, debating various issues of national policy and the right model to ensure rapid development and progress in Nigeria. Such sessions were always intellectually stimulating.

Allison Ayida more than acquitted himself well on such occasions. There is no doubt that the conclusions of those sessions helped in the articulation of Government Policy at the time. However, the main issue here is the tradition of civil servants' intellectual exchanges with academia in patriotic comradeship and without complexes - a tradition which most unfortunately ended after the 1975 decimation of the Civil Service following the Military Coup that terminated the Administration of General Yakubu Gowon.

Allison Ayida earned his full colours in soccer as a regular member of King's College Lagos 1st XI. He was also good in athletics and represented the college in the Grier Cup Athletic Competition for secondary schools in Western Nigeria. At Oxford, Allison played in the Queen's College soccer 1st XI. Except for lawn tennis and to a lesser extent table tennis, we were not sporting companions, as my own special games were hockey, cricket and squash racquets.

As regards cultural activities, Allison Ayida was elected to the King's College Society - mainly a debating society but it also organized an Annual Tea party and Dance at the end of Trinity Term in June. This was always a great social occasion for the senior classes in selected secondary schools in Lagos. It was a mixed-sex affair and invitations were rationed out in quotas to the deserving Boys' and Girls' Schools to be invited. King's College Society itself in our days at King's was rather exclusive — confined to classes IV to VI. Only a given minority number were elected from class IV each year to join the Society. There was great excitement in the days leading to the Annual Event you could see everywhere boys practising their dance steps in order to acquit themselves well. Apart from this our version of the Summer Ball, the Society also organized excursions to interesting places and industrial establishments, etc. I remember Allison Ayida as an active member of the Society. There were no cadets in our days at King's. If there were, I am not sure that Allison would have joined.

At Oxford I recollect that he and I were members of several clubs and societies: Ikwan-Es-Safa - an international club of all races promoting international and interracial goodwill; Labour Club; Socialist Club; The West African Students Club of which he became President. The West African students in Oxford in my time rejected the idea of establishing branches of the Nigerian Union, Ghana Union, etc. as we felt we were too few and in any case did not like such divisions. Many of us, certainly Allison and myself, still hankered after the Pan Africanism of Zik, George Padmore, Nkrumah and others. I remember we were also hostile to the demands of Dr Busia for Federalism in Ghana. Indeed for Nigeria, we preferred the ideas of Zik's N.C.N.C. about the need for a strong Federation to the ideas of Awolowo's Action Group for a looser Federation. Still less did we like the wishes of Alhaji Ahmadu Bello and the Northern Peoples Congress for what would amount to a Confederation.

I can remember that we both participated in many social activities in Oxford with great verve. We did, of course, pay adequate attention to our studies which were our primary reason for going up to Oxford. But we often joked that with the many house parties, dances at Arlosh Hall, Carfax Assembly Rooms, etc we seemed to be at dance parties eight nights a week!

At Summer we would spend a few weeks in work-camps — mainly canning vegetables and fruit together with students from other universities and from many different countries. Both of us would save up quite a great deal from our labours only to spend all the money within two or three weeks enjoying ourselves in London with one or two friends like Dr Eben Ikomi and Engineer Frank Ogbemi. We enjoyed many youthful escapades together.

I did not obtain a post-graduate scholarship from the

Western Region Government to do what I wanted at Oxford and I left Oxford in December 1956 and took up a job at the London County Council intending to study Law as a private student. Ayida was already in London at LSE. We spent a few months in London together. In April 1957 having been offered a position in the Nigerian Foreign Service which was just being established, I decided to return to Nigeria. Allison Ayida was among one or two friends who saw me off at Euston Station, where I took the train to Liverpool to catch the boat which brought me back to Lagos. I did not know then that within a few months Allison would decide to return to Lagos and join the Nigerian Civil Service!

We spent only a few months together in Lagos before my Foreign Service assignments took me abroad. From 1958 to January 1963 I was abroad, posted successively to London, Canberra, Wellington, Tours and New York. We kept in touch. We sailed back together from England in 1959 in one of the last mail boat voyages to Lagos when I came home on leave, and in 1960 as a member of a Delegation led by the then Minister of Finance, Chief F. S. Okotie-Eboh, Ayida was my guest in New York.

However, I returned to Nigeria in January 1963 and in August 1964 I moved from The Foreign Service to the Home Civil Service as Deputy Permanent Secretary of the Ministry of Lagos Affairs. Allison Ayida had been assigned in June 1963 as Permanent Secretary of the Ministry of Economic Development in a bold recognition of talent and appointment of a "young" officer to the high office of Federal Permanent Secretary by Mr S. O. Wey, then Secretary to the Prime Minister and Head of the Federal Civil Service.

In April 1965 I was posted as Permanent Secretary of the Federal Ministry of Health but I had first to set up the new Ministry of Industries. From then on as Permanent Secretaries and as members of the Economic and Finance Co-ordinating

Committee which, with the Secretary to the Prime Minister as its Chairman, advised the Prime Minister and Cabinet on matters referred to it, we both worked very closely together. But then it was not all work alone. As I shall show later we contrived to spend together with a few other friends our leisure time partly in creative activities and partly in sporting activities.

The post-independence political crisis had begun in earnest in 1962 with the break-up of the Action Group into the Awolowo and Akintola factions and the eagerness of the ruling coalition of N.P.C. and N.C.N.C. to exploit the division. At the same time the continuing revolt in the Middle Belt had obliged the Federal Government to deploy soldiers to help restore law and order. Then the Zik-Balewa face-off following the clumsy, ill-calculated boycott of the 1964 Federal Elections by the UPGA coalition which they might have conceivably won if they did not boycott the elections. Then the final straw of the massively rigged 1965 Western Region elections and the subsequent break down of law and order. Thus the National Crisis situation continued to deteriorate until the Military Coup d'etat of January 15, 1966 and the end of the First Republic.

The National Crisis from 1962 onwards and particularly 1966 to 1970 - i.e. from the military overthrow of civilian government till the end of the Civil War were most testing times for the Federal Civil Service - its competence, loyalty to its oath to uphold the Federal Constitution, its non-partisan objectivity, its national standing, its international recognition, its adaptability and innovativeness. The Civil Service ethos to which we were both heirs included the following core values - hard work, adherence to the highest possible international standards of efficiency and integrity, the scrupulous observance of Civil Service Rules and Financial Instructions to ensure probity and frugality in the use of public funds. It also embraced the values of being caring custodians of public property, defence of the public interest and proponents of the public good. I found

Allison Ayida throughout our years in the Civil Service a great adherent of this noble ethos.

In those days when you joined the Civil Service you would very soon identify a few pre-eminent officers — pre-eminent in competence and efficiency, in clarity of articulation of issues in their minutes and of their directives, in their integrity and in the respect they commanded from their civil service colleagues and from the political bosses alike. You would choose one of such officers as a role model and would emulate him and try to attain his standards. I am sure that Allison Ayida became such a role model to many young officers.

Allison Ayida has truly recorded in his 'The Nigerian Revolution Reconsidered,'

> When the military first seized power, one of their first suggestions was to draw members of the Federal Cabinet from the military, the universities and some Federal Permanent Secretaries. We declined to serve and preferred to retain our traditional role as advisers.

But there were enormous challenges before the country and although the Military had assumed all executive and legislative powers, managing political processes and administering a country, let alone one as complex as Nigeria, was not what they were trained to do. There was the critical need to carry on the business of government and to prevent the situation from degenerating into chaos; to re-establish and guarantee one-Nigeria economy as a pre-condition for rapid growth and development.

After the counter-coup or second coup of July 29 1966 the situation deteriorated seriously with Ojukwu refusing to accept Col. Gowon as he was then as Head of the Federal Military Government and Commander-In-Chief of the Armed Forces. Strategies had to be devised for obtaining national consensus on Nigerian unity, for abolishing the resentment of one Region being so dominant as to be able to rule alone or overawe the Federal Government which was so prevalent during the First Republic, and should the nation be faced with the secession of the Eastern Region, strategies for containing the secession and preserving Nigerian unity.

It was not until June 1967 — eighteen months after the Military assumed power that they agreed on the insistent advice of the Permanent Secretaries, to appoint some leading politicians and other civilians to head Federal and State ministries as Federal and State Commissioners.

The duty of planning, providing policy advice to the Military Government assuring day-to-day administration of affairs, preparing for the prosecution of the war in terms of funding, logistics, procurement, etc fell on the Civil Service while the Military were fully engaged in military expansion, training and all that is entailed in military operations.

In human affairs the vast majority prefer to play it safe. They prefer the role of passive unoffending citizens carrying out instructions. It is given to only a few when confronted with danger to seek even at the cost their lives to rise to the challenge and proffer solutions to assure the safety of the people. It was inevitable given the circumstances that an activist pressure group should arise from within the rank of the Permanent Secretaries to act beyond the call of routinely defined duty. Ayida, Joda and myself with the co-option of a few others from time to time as necessary formed such a group. It is to the credit of late Andrew Ejueyitchie, the Secretary to the Federal Military Government from 1966 till the end of the Civil War and his successor, Abdhul Aziz Atta who died prematurely in 1972 that they agreed to lead the Group on many occasions to see and urge certain policies on the Head of the Federal Military Government in the national interest. It is especially to the credit of Gen. Gowon as Head of the Federal Military Government, that he had the disposition to listen to and accept objective advice. We would often work very late into the night until the early hours of the morning causing our wives in the process great fears and anxieties.

The creation of states was agreed upon and eventually 12 states were created by General Gowon's broadcast and Federal Decree on 27 May 1967 on the eve of the formal declaration of secession of Biafra by Emeka Ojukwu. Among the states created were South-East and Rivers States, thus responding to decades of agitation by COR (Calabar, Ogoja, Rivers) state movement. Failure of the Biafran leadership to offer a prospect of autonomy within a Federation to the people of those areas cannot have helped the secessionist cause.

Our small group was also engaged in many overseas tours explaining the Federal position and policies and post-war reconciliation and rehabilitation plans to overseas audiences and to Nigerians abroad. At home we undertook several visits to the war front with or without accredited journalists. The visits to the front not only showed that civilian officials at home cared for the sacrifices and exertions of the troops but also helped to enhance compliance with the code of conduct issued to the troops.

Allison Ayida played a very prominent role in the aborted negotiations with the Biafran Secessionists in Uganda during which his personal secretary was abducted and murdered. He put a great deal of hard work into the planning for post-war rehabilitation and reconstruction.

Throughout this most trying period of our modern history I found Allison Ayida a man of high intellect and resourcefulness and of great courage. He was most industrious and was able not only to conceive solutions to problems but also to organize and implement agreed solutions.

It was tragic that under Chief C. O. Lawson the small pressure group collapsed. He explained that he was available 24 hours a day to answer any call of the Head of the Federal

Military Government but he would not lead any group to pressure him whatever the situation. It was not in the Civil Service tradition to bypass the SFMG and Head of Service, especially in peace time, to see the Head of the Federal Military Government on matters which would result in him issuing directives to SFMG. Everyone then kept strictly to running the affairs of his ministry only. This partly explains the seeming drift in the two years leading up to the coup of 1975. By the time Allison Ayida became SFMG in April 1975, the die was already cast!

General Gowon was overthrown in a bloodless coup on 29 July 1975. In the course of time historians will give full account of the reasons and objectives of the coup which has been a watershed in Nigeria's modern history. The immediate successor of General Gowon, General Murtala Mohammed, and his successor, President Olusegun Obasanjo were members of General Gowon's last Federal Executive Council. They were privy to the assumptions, the policies and the programmes that formed the Third National Development Plan, 1975-1980 and they were exposed to some of the leading Permanent Secretaries.

I did observe in my paper in 1997 given at the National Workshop in Abuja on 'The Civil Service and Vision 2010' that:

> The structure and role of the Civil Service did not change under the military rule from 1966 to 1975. However, because of certain reasons the public image of the Civil Service changed radically during the period leading to resentment with such dire consequences for the Service in 1975 and the history of economic development of the country subsequently. The reasons included the heightened profile of Permanent Secretaries with the suspension of Parliament and the absence of Ministers from

> January 1966 to May 1967. This was compounded by the public role played by some Federal Permanent Secretaries in countering widespread political demands for confederation before the Biafran declaration of secession and the Civil War. Even when politicians were appointed Commissioners, they were happy to serve Nigeria but eagerly looked forward to the earliest possible end to military usurpation of their offices and they suspected that Civil Servants were happy to aid and abet the military. The academics, the media, and the businessmen had their own grouses. Meanwhile, the Permanent Secretaries being unused to political public relations failed to see the dangers and to explain their real role especially that they were not involved in the postponement of the 1976 date for restoring Civil Rule.

Yet, with all this said, I cannot even today fully understand the justification at the time for the mass purge and decimation of September to December 1975 when over 10,000 officials all over the country were dismissed or retired without due process and with much injustice — engendering in its wake massive discontinuities in economic policies and project implementation and monitoring thus creating many of the problems still affecting the country today, including demoralization of the Public Service, poor productivity, insecurity and corruption.

Several questions have bothered me ever since those traumatic events almost three decades ago. I have not discussed them with Allison Ayida. Could the purge and virtual destruction of the public service as we know it have been avoided by a principled, courageous stand against lack of due process and arbitrariness and secret accusations against which neither explanations nor defence were allowed? A resolute stand against injustices and insistence on following lawful procedures by the Senior Permanent Secretaries who were not the immediate target of the displeasure of the leaders of the 1975 coup? Again why was it not possible to rescind some of the unfair and destructive decisions after the findings of the Pedro Martins Panel?

The Nation has experienced since then a long sad period of twenty-nine years of decline in standards of governance. Knowing our near identity of views when we were both in the Civil Service and our occasional observations on the current state of the Civil Service and of national governance I believe that Allison Ayida must be as saddened as myself. It is indeed very sad to see one's lifetime endeavours and dreams seemingly crumble before one's eyes. In terms of economic indices and human welfare indicators Nigeria is 40 years behind where it should be. There is no reason why Nigeria should not be as well of today as the Asian Tigers if the 1975-1980 Plan were implemented and built upon. Nations less endowed with natural and human resources which had not produced as sophisticated plans for national development in the 1970s but whose leadership maintained policy stability and focus and empowered competent technocrats and managers to deliver rather than resent their prestige and influence derived from performance have been successfully led out of the poverty trap to international significance.

Ayida retired from the Civil Service in 1977. He soon became active and successful in the private sector. We both remained active in the Nigerian Economic Society and continued to interact with our old friends in academia. The military governments, particularly that of General Ibrahim Babangida, continued to appoint academics as ministers but the old close collaboration with civil servants who could translate their views and prescriptions into elements of important national policy was no more. The nation is poorer for it.

As in the old days when even at the worst periods of the National Crisis and Civil War we integrated exercise at Lawn Tennis three times a week into our time table, leading some disgruntled fellows to quip that national policy seems to be determined on the tennis court; we continued playing tennis regularly at the Lagos Lawn Tennis Club. Ayida tried to play golf immediately after retirement but gave it up and continued with tennis until a few years ago. I played tennis regularly until arthritis in both knees made it increasingly difficult and since starting to play golf in 1989 I have practically stopped playing tennis. I believe that Allison Ayida still keeps to his old routine of going to Wimbledon every summer to watch the major matches of the Wimbledon Open.

I have the most pleasant recollections of many happy journeys undertaken together over the years visiting friends in different parts of the country — to see Tayo Akpata in Ibadan and later in Benin City. Oje Aboyade in Ibadan and once in Awe his birthplace. There were also the visits to Adekunle Sansi, now *Ebelu* of Esure, in Oyo, and Dr Femi Bucknor in Okitipupa; to Ibrahim Damcida in Biu and with Ahmed Joda to Yola, Jalingo and Mambila. Memorable and pleasant were also the sessions of the Nigerian Economic Society at Lake Bagauda Resort near Kano and at Enugu and the visit with Grey Longe and Ime Ebong to see the road construction in progress from Idiroko to Porto Novo to join the road to Cotonou. We then spent the night at Avrankou camp built for the project.

There are recollections of a band of happy confident young people, working hard, joking and playing merrily together in those hopeful years of recovery and expansion before the fall of Gowon in 1975.

I should not end my impressions of Allison Ayida without a few words about him as a family man. After the death of his father, Allison cut short his post-graduate studies in London married the then Miss Remi Cheke, SRN, SCM, and returned to Nigeria to join the Federal Civil Service in 1957.

Allison has been richly blessed with a very hardworking, loyal, devoted and religious wife. Mrs Ayida had a very successful career in nursing retiring as Matron but she also found time to bring up her three sons and two daughters very well. Allison was equally a caring and devoted father who ensured that his children received the best education possible. Indeed his two daughters went to Oxford and he has encouraged and guided his children to embark on good careers.

I still have in mind the pictures of his children and mine who were younger, and of course, photographs are always there to remind us should memories dim, pictures of the numerous week-end trips to Agaja, Ibeche and beyond playing with the children on the lovely Lagos beaches in total security which then prevailed. I also remember the numerous overseas holiday tours and courses which as a good father he made time to undertake with his family. I believe that with the unceasing exertions and prayers of Remi and with his support both succeeded in creating a very happy family. I am also glad that they have continued to play the role of model grand parents.

We all shared the dream eloquently summarized in the five national objectives of the 2nd National Development Plan 1970-74 of seeing Nigeria become:

- a united, strong and self-reliant nation
- a great and dynamic economy
- a just and egalitarian society
- a land of full and bright opportunities for all citizens
- a free and democratic society

Perhaps, more so in the history of nations than of individuals applies the saying "Better late than never" I am sure that Allison Ayida still has this dream. So have I and we pray that despite the raging tempests still buffeting the Nigerian state it will sail through it all and that the dream will be realized.

11

Allison Ayida: the crusader

- Chief Tayo Akpata

Former Trustee/Secretary, Petroleum (Special) Trust Fund

Some Nigerians tend to perceive "super permanent secretaries" as a special class of public servants with considerable influence and power, a status attained not necessarily on merit. Yet, others admit that these public servants attained and kept the dizzy heights of their careers by sheer ability, competence, diligence and unflagging commitment to overriding national interests. Allison Ayida, in many ways, personified this latter genre of public servants. He adorned the higher civil service, notwithstanding the unjustified reservation of less informed persons. Thus, he could be said to be a charismatic professional and competent technocrat. Understandably, in a country besotted with "wheeling and dealing" in most facets of life, where ascription, "god-fatherism" and various non-achievement criteria obtain in determining career mobility, even within a bureaucracy that should be achievement-oriented, success in the public service tends to be ascribed to Machiavellian practices and other less endearing, non rational factors. At best, successful public servants may be considered "lucky." But, alas, has Allison Ayida been merely lucky in his public career? Was he just in the right places at the right time or, did he possess the sterling attributes indispensable to a conventional public servant? Put differently, did he possess the charisma, competence and discretion of a technocrat?

A careful assessment of his early educational career, through the public service to his post-retirement hibernation, will tend to show fairly conclusively that the height he had "reached and kept" in the service had not been "obtained by sudden flight" or by mere fluke. The markings were all there when, at King's College, Lagos, he spent only four years to obtain his School Certificate, with flying colours, and went on, in a record time, to pass the General Certificate of Education at advanced level and the Higher School Certificate, too. By going on later to study for his bachelor's and higher degrees at Oxford and at the London School of Economics, with the same zeal and brilliance, he was merely confirming the potential he had shown very early on. Equally, Allison Ayida was not found wanting in sports and social grace. He bestrode ethnic and social barriers and related effortlessly with different strata and generations of persons of all races. These qualities have undoubtedly been crucial to the invaluable contributions he has made, as a higher civil servant, to the socio-political development of Nigeria.

His success and that of his classmate and soul mate in the pre-1975 Federal Service was, for several days, the subject of broadcasts on the defunct Nigerian Broadcasting Service (NBS) which had their achievements blazoned on to the world stage. From then on Allison Ayida, who is publicity shy, could no longer avoid public glare; he had been launched on the national and international scene. Some of his trail-blazing policy initiatives were to form the bedrock of government action. For example, the speech he delivered in Calabar in 1971 foreshadowed the Federal Government's intervention in the expatriate-run banks. This type of initiative or 'pace-setting policy thrust' would constitute the hallmark of his career in the Service.

Unfortunately, some of his fears and reservations about the

political culture of Nigeria and the behaviour of the ruling elite at various times would seem to have materialized. Well-articulated political manifestos and professional development planning are now things of antiquity in the Nigerian body polity. Owing to Allison Ayida's deep and wide knowledge of events, as well as his passion for the role of the public service in national development, he had a most visible profile in the Service. He became a role model and a mentor to his junior colleagues. He was uncompromising on the professionalism of the Service, its non-partisanship, loyalty and adherence to due process and patriotism. If ever he had doubts about these norms, his experience of the "rising grass" incident in the testy days of July 1966 put paid to such doubts. His exposure of "contractor and supplier credit" was penetrating. It exposed the blatant fraud inherent in a practice that was meant to be a progressive mode of economic development.

In some respects, Allison Ayida's entry into the public service in 1957 was at a unique time when Nigeria was in the throes of terminal colonialism. Cynicism about the capability of the black man to assume the mantle of bureaucratic leadership was rampant. As Allison Ayida had observed, the departing expatriate officers, who were "lords of the manor", tended to pamper the political class in the interest of the former. It will be observed that, historically, from 1954 to independence, there was an increasing identity of interest between the ruling Nigerian political class and the colonialists. It was not long before Ayida, as an assistant secretary in the Federal Ministry of Education, found himself in a little "storm in a teacup," which he survived. The incident showed him very early in his career that security of tenure and the in-built factors to protect loyal and diligent civil servants actually worked.

Later on, Allison Ayida was to serve as Permanent Secretary in the Ministries of Finance and Economic Development, as well as Secretary to the Federal Military Government and Head of Service. His relevance in the history of the Service and this country lay mostly in his contributions to development planning and the political evolution of the country. His tireless advocacy for the preservation of the territorial integrity of Nigeria at all times, especially during the civil war years, was unequalled. Ayida was a superb public relations man, although prone to occasionally uttering subtle and withering broadsides. He had the uncanny penchant for catching them "fresh and young" from academia: Hardly any other occupant of the positions Allison Ayida held in public service did so much to promote and involve academics and other professionals in economic planning and the development of the country. It was no longer *Planning Without Facts*. His attitude to planning was the result of his deep conviction of the critical relationship between well-researched facts and policy formulation, with the eventual disinterested implementation of public policy to advance the cause of sovereign public interest being always paramount. At one time or another, academics were either on sabbatical leave in the Ministry of Economic Development or involved in some *ad hoc* assignments on behalf of that Ministry. He kept the Nigerian Institute of Economic and Social Research (NISER) ever so busy with socio-economic policy matters. Indeed, the Ministry of Economic Development became a mini-university where senior academics and students on vacation had a ready laboratory to test their accumulated or inchoate knowledge. Thus, they became participant/observers in the exciting and revitalizing world of national planning and development - a clear lesson that scientific knowledge is critical to a properly conceived and understood modernization process.

It was no surprise, therefore, that Ayida had foreseen the problems that were likely to arise in post-civil war Nigeria, and had convened a National Conference on Reconstruction in Ibadan in 1969. The conference considered and made far-reaching recommendations on political and socio-economic issues, and was generously supported by politicians, academics, public servants and participants from the private sector. Later, the recommendations of the conference were published and edited jointly by Professor Ajibola Onitiri, Director, NISER, and Allison Ayida. The publication became the basis of the *Second National Development Plan, 1970-1974*, a truly endogenous development plan crafted by an all-Nigerian 'crew', with Professor Ojetunji Aboyade as its leader. As usual, the Asiodus and the Ebongs, etc., had their inputs. For the first time, Nigeria's development plan contained social objectives with a putative manifesto. It is hardly surprising, therefore, that the declaratory objectives contained in the *Plan* have found their way into successive Nigerian constitutions since 1979.

Among other things, Ayida had advocated a National Planning Commission, as in India, to be staffed by professional planners. Unfortunately, much of what we see today in the name of national planning has, at best, been vulgarized and stood on its head. In seminars, conferences and brain-storming sessions up and down the country, Allison Ayida and his 'gang of three' were ever present with academics on university campuses, organizations and institutions contributing forcefully and informatively to public debate on national issues. The thrust and essence of their contribution was a strong advocacy for the promise and vitality of a properly managed Nigeria. No opponents or 'doubting Thomases' were too formidable to be engaged in rational discourse on the Nigerian economy, anywhere and at any time. As has been observed, Allison Ayida came to his own and won his spurs as a great, committed and unwavering advocate of the oneness and indivisibility of Nigeria before, during, and after the civil war years and has remained unchanged since. This writer, who utterly shared his conviction on this fundamental issue, was often with him on the barricades, or in the trenches, trying to convert others to our cause. In the process, Allison Ayida and his gang were called names, including the sometimes derogatory 'super permanent secretaries.' Yet, many converts to the Nigerian project were won over, although the battle continues. Thus, despite his continuing cerebral and polemical advocacy, the birth of "the Nigerian Revolution" is yet to become a reality.

Allison Ayida's crusade for scientifically driven policies was not confined to Nigeria, as his participation in overseas seminars demonstrated. For example, in his valedictory speech as Chairman and Leader of the Nigerian Delegation to the ninth session of the United Nations Economic Commission for Africa (ECA), he submitted that it would be wrong for the ECA to perceive its function as an organization that merely accumulated and disseminated knowledge. Rather, he enjoined the ECA to "become a dynamic institution for fostering the rapid development of African countries," and to ensure it had the resources to do so. He was hardly sparing in his blunt admonition of African countries which relentlessly pursued foreign aid for their development programmes, instead of concentrating "more on self help and expanding mutual trading opportunities" between and among them. "How can a country which depends overwhelmingly on foreign aid be safe and independent", he had queried? The remarkable point about many of his incisive and outspoken pronouncements, such as those on public affairs, is that they remain as relevant and evergreen today as they were a couple of decades ago when he first uttered them. For example, Ayida had expressed fear that unless the "leakages and mismanagement" in our finances were "plugged" and replaced with prudent financial management, our financial plight would persist. At that time, little could he have foreseen the current muddle in Nigeria's foreign debt, deficit budgeting, bloated bureaucracy, and rampant "resource misallocation and abuse of office."

If there are still as knowledgeable, experienced and committed public servants in this country as Ayida's career has demonstrated, why does Nigeria seem to continue groping in the dark and seemingly condemned to crude power calculations by all sorts of questionable actors? Almost three decades after Allison Ayida fired his first salvoes at home and abroad, the neo-military 'democrats' continue, relentlessly, to roam round the world in search of the elusive foreign aid. Although Allison Ayida believes that Nigeria possesses one of "the warmest investment climates in the Third World," where is the committed visionary and capable leadership to maximize the use of such investment? Instead, it seems that the idea is being utilized to skew the developmental process. Consequently, the obsession of the Nigerian ruling elite with foreign aid has become wasteful of existing national resources, counter-productive, fraudulent and, at best, needlessly diversionary. The whole policy has become a bogey and opium for a people who yearn for genuine development. Compared with the pre-1975 years, Nigeria now seems to be trapped in a syndrome in which "it is relatively easier to manage an empty treasury than to ensure financial discipline and control in a cash-surplus situation," as Ayida once observed.

In the government-organized show debate on the imminent devaluation of the national currency (Naira) in the late 1980s, the red rag of the IMF had been mischievously waved. In spite of the professional advice of experienced and seasoned experts to the contrary, 'patriotic' economists who knew better had their way. Ayida and his soul mate at the time were on the side of the "devils" that is, non-devaluation. Today, the nation knows better with the exchange rate of the Naira hitting the roof, and Nigeria is now a haven for all sorts of imports under the guise of globalization – the euphemism for contemporary American imperialism.

Ayida had revisited this subject in his address entitled, *The Nigerian Revolution, 1966-1976* and had attributed the parlous state of the economy to the death of small- and medium-scale industries. Today, we may readily add globalization and de-indigenization of the economy, in effect, 'denationalization'. Instead of government, in our context, remaining on the "commanding heights" of the economy, it has taken to the foothills. With ill thought-out and ill-prepared, privatization and deregulation 'reforms', what is left of government's role in the economy, one may ask, as Ayida had often asked.

Allison Ayida had been upbeat about the change of government in 1966. In his "Nigerian Revolution, 1966-1976" lecture, he had concluded with the peroration of: "I am proud to be a Nigerian." He was optimistic that the prospects for a new dawn would result from the nine-point programme that the Federal Military Government had promulgated in 1970. The programme was aimed at sanitizing the socio-economic-political culture of a people emerging from a devastating civil war. Today, we may cavil about a non-listening government. For Allison Ayida, this could not be so. He was convinced that the military was receptive to well-articulated and informed ideas drawn from a wide variety of sources, such as the universities, the civil service, and the organized private sector, thereby enjoying a certain level of legitimacy. In such context, Ayida saw the role of the civil service as pivotal to national development and had wondered aloud whether the military, with its self-imposed mission to sanction errant civil government, would ever return to the barracks. If this was the million-Naira question in 1976, it was answered in December 1983 when the military seized power from an elected government, yet again.

As it happened, Nigeria has experienced a much longer military than civilian rule, with dire consequences for nation-building. The earlier genre of military rule in Nigeria, which had tempted supreme optimists to quote Alexander Pope's immortal words with gusto, is no more! It seems as if every military or civilian regime in Nigeria has been progressively worse than its predecessor, a view amply shared by Ayida. The dream of the optimists about a "Nigerian revolution" being championed by the military could be compared to that of the socialist internationalists during the Spanish civil war. The socialists had thought that the enthusiastic fervour aroused by the intervention of an international brigade, led by General Franco, would be overthrown and that a brave new dawn would replace it. Rather, a ruthless fascist dictatorship was unleashed on Spain for many years. Oakeshott, in his *Rationalism in Politics,* had mockingly proclaimed, "See how history made a fool of John Stratchey!", Stratchey being one of the socialists who had fought in the Spanish civil war. Let us hope that history rather than make a fool of Nigerian optimists, such as Allison Ayida, will eventually vindicate them!

It would be no exaggeration to argue that the tenure of Allison Ayida's civil service career and his contribution to national development deserves a multi-disciplinary appraisal. In his activities and pronouncements, he remained a solidly creative, thoroughly loyal and non-partisan civil servant. Of course, as in every sphere of life, success tends to evince adoration as well as abhorrence, even amongst peers. Allison Ayida was well imbued with the public service ethos. It would be hard to cite examples of his derailing from the letter and spirit of the game, except for good, verifiable causes and always in the interests of the nation. From very early in his short career, he had realized that there was virtue in sticking to the rules of his practice in a delightfully dynamic and imaginative manner. He never considered government rules and regulations, especially the General Orders (GO) and the Financial Instructions (FI) as constituting an albatross or a cover for administrative and financial tardiness or incompetence, but as rules to be creatively applied while ensuring predictability in the management process. His admiration for and defence of the Service in the Nigeria body polity, especially in a crisis situation, knew no bounds. Allison Ayida was not hesitant to give full marks to the federal and state civil services when he declared that "the part they had played in the civil war and the aftermath of the crisis will go down in our history as one of the decisive elements in Nigeria's quest for survival as a nation."

Allison had played the critical role of a 'Goebel' during the Nigerian civil war by disregarding the views of the Nigerian Head of State and dishing out 'disinformation' to the world on the status of the war. Whereas the Biafrans were marching on Lagos and the Ore Bridge had been blown off by the federal forces in order to halt the advance of the Biafran army to Ibadan and Lagos, Allison Ayida and Ahmed Joda, another "super permanent secretary," were actively concealing the facts at a world press conference. In truth and fact, the federal troops had been overrun in Akure. If the "truth, and nothing but the truth" of the situation had been told, there might have been utter chaos and panic in Benin City and its environs. One wonders if Ayida and Joda could have got away with playing such a role in the present dispensation. Nor, indeed, could one of the 'higher civil servants' who had reportedly snapped at General Gowon, the Head of State, by saying: "I am not your Secretary but Secretary to the Federal Military Government" during a particularly tense face-off on a point of principle. We may compare the Ayida/Joda role with that of the hapless permanent secretary who, in 1985, reportedly predicted, correctly, who would be his new military boss in a paper he delivered at a conference and was literally booted out his office within minutes of his presentation of the paper!

Paradoxically, Allison Ayida's enthusiasm for, and commitment to, the civil service and its rational norms received a mortal blow in 1975 when the mass retirement of public servants was carried out nationwide, with him as the Head of Service. For various reasons, some salacious, many public servants, without due process, lost their careers and means of livelihood as a result. "The immovables have been moved," a national newspaper had shrilled derisively. The retirees had no right of appeal. Pedro Martins, a Catholic soldier-priest who was charged with investigating the grievances of the retirees, found that most of them had been unjustly retired. His reward was that he, in turn, lost his commission in the Nigerian Army! Since then and several review panels of the civil service structure, retreats, seminars, etc., to the bargain, the basis of commitment to the public service and service to the nation seems to have been irretrievably compromised. The various 'reforms' of the 1980s finally brought the Service to its knees. The golden age when civil servants could stand their ground against political bosses in the national interest and expect justice seems gone forever. The Public Service Commission, except for its recruitment function, seems a ghost of its former power and influence.

In all this, the question remains: Why was the higher civil service so seemingly helpless when the pestilence of mass retirement struck the Nigerian Civil Service in 1975, a disease which has since become pandemic? Even the present post-military regime has not spared the nation the irksome experience of "retirement with immediate effect." Some of the victims of the pernicious practice have been recent recipients of national awards! It is a puzzle that members of the higher civil service, who won accolades for their professionalism, competence and commitment in the civil war years and immediately after, have not been on record to have taken a stand against the hounding dogs of war that have been unleashed on the Service since 1975. As a result of the 1975 mass retrenchment exercise, several decades of nurturing, which the colonialists and post-independence politicians had given the public service, have been rubbished. It is hardly surprising that in the rudderless body polity of modern Nigeria, the public service seems totally helpless. Its internal antithetical contradictions, such as its persistence on implementing the policy of 'federal character,' are almost as chronic as those of the ruling elite. However, it needs to be pointed out that a couple of individual senior public servants, both in the civil service and in the parastatals, heroically stood their ground against the heartless retirement directive. Ayida, in retirement, is on record as having publicly declaimed the palpably unjust and irrational exercise and its deleterious impact on the Nigerian public service.

Allison Ayida, a man of many parts, intellectually and professionally and also a diplomat but not infrequently given to incisive, hard-biting comments on public affairs, has 'paid his dues.' He could not be expected to have single-handedly 'carry the can' for the shortcomings of his beloved civil service, particularly after his premature exit from it in 1977. For the younger colleagues who joined the Service in the 1960s, Allison Ayida remains a role model. His capacity for bringing persons of different backgrounds and shades of varying opinions and disciplines to bear on policy formulation and implementation was remarkable. He remained a classic among his colleagues. One would always recall the heydays of his headship of economic planning with a sense of nostalgia. All over Nigeria and abroad, his professional mien won respect, admiration and impacted positively on the country and the regimes he was privileged to serve in. Luckily, Ayida's successive political, military and bureaucratic bosses have recognized the phenomenal talents of the soft-spoken Oxonian and have given his talents full reign. The well-earned opportunity to serve had enabled him to contribute immeasurably to Nigeria's development at a particularly critical period of its continuing evolution as a nation.

12

Allison Ayida: the making of a super perm-sec

- Professor Akin L. Mabogunje
former Chairman, Development Policy Centre, Ibadan

In the first half of the 1970s, the Nigerian press introduced the term "super perm-sec" into the nation's vocabulary. This was to describe four senior members of the Federal Civil Service: Allison Ayida, Phillip Asiodu, Ime Ebong and Ahmed Joda. The term was used in a rather disparaging manner almost to describe civil servants who did not know their limitations in the decision-making hierarchy of government and were ascribing more powers to themselves than they were entitled to do. But in truth the term was describing a phenomenon of public officers who, because they were well informed, knowledgeable and very confident of their views, gave advice which their political masters could not easily ignore. The super permanent secretaries, indeed, represented the best tradition of the civil service of any country. That this was so is well illustrated in the post-service career of each of the four individuals mentioned, although Ime Ebong died before this could be established in his case. Each of them, even after their civil service career was mistakenly truncated in the great purge of the later part of the 1970s, continued to play distinguished leadership roles both in the private and the public sector of national life.

This brief testimonial is in respect of only one of the quartet although in some ways his career was never as singular as it might appear. Allison Akene Ayida was born in Gbelebu, Siluko, on June 16, 1930, in what was then the Delta Province of the Colony and Protectorate of Nigeria. Because of the shifting nature of employment opportunities in those days, many parents had to live a somewhat peripatetic life with consequent impact, among other things, on the schooling of their children. Thus, Allison started schooling at the United Native Africa Church Mission School in Gbelebu, and had to transfer to the Roman Catholic Mission School, Ubiaja in the then Benin Province and back again to Ogitsi Memorial School, Okere, Warri in the then Delta Province. It was from here that, given his natural intellectual capacity, he got admission to King's College, Lagos in 1947 where he was to spend the next four years reading for the Cambridge School Certificate Examination which he passed with flying colours by 1950, and the Higher School Certificate Examination in 1952.

In this testimonial reflection, it is important to note how Allison used the opportunities presented by the changed circumstances of the country to become a public officer who was regarded as above the common run and one of the most distinguished Nigerians of this generation. A good number of my generation went through the same experience. Sometimes our paths crossed; sometimes they didn't. But whether they did or not, on hindsight, it is now difficult not to acknowledge the transforming significance of the period in the lives of all of us leaving school in the late 1940s or early 1950s. I have, therefore, divided this reflection into four parts, starting with the effervescent atmosphere of political development in Nigeria, especially Western Nigeria, in the 1950s, years when Nigeria enjoyed what was called internal self-government. The second part then examines Allison's role as a civil servant in using the privileged educational opportunities which he had enjoyed with a relatively small but growing band of young men and women in promoting the development process of the country. In the third part, I consider Allison's role in helping to forge and sustain national unity in the decade that almost saw the break-up of the country and the waging of a 30-month civil war. In the fourth part, I look at the way Allison worked with some of his contemporaries to see whether an institutional legacy of his rich, and what now looks like a peculiar, experience can be left for future generations. I then conclude by examining how all this helped in making Allison Ayida really and truly a "super permanent secretary".

The development effervescence of the 1950s

The late 1940s saw the beginning of serious changes in the political landscape of Nigeria. These were changes which, although essentially political, had tremendous implications for virtually every other aspects of life of the average Nigerian. The period could be said to begin with the return of Dr. Nnamdi Azikiwe to the country. Although the nationalist struggle in the country had already begun, his return gave a remarkable fillip to the movement. His educational career in the United States made him less anxious to be cast in the mode of the British colonialist. His short stint as a journalist in what was then the Gold Goast (now Ghana) made him appreciate the importance of the newspaper in fanning the embers of nationalist protest. Not unexpectedly, Dr. Azikiwe's major effort was to establish a daily newspaper, the *West African Pilot,* in Lagos and to work with Mr. Herbert Macaulay to form a political party, the National Council of Nigeria and the Cameroon (NCNC).

The *West African Pilot* became the most effective champion

of the nationalist struggle for the political emancipation of Nigeria. It not only strove to portray how unnatural and unacceptable colonialism was, insisting that it was man's inhumanity to man, it also worked to fire the imagination of Nigerian youths that higher education was central to the task of decolonization. Although the readership of the newspaper was largely in the Lagos area, copies did manage to get to most parts of the country. The flamboyant language of the newspaper found resonance in the bombastic inclinations of most Nigerian youths in their first encounter with the English language. It was, therefore, a favourite reading material for many youngsters whenever they could lay their hands on a copy. The newspaper underscored the fact that securing a good pass in the Cambridge School Certificate examination, even with an exception from the London Matriculation to boot, was no longer enough for the country's future leaders. The paper emphasized that the youths had to find various ways and means of going abroad for graduate and post-graduate education, a point vividly illustrated in the newspaper by using the imagery of the Greek mythology of Jason going in search of "the golden fleece." Those whose parents did not have the means of sending them abroad thought a lot about "stowing away" in the hold of cargo ships docking in Lagos. Various communities, especially in Igboland, came together to raise funds to award scholarships to youngsters to go abroad for higher education. The newspaper gave prominence to stories of young men who had managed to get abroad to study and were returning to the country. The arrival of such youngsters was usually a very special occasion for their families and their communities who saw it as a major indication of progress. Such returnees were usually taken to church for thanksgiving services in which relations and many members of the community participated, after which there was considerable merriment and jollification.

The United States of America had a special appeal for most

Nigerian youths at the time, but it was, invariably, the most difficult to get to. Its particular appeal was that, as a former colonial territory of Britain, it had much to teach about gaining political independence from that country. Besides, apart from Dr.Nnamdi Azikiwe, other budding nationalists being promoted by the *West African Pilot* included the likes of Dr. Mbonu Ojike, Dr.Mbadiwe and Dr. Orizu, all of whom were lead writers for the paper and whose fiery writings became almost daily reading for Nigerian students and youths. Then came Dr. Ikejiani, a medical practitioner with a post-graduate Doctor of Medicine degree from the University of Toronto, Canada. His arrival in 1947 and all the fanfare that went with it, as reported in the newspaper, also served to further inflame the ambition of Nigerian youths about going abroad to further their education.

By 1947, especially with the end of the Second World War in 1945, Britain had decided to set in motion significant political processes for the development of its colonies. The Colonial Government conceived of a *Ten-year Plan of Development and Welfare (1946-1956)* for Nigeria. At the same time, it also set in motion a number of dramatic constitutional changes, all of which were to impact significantly on the life of Allison and our generation in general. This constitutional reform began with the drawing up of a new constitution for the country in 1947 which came to be known as the Richards Constitution. The main provision of this constitution was the division of Nigeria into three regions, each with a Regional House of Assembly. It was the original intention that this Constitution would operate only for six years after which amendments would be considered. But Nigerian politicians used it to force the hands of Britain such that by 1949 the inadequacies of the Constitution had become very obvious.

A General Conference to review the Constitution was summoned for Ibadan in 1950. The new Constitution which emerged from the Conference came to be known as the

McPherson Constitution. It became operational in 1951 and was remarkable for conceding considerable executive powers to the Nigerian political class. For the first time, it proposed the election of members to each of the Regional Houses of Assembly. The election was, however, on the basis of electoral colleges and involved a series of intermediate stages, beginning with primary elections at which all male adult taxpayers were allowed to vote. Delta Province, the home province of Allison Ayida, was then a part of the Western Region. Election to the Western Regional House of Assembly was fought bitterly between the better known political party of Dr. Nnamdi Azikiwe - the National Council of Nigeria and the Cameroon (NCNC) - and the less well known but much better organized party of Chief Obafemi Awolowo, the Action Group. In the ensuing electoral college election, the Action Group emerged as the numerically superior party and moved on to form the party in power in the Region.

As a political party, the Action Group proved itself unique among the two parties forming the governments of the other Regions in that it came to power with a well-articulated set of policies on virtually every aspect of government. Its policy on education was perhaps the most revolutionary at the time, not only in Nigeria but also in Africa. The policy proposed to make primary education free for every child in the Region on attaining the age of six years, starting in January 1955. To prepare for it, a wide-ranging programme for capacity building was initiated in the Region. It began with establishing, in 1953, numerous two-year teacher training colleges whose products were meant to be ready by January 1955 to teach in the new primary schools all over the Region. Four-year teacher-training colleges were also established to prepare teachers for the Higher Elementary Certificate examination and equip them to teach the higher classes in the new primary schools.

Graduates were also to be trained not only to man these

teacher-training colleges but also to provide high-level manpower for various other departments of government. In this regard, it is noteworthy that the opportunities for post-secondary education within Nigeria itself had been changing, in consonance with the spirit of the colonial development process embarked upon by Britain after the Second World War. Instead of the earlier limitations placed on the educational ambition of Nigerians by the establishment of the Yaba Higher College in the 1930s, the British Government set up the Elliott Commission in 1943 to review the state of higher education in its West African colonies and make appropriate recommendations. In spite of the existence of Fourah Bay College in Freetown, Sierra Leone which had been established by the Church Missionary Society in the 19th century and was affiliated to the University of Durham in Britain, the Commission recommended that the whole West African Region needed only one other University College which was to be sited in Ibadan, Nigeria and to be in special relation with the University of London.

The University College in Ibadan opened its doors to students in October 1948 by taking over most of the students of the Yaba Higher College. From 1949, however, it began taking in directly young school leavers with the Cambridge School Certificate with exemption from London Matriculation, but only after they would have scaled through a highly competitive entrance examination. University College Ibadan in its early years provided mainly courses in Arts, Science and Agriculture. Students admitted to read for other professional courses, particularly in Medicine and Engineering, were sent abroad after taking their Intermediate Bachelor of Science or their Second Bachelor of Medicine, Bachelor of Science examinations.

By the end of its first five years when University College Ibadan had graduated the first batch of students admitted as fresh men in 1949, its total student population was then just about 300 and those of them enjoying government scholarships or bursaries were fewer than 50. Most of the students were either being sponsored by their parents, school proprietors, communities, or various ethnic associations, such as the *Egbe Omo Oduduwa*. In spite of the relatively small number of its total enrolment of students, the emergence of University College Ibadan had served to fan into a huge conflagration the embers of a burning ambition for higher education among Nigerian youths, and the *West African Pilot* and other Nigerian newspapers had kept it smoldering over the decades. Higher education was no longer seen just as an adventure or the search for "the golden fleece;" it had become the great key that opened the door to transforming the life chances of any and all Nigerian youths who could successfully complete their secondary education.

Given the Action Group's commitment to education, it was little surprise that the party launched a massive programme of offering scholarships and bursaries to most indigenes of the Western Region who passed the entrance examination to University College Ibadan. Moreover, the party also decided to award 200 scholarships annually, tenable in overseas universities, to students whose course preferences were either not available at University College Ibadan or who wanted to do post-graduate studies. Given the Nigerian bias for the British educational system, it was not surprising that most of the scholarships were tenable in British universities. And since the discipline of Economics and the Social Sciences generally were at that point in time not offered at University College Ibadan, all students desirous of studying Economics had to be sent to overseas universities. Allison Ayida's decision to study Economics thus meant that soon after leaving King's College in 1950 and staying on for the two-year Higher School Certificate examination, he got admission, in 1953, to Queen's College,

University of Oxford to read for the PPE (Politics, Philosophy and Economics) Bachelor of Arts (Honours) degree which he successfully completed in 1956.

By that time, I too had completed my first Bachelor of Arts (General) degree at the University College Ibadan and had secured, in 1954, a Western Regional scholarship to do a Bachelor of Arts (Honours) degree in Geography at the University College, London. Since I was allowed to do that degree in two years, I too graduated in London in 1956. Thereafter, I stayed on at University College London to do a Master's degree. This was at the same time that Allison moved on to the London School of Economics & Political Science (more popularly referred to as LSE) to do a postgraduate course in Money & Banking. The University of London ran a number of inter-collegiate programmes which provided opportunities for students from different Colleges in London to get to meet. Besides, the London School of Economics & Political Science kept a library from which students were not encouraged to borrow books to take home. Consequently, I found myself working often in that Library and getting to meet many of the Nigerian students at LSE. And that was how I first met Allison Ayida.

I remember my first impression of Allison as an unhurried student who, in general discussion or in argument, took pains to make his point and to articulate it with much controlled passion. As students, then and now, political goings-on in Nigeria were always of abiding interest. Occasionally, I would run into Allison in the company of other Nigerian students, such as Bola Onitiri or Sam Aluko or late George Ijewere. LSE had a sizeable colony of Nigerian students (in contrast to University College London where I was studying) and it was always a lively group when they met in the College's restaurant. I enjoyed my time there on the few occasions when I was part of the group. But Allison soon dropped out of the group as he abruptly terminated his course and returned to Nigeria in 1957 when he was appointed into the Federal Public Service as an Assistant Secretary. In this position, he was soon to be sent to the United States to spend some six months between October 1958 and March 1959 at both the Chase Manhattan Bank and the Federal Reserve Bank in New York.

Ayida and the challenge of national development

Allison joined the Federal Civil Service at a most critical time for Nigeria, both politically and constitutionally. The year before his joining the Service, in 1956, Chief Tony Enahoro, representing the Action Group in the Federal House of Representatives, had moved the motion for Nigerian political independence from Britain. This had been opposed by representatives of the Northern Peoples Congress and a political and constitutional stalemate had resulted, forcing the British Government to propose another Constitutional Conference in London for 1957. That was to be the last of a series of such Conferences. But it was at that Conference that it was agreed that Nigeria would become politically independent on October 1, 1960.

In the interval and with respect to the Nigerian Civil Service, emphasis was to be on the recruitment of appropriate high-level, well-trained manpower. Because of the very dynamic and progressive set of policies being formulated and implemented in the Western Region at the time, most graduates of Western Region origin invariably looked to the Regional Civil Service for their careers. Allison must have read the long-term signals correctly by opting to move instead to the Federal Civil Service. His training in Economics started to show him off as out of the common run, a fact that must have been largely responsible for his being sent, within less than a year of joining the Service, for the special course at the Federal Reserve Bank in New York. At any rate, his general performance was so impressive that within less than six years of joining the Service, he had moved through the ranks to the position of Permanent Secretary in the Federal Ministry of Economic Development by 1963.

The promotion of Allison to the position of Permanent Secretary and particularly his posting to the Federal Ministry of Economic Development says much about Allison's involvement with the history of post-independence planning in Nigeria. With the political changes of the 1950s that saw Nigeria evolve as a federation of three Regions, the Colonial *Ten-Year Plan of Development and Welfare* had to be terminated prematurely in 1954. In its place, an *Economic Development Plan (1955-60)*, which was later extended to 1962, was crafted with the assistance of the International Bank for Development and Reconstruction (otherwise known as the World Bank). Because of the regional emphasis of development at the time, it was necessary to establish, in 1955, a National Economic Council comprising representatives of the Central Council of Ministers, the Regional Executive Councils and the Executive Council of the Southern Cameroons, under the chairmanship of the Governor-General and, later, the Prime Minister. In 1958, the Council set up a Joint Planning Committee as its operational arm. The Federal Ministry of Economic Development served as the Secretariat for both the National Economic Council and the Joint Planning Committee. It was also the planning agency for the Federal Government, in addition to its responsibility for co-ordinating all technical assistance and external economic relations of the country.

It must be obvious from this overview that whoever became the Permanent Secretary of such a Ministry would occupy a most strategic position in the affairs of the country. It is, however, one thing to occupy a position; it is another to make an indelible mark in the position. Allison clearly achieved that distinction.

Soon after political independence, the Nigerian Government had, in 1961, invited Professor Wolfgang Stolper of the University of Michigan to help in the preparation of the *First National Development Plan (1962-68)*. To this end, he was made to head the Economic Planning Unit which had been established within the Federal Ministry of Economic Development to take care of the technical aspects of policy work and economic planning generally, as well as plan co-ordination among the various economic planning and development agencies of the country. Professor Stolper brought together a team of young but brilliant Nigerian economists from within both the Federal Civil Service and Nigeria's academia. Allison Ayida was easily one of the best from within the Service whilst late Professor Aboyade was invited to join the team from University College Ibadan. It was no doubt in recognition of his role in the articulation and preparation of this first national development plan that Allison, at the tender age of 33 years, was made to take charge of this crucial Ministry whose responsibility was to foster and promote economic development throughout the country.

It is not easy today to appreciate the importance of this Ministry, given current practices in the Federal Civil Service. But in those days, no item of the capital budget of any Ministry of the Federal Government could come before the National Executive Council for consideration and funding unless it had the support and concurrence of the Federal Ministry of Economic Development. The Ministry, quite clearly, was the monitor of government for plan discipline and for ensuring that all other Ministries kept their focus on the implementation of their various plan proposals. Consequently, to be the Permanent Secretary of such a Ministry was not only to become well-informed as to the prospects and processes of development in the country, but also to acquire great influence and power in the execution of government's projects and programmes.

All this could be a very intoxicating concoction, especially if you are vain and power-hungry. To keep himself from yielding to such temptation, Allison decided to build around him a coterie of advisers, formal and informal. Many of his informal advisers were at the University of Ibadan (until December 1962, the University College Ibadan). Allison, often in the company of Philip Asiodu and several others, started spending his weekends in one of the suites at the University Guest House, consulting with many of the staff members of that institution. Such interaction between, as it were, town and gown, was actively fostered by Professor Kenneth Onwuka Dike, the first Nigerian Vice-Chancellor of the newly chartered University of Ibadan.

But by then Nigeria was entering into its era of political instability. With the crisis of the Action Group in 1962, the controversy over the 1962 Census, the politically-loaded creation of the Mid-West Region in 1963, the inconclusive Federal Elections of 1964, and the combative Western Regional Elections of 1965, the scene seemed set for the intervention of the military into the politics of the country. The military coup of January 15, 1966 saw the assassination of prominent Nigerians, including the Prime Minister, Alhaji Tafawa Balewa, Chief Okotie-Eboh, the Federal Minister of Finance, Sir Ahmadu Bello, the Sardauna of Sokoto and Premier of the Northern Region, and Chief S. L. Akintola, Premier of the Western Region and a number of the top brass of the Nigerian Army. The situation in the country further deteriorated with a second military coup in July 1966 and the killing of Major-General Aguiyi-Ironsi, the Head of the Federal Military Government, Colonel Adekunle Fajuyi, the Military Governor of the Western Region and a large number of military officers, largely of Igbo origin. Attempts to solve the national crisis by correcting the political imbalance in the country through the creation of twelve states from the four Regions, in May 1967, simply led to a further downward spiral of the political crisis, culminating in the declaration of secession by the leaders of the Eastern Region, the establishment of the Republic of Biafra, and the launching of the country into a thirty-month civil war. The war was fought ferociously and with considerable devastation, especially of infrastructure facilities in the Eastern Region. It eventually ended on January 12, 1970 with the capitulation of the seceding Region.

There is, of course, no gainsaying the fact that the political crisis that had lasted most of the second half of the 1960s had totally derailed the *First National Development Plan*. Although Nigeria had succeeded in fighting the civil war without having to seek foreign loans (thanks to the prudent management of the national resources by Chief Obafemi Awolowo) it was not possible to pursue the full implementation of the *Plan*. Indeed, there was nothing the country could do except leave the implementation of the *Plan* in abeyance until after the end of the war in 1970. After the war ended, the challenge facing the Federal Ministry of Economic Development became not only the development of the country, but also the reconstruction and rehabilitation of the severely damaged infrastructure facilities of the Eastern Region of the country. The Ministry, in consequence, changed its name to the Federal Ministry of Economic Development and Reconstruction.

Allison Ayida remained the Permanent Secretary of the Federal Ministry of Economic Development throughout this period of national crisis. He had to cope with a situation in which both the National Economic Council and the Joint Planning Committee became unoperational, given the dissensions that were tearing the country apart. The initial effort, in 1966, to establish a ten-man National Economic Planning Advisory Group of eminent economists, under the chairmanship of Chief S. O. Adebo, also failed to resolve the situation. Indeed, the situation became more complicated with the need to co-ordinate economic planning in the twelve states created out of the former four Regions. Consequently, it was decided that the Supreme Military Council on which all the Military Governors of the States sat, under the chairmanship of the Head of the Federal Military Government and Commander-in-Chief of the Armed Forces, provided the best forum for harmonizing the various planning proposals at the inter-governmental level. At the official level, a Joint Planning Board was established under the chairmanship of the Permanent Secretary, Federal Ministry of Economic Development and comprised, among others, the Permanent Secretary, Ministry of Economic Planning in each of the twelve States. The Economic Planning Unit was then transformed into a Central Planning Office staffed by a cadre of professional planners outside the general pool of administrators, with Professor Ojetunji Aboyade of the Department of Economics, University of Ibadan being invited to head the Office in its first few years.

As Chairman of the Joint Planning Board, Ayida demonstrated his belief that the quality of any National Plan is a function of the richness of its conceptualization and the innovative ideas that underpin its formulation. Consequently, Allison deepened the relationship of his Ministry with Nigerian universities and the Nigerian Institute of Social and Economic Research. Indeed, to ensure that with the end of the civil war, the *Second National Development* would exhibit such richness of conceptualization, the Federal Ministry, under Ayida's leadership, sponsored the holding, in 1969, of an 'International Conference on National Reconstruction and Development' at the Nigerian Institute of Social and Economic Research. The Conference brought together not only local experts but also a number of foreign scholars with experience of economic development in other developing countries. The proceedings of the Conference were of such quality that they were edited and published as a special volume preparatory to the formulation of the *Second National Development Plan*.

The *Second National Development Plan (1970-74)* represents, in many ways, the high watermark of Allison Aydia's years as the Chief Economic Planner of the Federation. Coming on the heels of the end of the Nigerian civil war, the *Plan* required a re-dedication of all Nigerians to the national enterprise of building a strong, united country. Consequently, unlike national plans before and after it, the *Second National Development Plan* had to get the leaders of the country to subscribe to a set of "National Objectives and Priorities" underpinning the *Plan,* as well as a strategy for achieving the objectives. It was in this context that, for the first time in the history of the country, an attempt was made to articulate five national objectives designed to establish Nigeria firmly as:

- A united, strong and self-reliant nation;
- A great and dynamic economy;
- A just and egalitarian society;
- A land of bright and full opportunities for all citizens; and
- A free and democratic society.

Giving concrete meaning to these objectives as well as ensuring their full realization have been the main purpose of every national plan since then. But no other National Development Plan since has been able to match the breadth and thrust of this particular *Plan*. In the first year of its implementation, the re-construction element, especially with the end of the civil war, became Ayida's major concern. Accordingly, he was also made the Chairman of the National Rehabilitation Commission and Chief Coordinator of Post-war Emergency Relief, Rehabilitation and Reconstruction. Much of the work of putting the Eastern Region back on its feet after a devastating war thus absorbed Allison's energy in the years immediately after the civil war. Nonetheless, one year into the implementation of the *Plan*, Allison was moved, in 1972, to become Permanent Secretary, Federal Ministry of Finance. In 1975, he was made Secretary to the Federal Government and Head of the Civil Service of the Federation.

Ayida and the challenge of national unity

The second military coup of July 1966 brought to power Lt. Colonel (later General) Yakubu Gowon. With the military governor of the Western Region, Lt. Colonel Adekunle Fajuyi having been killed in the coup, the affairs of the Region were run by the top civil servants under the leadership of Mr. P. T. Odumosu, the Secretary to the Regional Military Government. As soon as things settled down in Lagos, each of the four Regions was asked to send representatives to Lagos to work out the modalities "for keeping the country a little apart to allow for things to cool down."

I was one of the three representatives from the Western Region, in mid-August, 1966 at that meeting, under the leadership of Dr. S.A.Ajayi, the Solicitor-General of the Region. The meeting lasted for nearly a week in the chambers of the then House of Representatives, was remarkable in many ways. Essentially, its thrust was to re-organize Nigeria on a confederal basis. The Nigerian Army was to be regionalized and most of the other functions of the Federal Government were to be reduced to the barest minimum. Key positions in government and in the Foreign Service were to be shared out between the Regions on some agreed basis. Revenue was to be collected at regional level and an agreed proportion forwarded to the Federal Government for its services. The meeting adjourned at the end of August to enable each regional group to report back to its principals for further instructions.

Whilst the Lagos Meeting was still in adjournment, notable political changes were taking place in the country. First, news broke of another pogrom visited on Easterners in the northern part of the country. This made the delegation from the Eastern Region decide that it was no longer safe for its members to return to the Meeting. In the meantime, Lt.Colonel Gowon had decided to free from jail all political prisoners that had been imprisoned as part of the fall-out of the national crisis. Principal among such prisoners were Chief Obafemi Awolowo and Chief Tony Enahoro. With these two leaders released from prison, the Federal Military Government re-convened the Meeting of Regional Representatives, this time led by the two important political leaders who had just been freed. Consequently, Chief Obafemi Awolowo led the Western Regional team whilst Chief Tony Enahoro led the Mid-Western Regional team.

It was clear from the very first speech made by Lt.Colonel Yakubu Gowon on assuming office as the Head of the Federal Military Government that there were significant forces in the country wanting a much looser federation than had been in operation up to then. The meeting of Regional representatives, of which I was a part, reflected the preference of these forces. However, unbeknown to us, there was a group of senior civil servants simultaneously engaged in deliberating on how to manage the Nigerian crisis and prevent it from further deteriorating towards the dismemberment of the country. Allison was already Permanent Secretary in the Federal Ministry of Economic Development and was one of the very strong but quiet voices among this group. Coming from the Mid-Western Region, he worked closely with Chief Tony Enahoro to ensure that that Regional delegation took a stance in favour of consolidating the unity of Nigeria. Chief Obafemi Awolowo, during his years in prison, had also written a book on his vision for a strong and united Federal Republic. However, when the delegations re-convened in late October, 1966, the Eastern Region declined to return its delegation. Nonetheless, in the deliberations that ensued, the whole idea of a confederal structure for Nigeria was decidedly jettisoned.

The challenge of preserving the unity of Nigeria entered a new phase with the intransigence of the Military Governor of Eastern Nigeria, Colonel Odumegwu Ojukwu and his refusal to acknowledge Lt. Colonel Yakubu Gowon as the new Head of State of Nigeria. Things reached such an *impasse* that in February 1967, the Nigerian Head of State and all the military governors, including Colonel Ojukwu, were invited by the Military Head of State of Ghana, General Ankrah to Aburi, near Accra to discuss the situation and as "officers and gentlemen" arrive at some workable decisions. The Nigerian Head of State, Lt. Colonel Yakubu Gowon came back from Aburi with the text of the discussions and the various decisions taken. Not having as yet constituted a Federal Executive Council, Gowon found himself discussing details of this text both with his military colleagues in the Supreme Military Council and his "kitchen cabinet" of top civil service officers, including Allison Ayida. It was common knowledge in the country that members of this "kitchen cabinet" did not believe that some of the decisions at Aburi were in the long-term interests of the unity of Nigeria. Consequently, other types of domestic solutions were proffered for dealing with the pervasive problem of political disaffection and conflict in the country.

It had been widely acknowledged that one of the principal causes of the political crisis in the country was the lop-sided structure of the Federation. With one of the Regions having more than half the area of the country and its population, there was concern that this did not make for an equitable Federation that ensured that none of the constituent units could impose its will on the whole Federation. The position was further complicated by the fact that each Region had within it a majority ethnic group and a number of minority ethnic groups which were all agitating for political self-determination. The agitation of minority groups for Regions of their own had forced the colonial government to set up the Willink's Commission which reported in 1957, just when the nationalist clamour for political independence of the country was at its peak. In the Constitutional Conference in London in that year, Britain had put the proposition before Nigerian leaders that if they wanted Britain to deal with the problem of the minorities, then the issue of self-government in 1960 would have to be shelved for some time. The political leaders chose not to wait, but insisted on the political independence for the country in 1960. Now in 1966, with the threat of secession from one of the Regions, the Federal Military Government had to resolve the situation somehow if only as a means of securing the commitment of a greater proportion of the population to the Nigerian enterprise.

On May 27, 1967, the Federal Military Government announced the creation of a new Federation comprising of twelve states, six in what was the former Northern Region, three in what was the former Western Region (before the creation of the Mid-West State) and three in what was the Eastern Region. The new states granted minority ethnic groups states of their own outside of those of the majority ethnic groups in each of the three former regions. A few days after the announcement, Colonel Odumegwu Ojukwu declared the secession of the Eastern Region to form a new 'Republic of Biafra.'

At this point, Gowon's "kitchen cabinet" must have recommended the establishment of a formal Federal Executive Council of distinguished Nigerian leaders from all parts of the country which could help the Federal Military Government to steer the ship of state safely in the difficult years ahead. Such had been the impact of the advice and the personal relationship established between some members of the "kitchen cabinet" and the Head of State that even after the establishment of the Federal Executive Council, such notable Nigerians as Chief Obafemi Awolowo, Chief Tony Enahoro, Alhaji Aminu Kano, and Alhaji Shehu Shagari, most Nigerians felt that the quartet of top civil servants, including Allison Ayida, continued to influence important national decisions and policies. It was to this quartet that the Nigerian newspapers began to refer to as "Super Permanent Secretaries."

Whether this was a fair perception of the top civil servants or not, there is no denying the fact that, to a certain extent, Nigeria owes its continued existence to their wisdom and foresight. Allison and his colleagues helped in formulating policies through those years of political crisis and had to face the challenge of managing a surfeit of financial resources soon after the end of the civil war. The year 1973 was remarkable because of the Arab-Israeli War and its effect on the price of petroleum. Suddenly, with the price of oil moving from less than a dollar per barrel to US$3.00 and finally to US$13.00, Nigeria was awash with money. The least that could be done was to ensure that much of the windfall went into serious economic development. This gave rise to a strong feeling that Nigerians could now strive to develop their economy on their own. The State was to control the "commanding heights" of the economy whilst Nigerians were to take charge of much of what was left through an "indigenization decree" that sought to define areas where only Nigerian citizens could operate. The idea was good but it ran in the face of inadequate executive capacity in the country to spend the windfall money effectively. Moreover, with the military in firm control of the country, the plea for prudence in the circumstances was very difficult to sustain. Consequently, Nigeria swung into the era of a spending spree that promoted immense corruption and inefficiency in the system. By then, it was felt that the Federal Civil Service could be reformed to make it a more effective agency of policy implementation. A Public Service Review Commission (1972-74) was set up under the chairmanship of Sir Jerome Udoji. The Commission, described as the most comprehensive Public Service Review the country had ever had, found its reform mandate compromised. The implementation of a wage and salary review (which it had also been asked to undertake) came to becloud much of its recommendations on public service review and their impact on the Nigerian bureaucracy.

At any rate, Allison Ayida was promoted in 1975 to the post of Secretary to the Federal Government and Head of the Civil Service. It was thus to him that much of the responsibility devolved for implementing the Government White Paper on the recommendations of this Commission. But before much could be done in this connection, the country experienced another military coup which replaced General Yakubu Gowon with General Murtala Muhammed and, after his assassination in February 1976, with General Olusegun Obasanjo. Although Allison continued in his position over the period of the change, the relationship between the military government and its civil servants was no longer the same. For one thing, the top civil servants were no longer allowed to attend cabinet meetings unless specifically invited to do so. Consequently, their influence on policy waned considerably. The new regime also embarked on a massive purge of the Public Service on such grounds as "diminishing productivity" and "divided loyalty" among others. It was clear that the immense influence and power which some of the Permanent Secretaries had exerted on national policy and development did not go down well with some people in the polity. Consequently, as part of the relentless purge, Allison was forced to retire from his position as Nigeria's topmost civil servant and Secretary to Government in 1977.

But such was the experience and competence that Allison had acquired during his twenty years in the public service of the country that, on his retirement, he became prime choice for serving on the governing boards of various private sector and international organizations. Indeed, no sooner had he been retired than he was asked to be Chairman of Berger Paints Nigeria Plc. in 1978. In the same year, he was appointed to serve on the Board of Governors of Canada's International Development Research Centre in Ottawa. Today, Allison is still Chairman of a number of companies and a Board member of many others.

Ayida and the legacy of policy making

By the time Ayida was employed in 1957, the Federal Civil Service, perhaps more than that of any of the Regions, had a serious problem of lack of trained manpower. But the crisis that had loomed over the country for most of the first ten years of independence meant that not much could be done about the problem. Similarly, although the Report of a Manpower Survey for the Federal Civil Service commissioned by the Federal Ministry of Economic Development had been submitted in 1968, not much could be done so long as the civil war continued. Allison, as the Permanent Secretary of the Ministry at the time, had responsibility for overall manpower development in the country. As part of the post-civil war reconstruction effort, therefore, he challenged Nigerian universities to come up with practical training programmes that could help the country in building adequate capacity for planning its development and reconstruction effort.

In response to this challenge, the Faculty of the Social Sciences, University of Ibadan which was at the time under my

Deanship (!968-70), proposed the establishment of the Planning Studies Programme as a new initiative of the University sector in the *Second National Development Plan*. The proposal was sponsored basically by the Departments of Economics and Geography although other Departments in the Faculty were invited to participate in its activities. When it was eventually approved to begin in 1971, the Programme had as its Co-Directors Professor Ojetunji Aboyade from the Department of Economics and myself from the Department of Geography, with Drs. Edozien, Teriba and Kayode as our Deputies. The aim of the Programme was to offer short-term and long-term training courses in economic planning as well as in urban and regional planning. It also provided consultancy services in these areas to Federal and Regional Governments as well as to multilateral and donor agencies.

No sooner did the Programme take off in the 1971-72 academic session than it was challenged to undertake, during the long vacation of 1972, a series of short-term training courses for planning officers from all of the new twelve states of the Federation as well as from the Federal Government. The training was to equip them to be better able to monitor the implementation of the *Second National Development Plan* and prepare them for conceptualizing and articulating the *Third National Development Plan* for their sector and government. The courses included training in macro-economic policy analysis and planning for various critical sectors, such as agriculture, industry, transportation, education and health. Each course lasted five weeks. The local teams of trainers were supported by a few staff of the World Bank. The whole atmosphere was very stimulating particularly as it encouraged planning officers throughout the Federation to start sharing experiences and having a convivial sense of fraternity.

The Planning Studies Programme continued to enjoy a very close and cordial relationship with the Federal Government even after Allison Ayida had been moved to the Federal Ministry of Finance and much later when he became the Secretary to the Federal Government and Head of Service. But with the "purge" of the Civil Service in the 1975-1977 period, a lot of experienced planning officers either lost their jobs or retired from the Service. With time, the negative effect of this erosion of trained manpower began to tell on the quality of policy analysis and policy development in the country. As the period of military rule became prolonged, extending over most of the 1970s and 1980s, the situation deteriorated further. Indeed, all over Africa, the 1980s came to be known as the "lost decade" because of the economic mismanagement that forced most African countries to have to submit to structural adjustment programmes initiated by the Bretton Woods institutions.

By then, various donor agencies were already worrying about the direction of development in most African countries with the capacity for serious macro-economic policy analysis having been so widely eroded. The outcome was the decision by these agencies to establish the Africa Capacity-Building Foundation (ACBF), based in Harare, Zimbabwe. The Foundation set out to encourage the establishment of policy analytical institutions in different African countries so as to start re-building capacity in this field. With Professor Ojetunji Aboyade as a member of the Board of the Foundation, it was not unexpected that the deteriorating policy analytical situation in Nigeria would get to be discussed by a group of us who had promoted the surge of initiatives in this field in the country in the late 1960s and had painfully to watch the erosion of capacity in the late 1970s and 1980s. What to do to arrest the situation was often the topic of discussion whenever we met. On one such occasion, it was proposed to capitalize on the possibilities being offered by the African Capacity Building Foundation. The support of the Foundation was to be secured to establish the

Development Policy Centre in Ibadan which was to serve as our legacy to coming generations of policy analysts and development specialists in Nigeria.

The idea of establishing such a Centre received wide concurrence among many of those who had worked with Allison Ayida during those halcyon days of preparing the *Second National Development Plan*. Ladipo Adamolekun, for instance, who was with the World Bank, worked to ensure that the Bank supported the idea. Indeed, he succeeded in getting the Bank to finance the management consulting firm of Omolayole & Associates to investigate the feasibility and viability of such a Centre in the context of other similar institutions in the country. The Report of the consultants underscored the need for such a Centre in the country at the time. It particularly stressed the wisdom of ensuring that the Board of such a Centre paid attention not just to the geographical spread of its members, but also to their experience in the public, private and university sectors of the country. It was thus not unexpected that in constituting the membership of the Board of the new centre, Allison Ayida would have an honoured place representing years of experience of policy analysis and development in the public sector.

The Development Policy Centre, Ibadan was thus part of a legacy that Allison Ayida and the rest of us believed needed to be left to posterity. The Centre was established in November, 1993 with a Governing Board of nine members. Three of the members were non-Nigerians representing ACBF-sponsored sister institutions in Ghana, Kenya and South Africa. Of the remaining six Nigerians, Professor Ojetunji Aboyade was Chairman and I represented the second member from the university sector. Mr. Allison Ayida and Engr. Vincent Maduka represented individuals with largely public sector experience, whilst Dr. Michael Omolayole and Alhaji Umaru Ndanusa represented individuals with essentially private sector experience. The Board was still overseeing the recruitment of staff, the articulation of programmes and the physical development of the Centre when its first Chairman, Professor Ojetunji Aboyade died in December, 1994.

I then took on the challenge of guiding the Centre through its difficult formative years. Although the first Managing Director of the Centre as well as the Financial Controller and Librarian had been appointed before the death of Professor Aboyade, the inability to complete the construction of the major buildings of the Centre meant that other full-time staff could not be appointed. The part-time research staff that were appointed did most of their work away from the Centre. With the completion of the physical development of the Centre in late 1995, the recruitment of full-time staff and the articulation of programmes began in earnest. By then, the ACBF had expressed concern that the capability and effectiveness of the management of the Centre was below expectation and wanted to see some drastic changes in this respect. In the circumstance, I was persuaded by the Board to take over the direct management of the Centre as its Executive Chairman in September 1996.

Throughout the four years I spent in this position, Allison was a real tower of strength. His abiding reputation within the Nigerian Public Service meant that his name as a Board member opened doors that would otherwise have remained closed. Indeed, it was interesting that at the first meeting of the Board with the then Secretary to the Government of the Federation, the latter indicated that, although he was slightly indisposed, he had to keep the appointment because of the name of his boss, Allison Ayida, in the delegation. At Board meetings, Allison's voice could always be relied on to point out the areas in which the Centre should be seeking to make its impact. His quiet interventions in moments of crisis often served to calm ruffled feathers. Allison spent his full nine year-term as a member of the Board and retired only because his term had come to an end. It had been a wonderful experience working together on what was essentially a labour of love since there was really no remuneration attached to the task.

Conclusion

In concluding this short testimonial, the question may be asked: What makes Allison a Super Perm-Sec? I believe the answer to the question is really threefold. First, there is the quality of training and education that Allison had imbibed. This ensured that he was intellectually and intrinsically prepared for the task of being at least a successful Permanent Secretary. Second, there is his emotional appreciation of the importance of knowledge and of continuing self-education if one were to rise above the common run of things and people. For me, this was perhaps the most important factor in Allison's extraordinary success in the Nigerian Public Service. Instead of the common experience of finding civil servants who believe that, on appointment to the highest position in the Service, they have nothing more to learn or even to read outside of files and newspapers, Allison showed an unusual commitment to keeping himself as much as possible a member of the knowledge community. His love of learning made him want always to rub his minds against those of his colleagues who were actively engaged in the pursuit of knowledge. His concern with deepening his professional competence as an economist saw him rising to the position of being elected President of the Nigerian Economic Society for the 1972-73 year. He was made a Fellow of the Nigerian Economic Society and later Fellow of both the Nigerian Institute of Management and the Institute of Directors. It is all of this and more that go towards making Allison a "super" within the Civil Service.

But, perhaps, of greatest importance is the third factor of a wisdom that allows Allison to relate cordially not only to his colleagues but also to his superiors as well as to his staff. Allison's human relations is really of the best and enables him to advise without being patronizing or condescending and to caution without being censorious. Of course, he can at times exhibit a wry sense of humour and normally does not suffer fools lightly. But, notwithstanding, his generally friendly disposition made him get on very well with his military "masters" who needed some guidance in the art of governance during those critical years of late 1960s and early 1970s. It is this attribute that for me sums up Allison's personality. Indeed, I believe the most fitting testimonial for him is best captured in the following celebrated lines of Rudyard Kipling:

> If you can talk with crowds and keep your virtue,
> Or walk with Kings nor lose the common touch.
> If neither foes nor loving friends can hurt you,
> If all men count with you, but none too much;
> If you can fill the unforgiving minute
> With sixty seconds' worth of distance run,
> Yours is the Earth and everything that's in it,
> And - which is more - you'll be a Man my son.

Ayida was all of this and more; they sure made him a "Super" Permanent Secretary.

13

Allison Ayida: administrator and development expert

– Dr. Michael Omolayole

Introduction

I received an invitation towards the end of 2003 to write a few lines about Mr. Allison A. Ayida as I see him. I did not hesitate to accept this pleasurable assignment because I happened to have interacted with Allison in different spheres of human endeavour for over five decades.

First and foremost Allison, sometimes referred to as 'Triple A', is a man of many parts. He was an exceptionally brilliant student at the prestigious King's College, Lagos in the late 1940s. He, in fact, became the President of King's College Old Students Association, after the late Chief Adeniran Ogunsanya who regarded that position as the most worthy one on earth. Up *Floreat!*

My first contact with Allison was when he was at King's College. Initially, I knew of him only by reputation as someone who was so brilliant that he had been given a double promotion at King's. Somehow through my cousin Kamoru Sansi, who was a classmate of Allison, I had met both Allison and Philip Asiodu, because the three of them were very close. (Kamoru Sansi is now Dr. K. Sansi, the *Obelu* of Esure in Ijebu Imusin.)

Between the time that I finished at St. Gregory's College, Lagos in 1947 and my admission to the University College, Ibadan in 1948, I lived at No. 36 Okesuna Street, Lagos, the home of the veteran King's College tutor, Mr. D. Ade Onojobi whose son, Sola, now Dr. Onojobi, another classmate of Allison, was close to me.

However, my first memorable encounter with Allison Ayida that I remember very well as if it were yesterday was in November/ December 1952 when he was sitting for the examinations of the Cambridge Higher School Certificate at King's College Hall. I was one of the two invigilators for that centre which served both King's College and Queen's College candidates for the Cambridge School Certificate and the Cambridge Higher School Certificate examinations. I saw him practically every day for about three weeks during the examinations. If I remember rightly, apart from the General paper, he and Philip Asiodu took three subjects each, namely, English Literature, Latin and History. Incidentally, the chief invigilator was Mr. D. Ade Onojobi, the former veteran tutor at King's College who had retired, and I was his assistant from St. Gregory's College, Lagos where I was a science master. Allison Ayida and Philip Asiodu must find it difficult to remember now who the invigilators were, but I have made sure that whenever the occasion demands it, I will never let them forget.

A year later in 1953, Allison, Philip and myself were at Oxford University. I had gone up during the Trinity term in March 1953 to Corpus Christi College to do a postgraduate course in Education. Allison and Philip came together during the Michaelmas term of 1953/54 in September 1953 to Queen's College, almost like Siamese twins, to read PPE (Modern Greats). I saw a lot of them at Oxford for one year. Then I finished in 1954 and returned to Nigeria.

Allison Ayida as Administrator in the Federal Civil Service

After graduation at Oxford, Mr. Ayida registered for a Master's degree in Economics at the London School of Economics. He soon gave it up and returned to Nigeria to join the Federal Civil Service because of the strong pull on him: Nigeria was then marching rapidly towards independence. He joined as an Assistant Secretary in the Federal Ministry of Finance where he rapidly made his mark, so much so that by the early 1960s, he had been transferred to the Ministry of Economic Development as acting Permanent Secretary.

We again linked up when he was in that Ministry because the Permanent Secretary, Ministry of Economic Development was the chairman of the National Manpower Board. I was representing employers, the Nigerian Employers Consultative Assembly (NECA) on the Board. By then I had become Personnel Director of Lever Brothers Nigeria Ltd., having joined the company in 1958. Coincidentally, there was a mutual friend of Allison Ayida and myself who was also a member of the National Manpower Board. He was the late Professor Ojetunji Aboyade who had returned from Cambridge after his Ph.D./Economics in the early 1960s. He was an exceptionally brilliant and charming man who had the gift of making the studying of Economics very easy for his students.

In those early years after the establishment of the National Manpower Board, it was really very effective under the leadership, first of Mr. Ladner and later Mr. Ayida. To my mind, the Board has now ceased to be a planning tool, very much a part of the era described by Prof. Stolper as *Planning Without Facts*.

Mr. Ayida's meteoric rise in the Federal Civil Service continued during and after the Nigerian civil war. A few of the federal Permanent Secretaries constituted the main "Think Thank" for the Government of General Gowon and Mr. Allison

Ayida was certainly one of them. They came into prominence in the years when the Federal Government had neither civilian nor military cabinet Ministers. General Gowon was very young and relied very heavily on their advice. Hence the retired General, up till today, is still very friendly with many of them. In addition to Allison Ayida, there were the following members of the group: Philip Asiodu, the late Ime Ebong and Ahmed Joda.

Mr. Ayida as Negotiator

During the Nigerian civil war, the responsibility for properly advising the Federal Government readily fell on the shoulders of the inner caucus of Permanent Secretaries, "The Think Thank." Also when it became necessary to negotiate, the responsibility fell on fewer members of the caucus and one person who was very prominent and effective in the group was Allison Ayida. Because he is easy-going and naturally soft-spoken and deep-thinking, he could always be relied upon to pull the chestnut out of the fire. As a keen tennis player who obviously observes the spirit of sportsmanship even outside the lawn tennis court, he was a naturally gifted negotiator. And so he went everywhere with Chief Tony Enahoro, another *floreat*, to meet yet another *floreat* on the Biafran side, Justice Mbanefo, sometimes at great personal risk.

Consequently, after I had become the first Nigerian Chairman and Managing Director of Lever Brothers Nigeria Ltd. (now Unilever Plc.) and felt that the company needed the first independent non-executive director, I did not hesitate to recommend Allison Ayida to the shareholders (core and non-core) and to persuade Mr. Ayida to accept. I am, indeed, proud to say that it was his first Board appointment to a publicly quoted company in Nigeria after his retirement from public service in 1977 when it was obvious that there was still a lot of energy in him. Even now, there may be snow on the rooftop, but there is still a lot of fire down below!

Allison Ayida went on to serve with distinction on the Board of Unilever Nigeria Plc for 23 years thereby exceeding my own record by 3 years. In dealing with Mr. Ayida as adviser or negotiator, one must never ever forget that slow-moving water runs very deep!

Post-Civil War career

Just before the civil war ended in January 1970, Mr. Ayida, then as Permanent Secretary, Federal Ministry of Economic Development, organized a high-level seminar at the University of Ibadan which brought together a lot of Nigerians and international experts, and chaired by the late Chief Simeon Adebo, to deliberate on the shape of Nigeria's post civil war political economy. The preparation was typically very thorough and the deliberations, which were very exhaustive, led to the preparation of the *Second National Development Plan* and its publication as a book. I was glad to have participated as a discussant at the Seminar, especially since I was then also a Visiting Professor in Industrial Relations and Personnel Management at the University of Lagos, in addition to my regular job as Personnel Director at Lever Brothers Nigeria Ltd.

Not long after that successful seminar, the civil war ended. A few years later Allison Ayida was moved back to his former Ministry, the Ministry of Finance, as Permanent Secretary. By that time I had become the Vice-Chairman of Lever Brothers Nigeria Ltd. and given permission by Unilever, London to be the non-executive chairman of National Bank in Nigeria, which was in a very bad shape. I arranged to hold a discussion with Mr. Ayida on the state of the Bank and to know whether the Federal Government could provide assistance as it had done to the Africa Continental Bank (ACB) immediately after the civil war. Mr. Ayida commiserated with me for taking on a terrible job. He said if I had consulted him he would have advised against it. He told me that the Federal Ministry of Finance, quite emphatically, would not help. He didn't believe in throwing good money after bad. But he was very polite about it. The discussion was cordial but achieved nothing for me. However, because of the nice way he had put it, our relationship has remained strong and cordial ever since.

We ended the meeting on the note that I would give the job my best shot. To my greatest and pleasant surprise when, by another route, a memorandum had gone to the Supreme Military Council requesting assistance for the same National Bank, the Bank of the North, and additional assistance for ACB, on the premise that the National Bank had been recently re-organized and I had become its chairman and late Mr. J. Court, an expatriate, its M.D., the Supreme Military Council approved. Notwithstanding Mr. Ayida's original objection, he was the first to telephone from the Ministry of Finance asking me to come over and discuss how the National Bank wanted the approved sum of ₦34 million disbursed. I felt that Mr. Ayida was a very great civil servant in the mould of the great Chief Simeon Adebo. Once a decision was taken, even if it was against the civil servant's advice, it was implemented in good faith.

My last encounter with Mr. Ayida in the Federal Ministry of Finance was in connection with the importation of palm oil. For the first time in 1974, Lever Brothers Nigeria Ltd.'s stock of palm oil was going to run out. The company's bulk oil plants did not have any and we had applied to the Federal Ministry of Finance for permission to import. Mr. Ayida, as the Permanent Secretary, could not believe what he was reading so he invited me for a discussion and invited Mr. Funke George, the General Manager of Produce Marketing Company, a federal government parastatal. When Mr. George read our application he went ballistic! He would have none of our request, but Mr. Ayida adjudicated in a nice and inoffensive manner by asking both of us to go to the field again and come up with new figures in two weeks. When we went back after doing extra field work, Lever

Brothers reported that there was still no palm oil available and the Produce Marketing Company, once more, had no figures to report. There and then, it was agreed that Lever Brothers should be given permission to import for three months after which the situation would be reviewed.

By the review date, Mr. Ayida had already been promoted to the post of Secretary to Government and Head of Service, the third Oxonian in an unbroken succession to occupy the post. It so happened that I had been at Oxford at the same time with all the three of them who had occupied that prestigious position. The first was the late A. A. Attah who went back to Oxford for his second Devonshire course in 1952/53; the second was Mr. Tunde Lawson who finished PPE at Oxford in June 1953 and the third was Mr. A. A. Ayida who went up in September 1953 and so didn't meet either Attah or Lawson at the University. Surprisingly, all the three of them had read PPE (Politics, Philosophy and Economics.)

The Civil Service purge of 1975 and Mr. Ayida

The period of the civil service purge coincided with the beginning of the tenure of Mr. A. Ayida as Secretary to Government and Head of Service. Judging the situation from the outside, I could imagine how much anguish Mr. Ayida would have endured.

Some of the decisions at the time were totally illogical. What was even difficult to understand was the method and the timing of the announcements of retiring long-serving officers "with immediate effect." Like all human events, one would have to concede that the process must have done some good, and must also have done some evil. Nearly 30 years after the event, are we in a position to say whether the good outweighed the evil? Anybody who has listened to either Allison Ayida or Philip Asiodu comment on the situation would surely have no doubt where they would probably cast their vote in answer to the question.

My own dispassionate view is that subsequent events seemed to have confirmed that the baby would appear to have been thrown out with the bath water!! The situation can be put in a more dramatic way by using the anecdote involving two Hungarian peasant farmers. They both went out to the field to work and were returning in the evening after a rainfall. Peasant A had a donkey, but Peasant B was too poor to own even a donkey. As they walked along, frogs were croaking in the field. Peasant A said to B, "If you would dash into the field and swallow one of those frogs alive I will give you my donkey."

In a jiffy B dashed into the field, seized a frog and swallowed it alive. Thereupon A gave him his donkey. As they continued to walk back to the village, B was happy, but observed that A had become moody and refused to engage in any conversation. Soon, B started feeling uncomfortable and said to A, 'If you would dash into the field, seize a frog and swallow it alive, I shall return your donkey to you.' As quickly as in the first instance, A dashed into the field as well, seized one frog and swallowed it alive. So B returned A's donkey to him and their relationship was normalized.

The moral of the story is this: two peasant farmers had each swallowed a live frog, plus all the unpleasantness that goes with it but nothing had changed in their status! Great lesson!!

Mr. Ayida's post-Civil Service contribution to development

Mr. Ayida has now had 27 years of life outside the Federal Civil Service and continues to thrive. Therefore, there must be life after the civil service!

He has been invited to join several boards of companies since Unilever Nigeria Ltd. beckoned and has become chairman or retired chairman of several publicly quoted companies. On top of it all, he is chairman of a Nigerian bank. Wow! He has also raised up children who have become significant players in the industrial and financial sectors of the Nigerian economy.

His advice and inputs continue to be sought by local, state and federal governments alike He can be described as an excellent example of thinkers and planners who have also made a memorable impact as implementers. Ideas are wonderful, but tend to have legs to engage in flight. The doer, however, is the hero: Mr. Allison Ayida is both a thinker and a hero.

Epilogue

…flying with shackles…

14

The framework

It is important to appreciate, from the outset, the use of the analogy of flying as our choice of the title of this concluding chapter. It is a title capable of dual interpretation, namely, 'flying in spite of shackles', which might be an apt summarization of Ayida's performance in public service. A second possible interpretation would be the characterization of Nigeria's development performance as being 'second to none,' at best, or, at the worst, 'second to not-too-many'. Both possible interpretations would probably describe aspects of Ayida's performance, first as an individual and second, as a member of several teams steering the affairs of a country during twenty critical years of evolving nationhood. To appreciate better Ayida's role during the period, it would be pertinent to highlight a few of the characteristics of flying.

Flying is a fast mode for locational change. Such change usually involves large land masses of various forms and features, such as vegetative, climatic and water forms, even when the flight takes only a few minutes. Many of the changes that occur during a flight are not observed and, indeed, are rarely observable by the average passenger in an aircraft. All that the passenger may be capable of observing or experiencing is locational change, such as taking off in, say, Lagos and landing in Los Angeles or Las Pamas. To the occasional flyer, the experience could be something of a dream, a transformation that borders on the magical. To the frequent flyer, however, it is a normal and routine event, an effortless and convenient means of moving between two locations separated by thousands of kilometres.

The foregoing describes the possible experience of two types of passenger, an experience that may be totally different from that of the flight crew in the same aircraft. The cabin and cockpit crew is usually kept busy throughout the flight period: those in the cockpit keep their eyes on the instruments panel and are in constant communication with ground control, while the cabin crew takes care of passengers. Of special significance is the altitude indicator which shows the position of the aircraft relative to the ground, a critical indicator of aircraft performance. For example, it is said to have a nose-high altitude when climbing and a nose-down altitude when descending. Thus, a change in altitude would alter the performance of the aircraft which, in turn, would require a trade-off in speed: when an aircraft is in a nose-high altitude, its speed increases and vice versa when descending.

The aircraft analogy seems particularly appropriate in assessing the contributions of a natural flyer, Allison Ayida, to Nigeria's socio-economic development from the late 1930s to the late 1970s. Here was an economy that had all the potentials of a smooth take-off and a smooth flight to deliver the social and economic goods expected of a big, resource-rich, and vibrant nation. And here is a man who has been portrayed in the preceding chapters of this book as:

- One who had one of the best and most appropriate and effective preparations in his youth by going through the 'school of roughness and toughness';

- A student who went through his primary and secondary education in record time and emerged with flying colours, and then went to the best of universities;
- A civil servant with an uncommon grooming for high service;
- A daring 'super perm-sec' who was always looking for challenges and creative solutions to problems; and
- An 'officer' in the cockpit of an aircraft with one of the best engines (the Nigerian economy).

Why, despite the enviable attributes of Ayida as a member of several teams at the helm of affairs has it taken Nigeria such a long time to be fully airborne, especially when other 'economic aircraft' that took off at the same time seem to be requesting their passengers to fasten their seat belts for safe landing? What went wrong?

Providing answers to these and many other related questions is almost daunting, especially when the objective is not to praise or apportion blame. Our interest in this chapter is to distil the learning points that could assist in closing the gap between the enormous potential of an economy on one hand, and its relatively poor performance, vis-à-vis similarly endowed economies - to the extent that Nigeria's economy is now competing among the poorest in the world - on the other hand! The challenge of achieving a faster rate of development in future appears Herculean when it is realized that the chances of having the combination of another Ayida with the opportunities and responsibilities he had to move forward the Nigerian economy specifically, and society generally, are becoming slimmer. The lessons from Ayida's career may enable us to read better the instruments in the cockpit and those charged with managing them, and thereby control the craft better.

Put more succinctly, the objective of this chapter is to examine how the Nigerian project might have been handled differently to produce more tangible, more enduring results. Fortunately, Ayida himself provides many of the answers to the pertinent questions in our quest. His lecture, "The Nigerian Revolution, 1966-76" contains valuable ingredients that must not be overlooked and, indeed, must constitute the starting points of our post-mortem. The possible answers to the our questions, as contained in Ayida's book, may be classified into nine groups, including: indigenization, the "commanding heights" approach to development, the creation of more states and local governments, and the revenue allocation formula, among others. The nine points are programme-oriented and provide both performance indices and learning points. It is around these points that the shackles in Nigeria's development have been identified in our review.

Incidentally, Ayida's characterization of the development of the Nigerian society in terms of a "revolution" appears even more insightful than our flying analogy. Both types of characterization are certainly useful or, at least, can be used in a complementary way to promote understanding and assessment of the complex issues involved. Thus, the two concepts can be regarded as a double sieve for sorting out the variables in the performance of the Nigerian economy specifically, and of society in general.

We examine, in the remainder of this chapter, some of the issues raised in the development of Nigeria, by using the flight analogy, during the pre-1966, 1966-76, and post-1976 stages. We discuss the pre-1966 and the 1966-76 periods which Ayida has described as constituting the 'Nigerian Revolution,' but first, it would be helpful to summarize the characteristics of the flying analogy we have adopted, vis-à-vis the shackles of Nigeria's economic development.

Characteristics of the flying analogy

Only the salient features of flying are highlighted here by focusing on those that will aid our understanding of the progress, or otherwise, in transforming the Nigerian society generally, and the economy specifically. In other words, the focus is on those features that enhance our understanding of Nigeria's economic development, so far. Above all, our concern is on those that help in placing Ayida's contributions in proper perspective. But, even then, we can do no more than generate a few pertinent questions to guide our thinking on the subject, especially in further x-raying the attributes of the 1966-76 'revolution.'

Here, then, are some legitimate questions as we take the flying analogy further:

- Why have we chosen to fly? Where are we flying to?
- Do we have on board all that it takes for a smooth and successful flight? What are the assumptions of the needs of passengers during the flight?
- What particular aircraft have we chosen to fly in? What are its advantages and disadvantages? Do we have any contingency plans to handle the disadvantages?
- What qualities do we expect of the flight crew? What is the process of developing such qualities? What are the yardsticks and processes for determining them?
- What adverse weather conditions are the flight likely to encounter? What contingency arrangements are put in place to handle them?

The questions relate to critical issues that would determine as much the success or failure of a flight as they would any economic development programme. The questions may be further grouped into six categories of concern as follows: the flight destination, the aircraft, the flight crew, the condition of the cockpit, the passengers, and the external environment of the aircraft. Our brief comment on each should help us to understand how they may be applied to elucidate the Nigerian economic development situation, with profitable results.

The destination

The basic question here is: Where do we want to go as a nation? Who decides our destination and at what point (s) is the decision made? In a flight, this fundamental decision has to be taken before take-off and rarely changed. In the context of economic development, however, this is not necessarily the case and the realistic question may be: What do we do when we realise that we are heading towards an undesirable destination? Once this question is put, a host of other questions become relevant, such as:

- How do we determine the degree of deviation between where we want to go, and where we are heading?
- Who effects the necessary correction to ensure that we are heading towards our planned destination and how?
- Having chosen to fly, do we regard flying as an end in itself or a means to an end?
- Do we regard flying as a race? If the answer is 'Yes,' with which countries are we competing?
- Must we fly in the same direction as our competitors? If the answer is 'Yes,' must it be a race to catch up (with, say, the 'developed' countries)?
- If the answer is 'No', what should be our preferred destination and to what extent should we allow such a destination to be influenced from outside? etc, etc.

The distinction between the destination of an aircraft in flight and that of a nation in the process of economic development appear rather straightforward. In the latter scenario, however, one particular relationship - the horizontal and vertical - assumes a significance that is hardly ever taken into account in flying. In the Nigerian context, it becomes crucially significant to determine from the outset, as well as throughout the course of economic development, what type of vertical relationship we aspire to have with the developed countries - exploitative or a master-servant relationship which tends to result when a country relies more on its primary sector for economic survival and prosperity, rather than growing its industrial sector on the basis of its natural resource endowments.

The craft

This is essentially the structure of the Nigerian society. A number of pertinent questions need to be addressed in this regard, such as: What are the necessary components of the structure? (The three-tier levels of government - federal, state, and local - would be a key consideration here.) How well designed is it? Are the components and the design appropriate for delivering the social and economic goods in the specific Nigerian context? What tools (mechanisms) - National Development Plans, Perspective and Rolling Plans, Structural Adjustment Programme, etc. - would best deliver the goods? How effective have the tools been over the years and what parameters of effectiveness should be used?

In the final analysis, all other things being equal, the performance of the state structure would be a function of how its relevant parts have been identified and put together to function maximally in the unique socio-economic context of Nigeria.

The flight crew

The relevant questions here relate to the qualities of the crew and the instruments at their disposal. In a typical aircraft, members of the crew comprise the pilot, the co-pilot and the navigator – all well trained and well equipped for their collective responsibility of navigating the aircraft safety and landing it at the planned destination. A number of questions arise when we move from the analogy of an aircraft to the reality of a nation's economic development, such as: Who are the players in the cockpit of Nigeria's economic development? How well prepared are they for their roles, whether specialized or generalized?

With a well defined and an agreed destination at take-off, working as a team becomes rather easy for members of a flight crew. What happens in the course of economic development when the goal is not so well defined, or even agreed upon? And to make matters worse, how do we know what progress is being made, when different indices are being used to measure progress? Can such indices be reduced to one omnibus index, such that the targeted beneficiaries of socio-economic development can readily discern the similarities between the hijackers of an aircraft and the "state hijackers" in either a coup d'état or a democratically elected government?

The phenomenon of state hijackers introduces a series of questions, such as: How are the responsibilities of state governance shared among surviving crew members and the hijackers? Shouldn't the sharing of responsibilities be influenced solely by professional and patriotic concerns about the safe landing of the state structure at the planned destination? How should the rights and responsibilities of passengers (the beneficiaries) be respected, and even enhanced, in the process?

The passengers

The whole point of flying is to move passengers, who have duly paid their fares, from one safe location to another. In other words, the point of our earlier considerations, in the context of our analogy, is to identify the right components for an appropriate, well-designed and robust socio-economic strategy for moving Nigerians from an undesirable state of poverty to one of prosperity. Put differently, the desirable interests of the beneficiaries of socio-economic development must remain paramount at all times.

Once again, we have to address a number of pertinent questions, such as: Do the targeted beneficiaries have a say in Nigeria's socio-economic development programmes? If they do, how strongly are their views respected? Are the components of state structure being imposed or negotiated? If they are being negotiated, what criteria are being used and how well understood are they to the targeted beneficiaries? How frequently must we tinker with the components and what should activate the tinkering? Is there an optimum limit to the number of components, say, of local or state governments? What forms of effective relationships should exist between the components at various levels and from one level to another?

The external environment

This factor is totally out of control of the crew. The best that the crew can do is to learn to cope with it to ensure a safe and smooth flight for the aircraft and its passengers. Of course, the instruments in the cockpit and communication with ground control enable a reasonable measure of prediction of environmental changes and their likely effects on flight progress.

In the context of socio-economic development, the external environment comprises other societies and their economies.

Nigeria's relationships with such economies determine, to a large extent, what progress is possible in growing the local economy. But, such a relationship is a double-edged sword; it can promote, retard or even stunt our own progress. The challenge seems to be the ability to discern what type of relationship Nigeria wants at any point in time, essentially the ability to differentiate between a win-win and a zero-sum situation. It needs to be appreciated, however, that in a developing economy and nation like Nigeria, striking the right balance is not always easy.

We conclude this section by observing that virtually all the questions raised so far in our discourse have been raised and addressed by Ayida in his lectures and publications. Moreover, most of them were re-affirmed during the extensive interviews with him in preparation for the publication of this book. Here, we illustrate how some of the questions have been addressed by focusing on the 1966–76 period and the role of Ayida in it. A consideration of a few of the questions addressed by Ayida should guide our judgment on Ayida's verdicts in 1977 and 2003 on the same questions. Here then are a few:

- In 1977, Ayida contended that there had been many complex factors at play in Nigeria since the attainment of independence, and that between 1966 and 1977, the method and organization of the Nigerian society had undergone fundamental changes which, if not arrested, could qualify as the beginnings of a national revolution.
- However, a quarter of a century later and at another lecture delivered in far away Oxford University, his *Alma Mater*, Ayida observed, rather sadly that "with my head bowed and subdued, I can say with little hesitation that the Nigerian Revolution never took place." He then added, "alternatively, it did take place in the wrong direction."

- Ayida had predicted in a 1977 lecture that "unless a Vanguard can be evolved to provide the leadership and the impetus for the revolutionary forces at work, the Nigerian Revolution is bound to prove abortive."

In his judgement, Ayida seems to take the firm position that failure was traceable to deficiencies in the cockpit. Perhaps, but we believe that there are more fundamental reasons for failure, and we attempt to provide some examples in the next section.

An assessment of Nigeria's performance

Although Ayida has written most extensively on the 1966-76 'Nigerian revolution,' three phases of Nigeria's development are discernible: the pre-1966, the 1966-76, and the post-1976 periods. Recognition of these phases will help to sharpen our assessment of the 1966-76 'revolution' discussed later in this chapter. Meanwhile, we focus on the pre-1966 and post-1976 periods.

The pre-1966 and post-1976 periods

Fortunately, there is enough in the literature to show that some revolutionary seeds had been sown in the pre-1966 era. How else is one to describe the introduction of a new approach to government with its new system of justice and maintenance of law and order as encapsulated in Chapter One of this book, 'Perspectives of Nigeria's Public Service'? Particularly noteworthy is the observation that "... he has won our brothers, and our clan can no longer act like one. He has put a knife on the things that held us together and we have fallen apart."

The answers to the questions raised are blowing in the wind as well as further questions arising from those questions. It is important to recall our earlier observation to the effect that "admittedly, the civil service served the purposes of colonialism by providing the tools and principles and philosophy of governance." Some of the questions arising would be how inimical to the people's interests was that system of governance? Could it be argued, as we did earlier, that "whatever was good for the white man must be bad [or good] for the black man"? The question is particularly relevant, given that the black man was represented by a poorly educated class thereby creating a questionable but serious disconnect between the class and the people. This disconnect, which had its roots in the colonial days, was heightened during the military regimes with their exclusive and coercive use of power. Even though infinitely preferred to military rules, the civilian administration does not seem to be shortening this disconnect, as expected, given the doubtful process of effective participation by the people. We conclude with three questions. Firstly, can governance through the civil service not be regarded as a revolutionary seed, if not a revolution in itself? Secondly, can the role of the people, in this important organ of governance, which at best is marginal, be regarded as one of the seeds of the shackles to our socio-economic emancipation? Thirdly, should the concept of the black man being the master of his national destiny not be regarded as revolutionary itself? Ayida's thinking on this issue seems particularly illuminating:

> Just as the act of National Independence in 1960 marked the beginning of fundamental changes which could not be contemplated in the colonial days, the rule of the Blackman as master of his national destiny is taken for granted by the new generation of Nigerians, but it is not often realised that on the eve of national independence in 1960, it was regarded in many circles as a Leap in the Dark (Ayida, 1973:3).

The post-1976 revolution

The post-1976 'revolution' is well analysed by Ayida in two documents: The Nigerian Revolution, 1966-76 (1973) and The Nigerian Revolution Reconsidered (2003). The focus of the last sub-section of this chapter is the former, while this sub-section is concerned with the latter. In reconsidering The Nigerian Revolution, 1966-76, Ayida had observed hopefully that "with the benefit of hindsight, it [the revolution] can be accomplished." He had, however, added rather apologetically as follows: "with my head bowed and subdued, I can say with little hesitation that the Nigerian Revolution never took place," and, as we have noted, he then added, "alternatively, it did take place in the wrong direction" (Ayida, 2003).

Based on Ayida's conclusion, then, the Nigerian socio-economic aircraft was just about airborne, but flying in the wrong direction. The research team for this book identified this issue for intensive interviews with Ayida in which he basically repeated or re-affirmed the essence of his earlier publications on the subject. It is clear that Nigeria's post-1976 Revolution has been characterized more by flying with than without shackles. We will illustrate with a few examples, with a more detailed assessment reserved for the last sub-section of this chapter.

Of particular interest are the shackles associated with economic planning and the roles of the International Monetary Fund (IMF) and The World Bank in Nigeria's post-1976 development. Although he did not use the word 'shackles' to describe the effects of the two institution's on Nigeria's economic performance, Ayida counsels in his 1987 Convocation Lecture delivered at the University of Jos that Nigeria should "learn more from the lessons of history and experience and rely less on experts and economists from the IMF and the World Bank without practical experience or sufficient knowledge of the Nigerian situation."

Highlighting the not-so-positive effect of The World Bank on Nigeria's economic planning effort, Ayida cites the example of the Bank's advice to abandon the periodic planning approach in favour of rolling plans. He emphasizes that the planning process has all but collapsed as a result of adopting the rolling plan approach. Ayida further demonstrates the effect of the World Bank's advice on the quality of Nigeria's rolling plans by re-emphasizing his earlier observation in his lecture entitled, Nigerian Enterprise for Decision Makers (1987) as follows:

> ...these plans themselves were not phased; that is to say that the plans did not stipulate what would happen in the first year; what would happen in the second, third and fourth years. The plan [document] was just a statement of what was to happen for a 4- or 5-year period. So you have to judge the 5 years as a whole, whereas the progress reports tend to review each year in isolation. In the first year, nothing significant happens because you are mobilizing. The pattern then was that in the second, third years, you find a lot would happen, and then the executive capacity problem will crop up. The Government itself will stop the plan implementation and the organizational process in the 4th and 5th years because too much is happening and either that they cannot cope or they cannot finance the projects-in-progress (Ayida, 1987).

Many questions could be raised on the rolling plan approach to development planning in Nigeria. For example, given the distortions associated with planning in Nigeria, what happens when the plans are rolled over with the distortions? Plan distortions are defined by Ayida as those "projects that probably should never have been started [but]... have been introduced on political grounds or for non-economic reasons."

According to Ayida, distortions to plans have always been a problem in Nigeria. He believes that a better approach to the rolling plan would be to plan long (i.e., perspective planning) and implement long. With longer-term planning, Ayida further argues, a greater demand for plan discipline would be inculcated and the Head of State or President would become the embodiment of the plan, capable of integrating the various state-level plans with the federal plan. Ayida observes, however, that the President may not be able to achieve this objective if he is the source of plan distortions!

It is appropriate to conclude our assessment of Nigeria's post-1976 economic performance with Ayida's observation on the Federal Civil Service which, according to him, has disappeared. Without mincing words during the research team's interviews with him, Ayida, maintains that:

> The Civil Service evaporated and we have no civil service now; it [has] totally evaporated. Attempts are being made to put the Civil Service together again, but I am not sure the right things are being done. I thought about what it would take to put the Service back and concluded [that] it will be an impossible task. The public utilities and general services are in a shambles – the [Nigerian] Railways has evaporated as well as the [Nigeria] Airways. The Airways is gone and there is nothing to rescue it except you start a new airline.

Ayida is firmly convinced that the public sector constitutes the engine of Nigeria's economic growth, not the private sector. Explaining his rather strong position on the subject, he asks: "How do you explain [government] building a stadium when you are trying to privatize another stadium? Why can't the private sector do both? You sell one to them and the other one they build."

The issue of which sector - private or public - should

provide the engine of Nigeria's economic growth cannot be regarded as closed, however, especially if a distinction were to be made between ownership and management. By making such a distinction, a fundamental question would then arise: Would Nigeria's public sector enterprises and public utilities have collapsed if they had been managed by the private sector, with ownership remaining public? In the alternative, could management have remained public, but with a private sector style of management? Providing appropriate answers to these and related questions would provide useful learning points for the health of Nigeria's long-term economic growth and prosperity, we believe.

The shackles of Nigeria's development: some lessons

This final section of the chapter focuses on the 1966-76 'Nigerian Revolution' that wasn't; there are many candidate shackles to highlight and many lessons to learn from this period, but only a few have been selected. It is, of course, a matter for debate about how much of Nigeria's economic development in future would benefit from such lessons and how much it may have benefited from such considerations in the past. Our objective here is to sensitize all sections of Nigerian society about the importance of the lessons from Nigeria's development experience that has, no doubt, been very rich although often confusing. We continue with the flight analogy, drawing freely from some of the questions already highlighted and from some of Ayida's contributions to the subject.

Destination-related shackles and lessons

Ayida observes that there is a general consensus by all sections of Nigerian society about the validity of the five national objectives aimed at establishing Nigeria as a truly great nation state. The objectives are as follows:

- A united, strong and self-reliant nation,
- A great and dynamic economy,
- A just and egalitarian society,
- A land of bright and full opportunities for all citizens, and
- A free and democratic society.

By all accounts, these objectives constitute an excellent articulation of the desired Nigeria, or the Nigeria of our dream. The real challenge is how to operationlize them. Fortunately, the concept of a 'national value-added', as enunciated in the Second National Development Plan for assessing the desirability of projects of interest to the country, would appear to provide the key to most of the operational problems that may be encountered. Thus, the real challenge may have to do less with the appropriateness of stated objectives (the destination), and more with the mechanics of operationalization. Also, the challenge may have more to do with the degree of commitment to stated objectives by different sections of Nigerian society. As Ayida, has observed, "there is no nation without national objectives - it is a question of the single-mindedness with which its leadership pursues at all times the attainment of such objectives, principles and general ideas or philosophy of life." (Ayida, 1973: p.4) Ayida also emphasizes that

> What Nigeria lacked most in the past [and still lacks at present], has been the national sense of purpose, particularly in economic matters. The Federal Government will therefore occupy the commanding heights of the economy in the quest for purposeful national development and provide the leadership and honest administration necessary for the attainment of

> a national sense of purpose. Government intervention in economic matters designed primarily to protect and promote the public interest is therefore fully justified (Ayida, 1973:8).

We submit that Ayida's emphasis is a necessary but not sufficient requirement to ensure national commitment to a declared destination. To be sufficient, a number of conditions need to be satisfied, including the commitment of the peoples which, in turn, requires their understanding and acceptance of the national stated objectives. To facilitate all this, the objectives must be simply stated, preferably with a central focus, such as 'dependency reduction' (that is, the attainment of greater independence) that is sustainable. Furthermore, such central focus must be measurable to facilitate the monitoring and control of any deviations from the accepted objectives. It is in the context of such requirement that most of the questions raised earlier in our discussion of the destination of the aircraft are best appreciated. Of particular relevance are such questions as: Where do we want to go? Who decides where we want to go? How do we measure the progress towards reaching our destination? How do we correct any deviations along the way? Is development an end in itself or a means for reaching the nationally agreed destination?

It is pertinent to emphasize at this point that all aspects of flying affect the attainment of a specified destination, whether or not they were identified at the outset of the flight. For example, few flights ever factor the possibility of a hijack into pre-flight preparations. Corruption is definitely a major factor affecting the chances of Nigeria ever reaching it desired destination. Corruption (spelt with a capital letter) has become a malignant ailment in Nigeria's body polity and deserves the special attention accorded it later on in this chapter.

Aircraft-related shackles and lessons

An important component of the state structure (the aircraft) for attaining specified national objectives comprises the units at state and local government levels, as well as the assumed vertical relationships between them, that is, the relationships between federal, state and local governments. Another is the formula for sharing the resources among the various units of government, which has always been influenced by the assumed relationships. This explains, in part, why the assumed relationships, whether explicitly or implicitly stated, is always a major consideration in the controversies surrounding revenue allocation reports. The best example is provided by the Report of the Interim Revenue Allocation Review Committee set up in July 1968 under the Chairmanship of Chief I.O. Dina. According to Ayida, the Dina Report though one of the best documents on the country's fiscal system, has proved too controversial largely on account of its political assumptions summarized by the Committee as follows:

> We believe that fiscal arrangements in the country should reflect the new spirit of unity to which the nation is dedicated. No more evidence of this is necessary than the present war to preserve this unity at the cost of human lives, material resources and the radical change in this country's structure. It is in the spirit of this new-found unity that we viewed all the sources of revenue of this country as the common fund of the country to be used for executing the kinds of programmes which can maintain this unity (Ayida, 1973, p.8).

That the issue of resource sharing remains controversial is shown by the series of reviews since the Dina Report, culminating in the setting up of a permanent revenue commission, the 'National Revenue Mobilization, Allocation and Fiscal Commission.' The Commission has gone through a series of transformations in terms of size, tenure of membership - part-time or full time - political flavouring and focus, in terms of emphasizing sharing based on equity and effectiveness. There is little doubt that resource management has become a perennial problem in Nigeria, but more worrisome is its effect on the development process and, consequently, the rate of progress towards the attainment of national objectives. To a large extent, the not-too-satisfactory formulae for allocating federal resources have become a major cause of the agitation for the creation of more units at the state and local government levels, as well as the call for a redefinition of the vertical relationships between the units.

Ayida raises an alarm about the ballooning number of states and local governments in Nigeria. From the original three or four Regions then 12, now 22 and to 36 states, Ayida wonders if we will not reach 100, if the present trend is allowed to continue. As for the local governments, the current number of 774 represents only the constitutionally recognized ones. If the newly created local governments were included, the number would be well over 1000!

One may reasonably conclude from our discussion so far that the Nigerian aircraft, as presently designed and structured, has too many shackles impeding its flight performance. Ayida's observation, when interviewed on the subject, is that "Nigeria is not a craft, but several craft flying in different directions." The question is, can the present craft accommodate the size and heterogeneous demands of Nigerians and still cope with inevitable storming weather ahead, fly to schedule, and land safely? In other words, can a new system be worked out to provide a larger measure of independence for the component units, while ensuring that they are all in the same craft? Put more directly, can a more development-oriented system be distilled from the extremes of the pre-1966 and post-1976 units and structures of government? If so, why does it appear so difficult to come up with such a system?

One question appears legitimate: Which creates more problems for the development process, the ballooning number of units or perpetrating the inappropriate relationships between the existing units with the consequent demoralising effects? If, as we believe, the answer is more with the relationships than the numbers, then the Revenue Allocation Commission would appear to have more work to do in ensuring that the Federation resources are not just allocated, but mobilized and the units made to be more development-oriented. Although it is not our intention to go into details of revenue allocation in this book, we would still like to suggest that paying greater attention to the savings and stabilization aspects of allocation, as well as putting greater emphasis on internally-generated revenue would go a long way in reshaping the Nigerian craft which seems presently out of alignment. Indeed, the Commission has the means to creatively panel-beat the Nigerian craft which is presently in bad shape, until a more functional one is fashioned to replace it.

The endemic shackle of corruption

Corruption is a major source of leakage of vital resources from both the public and private sectors of Nigeria's economy. It is like the leakage of fuel from an aircraft in flight which could jeopardise its planned arrival at a destination. No matter how corruption is viewed, it remains a debilitating shackle on Nigeria's economic progress. A brief review of the nature and causes of corruption should assist in distilling the appropriate lessons to be learned as a basis for future action. Ayida's views on the subject provide a useful starting point.

According to Ayida, "as the 'petrol-Naira' flowed into the nation's coffers, so also did allegations of corrupt practices in the media." He adds that although corruption is a world-wide phenomenon, it has acquired a larger-than-life status in the Nigerian context. He then makes the following telling observation on the Nigerian version of corruption:

> The subject of corruption has always been one that I am most reluctant to comment on publicly, because the evidence is never visible and those who know don't talk about it when confronted. When I was in Government, I knew of many occasions when people refused to give confidential information on allegations of corruption. One feature I have noticed is that very few men of courage ever accuse the Government-in-power of corrupt practices. It is usually when the Government has fallen that allegations against its functionaries begin to flow; while they were in power everybody praised them and danced to their tunes. This is very unfortunate.
>
> I think it is appropriate to say that not only has corruption attained unimaginable proportions, but has gone beyond rational thinking. This applies both to the public and private sectors, and my observation is that it is even worse in the latter. Take the distribution of goods, for example. If you went to manufacturing concerns in the recent past and discovered what people paid some managers to become distributors, you will definitely call it Monumental Corruption. Corruption is more visible in the public sector especially at the top, but it permeates the entire system at high and low levels. It tends to thrive most in the midst of bureaucratic controls, inefficiencies and shortages in relation to demand situations. The answer is to enhance efficiency and reduce controls and artificial bottlenecks.

In giving an account of his experience of corruption in Nigeria, Ayida also suggests it can be managed by acknowledging its function and openly rewarding it. He points out that corruption would become an issue of paying a commission, using registered commission agents. The effective management of corruption would require that a ceiling be put on the amount of commission payable, and payment would be made only after specified services would have been rendered, he continues.

In support of his position, Ayida recalls a number of cases involving open lobbying for contracts by businessmen and their readiness to pay a commission, up to the cabinet level, during the first part of the 1970s. He recalls a particularly interesting case involving a senior cabinet member who had been lobbied by a businessman and who had, in turn, lobbied Ayida, the then Secretary to the Nigerian Executive Council (or Cabinet). The lobbying cabinet member had disclosed everything to Ayida, including the promised commission the businessman would pay the cabinet member. As it turned out, the quotation of the lobbying businessman was not the lowest, but he had also indicated his willingness to accept and execute the contract at the lowest bid. The discussion at the cabinet meeting, including the issue of a commission, had been open and frank. At the end, the lobbying businessman and the cabinet member lobbying on his behalf lost!

Ayida traces the origin of paying a commission (corruption) for the execution of public projects to the days of Chief Okotie-Eboh, Nigeria's first post-independence Minister of Finance, when the system was 'openly' managed. A fee of between five and ten percent was charged and shared among selected and trusted leaders across all political parties. The practice was abandoned, or at least stopped being similarly well managed, as soon as Okotie-Eboh was removed from office, Ayida submits. Subsequent attempts to institute a similarly well managed, open system had failed, even after a study had recommended the registration of commissioned agents and the payment of tax on commissions during Obasanjo's first term as Head of State, Ayida concludes.

The failure to upgrade corruption to the level of a 'commission' has, apparently, led to corruption getting completely out of control and doing untold damage to the cause of Nigeria's economic development. *A laissez-faire* attitude to corruption by successive Nigerian Heads of State then evolved; the management of corruption became personalized. Some Heads of State distributed 'patronage' generously to secure goodwill and support; others used it to secure other ends. At least one Head of State tried to discourage it by 'closing in' on some people while leaving others untouched, an approach tantamount to making scapegoats of a few and failing woefully to check corruption. Yet some other Heads of State were firm on any person found involved in corrupt practices, with the significant exception of themselves, members of their families and friends.

As might be expected, none of these arbitrary approaches arrested Nigeria's rampant corruption. Ayida maintains that effective and successful efforts to combat corruption would have to recognize that some of it is inevitable, so long as frictions and obstacles exist in any human system. He also points out that it is important to note that corruption seeks to reduce such frictions and obstacles to the mutual advantage of the parties involved. There is always a cost to a third party which, in most cases, is an organization or society. What is needed, Ayida insists, is to contain and curtail corruption by treating it as 'what it is', a price (commission) for some service rendered, and make it open and properly regulated. Ultimately, corruption would be eliminated or reduced to the level of mere tips, Ayida finally submits.

We conclude by highlighting one or two other issues that should be addressed in curtailing corruption in Nigeria. The massive oil revenue is regarded by many as the root cause of corruption in Nigeria as rent-generating activities seem to have been created at the pace of the magnitude of oil revenue. Furthermore, Nigeria's massive oil flood has apparently washed away most of the hitherto effective controlling mechanisms in the management of resources. One result is the ever-broadening of the areas of discretion available to those at the helm of affairs and the seemingly endless dishing out of goodwill which provides a rich bed for the growth and blossoming of corruption. The binding constraints of limited resources have been relaxed to such an extent that hard choices are no longer respected. The critical question is, can we device a means of harvesting the benefits of an oil boom and effectively combine it with the wisdom imposed by 'poverty' of resources at the same time? The answer may well lie in the way we allocate and use resources, especially among the units of government, irrespective of their number. It is critically important that available resources be consumed to promote growth and development rather than to enhance governance which has become the veritable fountain of corruption in Nigeria.

The external environment: a lever or shackle?

The external environment can affect, positively or negatively, the flight performance of an aircraft and, therefore, the time of its arrival at a planned destination. A pilot's ability to cope with the environment in his flight path is essentially an issue of the pilot's strategy, attitude, and preparedness to deal with all forms of emergency. Ayida's view on strategy, in regard to the use of external bodies in Nigeria's economic development, especially the role of The World Bank and IMF in planning, has been cited earlier in this chapter. Ayida had also taken the liberty to express equally strong views on this and related matters elsewhere. It is important to note that his position on the handling of the external environment in the management of Nigeria's economy has not changed. Essentially, he is strongly against the Federal Government relying more on international agencies and foreign consultants than on Nigerian agencies and experts. By extension, this position is also applicable to foreign ownership and control of Nigerian business enterprises.

We begin with an examination of his views as expressed at a lecture entitled, "Self-sufficiency: the Path to a Virile Nationhood" delivered during the National Day celebrations in 1988. According to Ayida, "self-sufficiency is an attitude of the mind. Until there is a radical change of attitude on the part of the Government and the governed, this nation cannot attain self-sufficiency in any significant manner." One of the conclusions of the lecture is the affirmation that, "the bottom line in the Agenda for the year 2000 and beyond is a nation which believes in self-reliance and radiates national self-confidence and mutual trust and, above all, integrity and leadership by good example."

Ayida's justification of government's intervention in business and the economy, using the 'indigenization' and the 'commanding heights' strategies, is difficult to fault. According to Ayida,

> Orthodox economics tries to show that markets allocate scarce resources according to *relative efficiency*; political economics tries to show that markets distribute income according to *relative power*. It is good to know about efficiency but in our world (Nigeria), it tends to be subservient to power. Power is usually enhanced by efficiency but the two are nevertheless quite distinct. *Economic power* ultimately rests on the ability to inflict a loss – *the stick*. A subsidiary form is the ability to bribe – *the carrot*. If economists paid as much attention to bribery and extortion as they do to marginal utility, we should be able to develop rough quantitative indices by means of which one could sensibly discuss

> the distribution of economic power in society. By failing to accord the distribution of income between labour and capital a properly central role, orthodox economics has become cut off from the central issues of our time...
>
> The dominant role of expatriate business enterprises in the Nigerian economy can thus be fully appreciated when this is related to their corrupting influence and power. Orthodox economics cannot justify the current crusade of indigenisation of certain expatriate businesses if we were preoccupied with efficiency and economic growth. We cannot ignore both in the long run, but there could be overriding considerations, such as distributive equity as between Nigerians and non-Nigerians.
>
> The other consideration is the necessity for the political system to apply to the private sector, strategies and yardsticks similar to those which necessitated the Nigerianisation of the public sector at Independence. Most of us would not have become Permanent Secretaries, and even University Professors, when we did, if the expatriate holders of such posts were not forced by the logic of the situation to surrender their jobs to us prematurely. A similar historical necessity prompted the Nigerian Enterprises Promotion Decree. The schedule of businesses in that Decree should be seen as a beginning in the process of indigenising and eventually controlling the private sector of the economy (our emphasis).

Ayida reaffirms, during the interviews to collect data for this book, his earlier assessment of the significance of the indigenisation exercise by repeating the now familiar words that, "the programme of indigenisation of the economy may yet turn out to be one of the most important landmarks of the military regime." This may be true. His concluding remarks that, "there is, therefore, no need for the authorities to continue to adopt an apologetic stance in a matter of historical necessity and national pride" may, however, not have been accepted by a subsequent military regime which rolled back the provisions of the Indigenisation Decree and opened up the economy, once again, to foreign investors. Ayida does not think opening up of the economy, even with privatization, is the right step. In a 2001 lecture entitled, *National Development Planning and the Market Economy*, Ayida has this to say:

> If privatisation is designed to encourage the inflow of foreign investment, not much of this has happened in Nigeria for many reasons. One, existing investors and companies have merely tried to expand their assets base and protect their markets by buying up privatised businesses, rather than brand new investors moving into the economy. Two, those investing are not bringing in fresh capital as they have easy access to local funds and credit facilities. Three, there is the continued fear of security of investment in an environment where contractual agreements receive little respect. And, four, the increasing insecurity of life and property and thus law and order considerations have discouraged potential external investment.

One final question on this topic would, therefore, seem in order: Given the way in which Nigeria is managing the 'external environment' of its economic development, should one regard that environment as a shackle to, or an accelerator of, development?

The cockpit crew: some lessons

In the cockpit during Ayida's days in government were: the

Head of State, the Chief of Army Staff, top Permanent Secretaries, Commissioners and a string of advisers drawn from the Universities, the Armed Forces, private organizations, and personal friends. The performance of successive teams in managing national development is largely a function of the complementarity of members as well as how they perceive and perform their functions. As would be expected, enormous differences were often recorded with regime changes. Some of Ayida's assessments of the teams are, nonetheless, useful in helping to determine the extent to which they aid or retard national development. Here, we focus on only three of the team members, namely, the top Permanent Secretaries, the Commissioners, and the Heads of State. We have deliberately left out members of the Armed Forces since, by tradition and training, they are not supposed to contest the rulings of their superiors.

The relationship between the Permanent Secretaries and the Commissioners was not always smooth. As Ayida explains,

> If civil Commissioners appear to exercise less power than the former ministers, it is not because their functions have been usurped by Permanent Secretaries and other senior [civil] servants. It is because authority now resides in the military. Commissioners and senior civil servants are fellow Advisers, with different roles, to the powers-that-be who sometimes receive their advice from outside the two groups, to their mutual frustration and suspicion. Commissioners were not appointed to run the government as political masters but as servants of the military, the new political masters. This is one of the reasons why some of them sometimes erroneously regard top civil servants as rivals especially where they are technocrats and not professional politicians by origin. Even as spokesmen for the regime, some of them sometimes seem most

> anxious to dissociate themselves publicly from the less popular measures of the military regime, presumably in the interest of their political career after 1976 (Ayida, 1973:11).

As Ayida further explains,

> The place of federal Permanent Secretaries in this set-up has been misunderstood for three historic reasons. Between 15 January 1966 when the military came to power and 12 June 1967, Federal Permanent Secretaries headed Ministries without Ministers until Commissioners were appointed at a later date. It is not generally realized that during this period, all ministerial powers were vested in the Federal Executive Council and not in individual Permanent Secretaries. When the military first seized power, one of their first suggestions was to draw members of the Federal Permanent Secretaries. *We declined to serve and preferred to retain our traditional role as advisers.*
>
> The second reason for the myth about Federal Permanent Secretaries is that during the civil war, *some of them were called upon to speak up for the Federal cause and to serve in varying capacities*, such as the Kampala and other peace talks. This misled many people to assume at the time that we were no longer playing our traditional roles. *They were grossly mistaken*.
>
> The third ground is that senior civil servants are now called upon to serve on the Boards of public corporations and other statutory agencies. It is not often realized that *a Permanent Secretary does not often sit on Boards* for which he is listed. Oftener than not, he designates a representative (our emphasis).

It is illuminating to note the views of Ayida on the Military in the cockpit during his tenure in government. Ayida's personal impression is that " the military rulers are very receptive to new ideas provided they are well articulated." As if Ayida is thinking of the shackles in our analogy, he adds: "What the country suffers from is the poverty of new ideas and well thought-out policy reform proposals, based on a full knowledge of the workings of the system." This observation remains as valid today as when Ayida first made it: "paucity of innovative ideas" remains a major shackle in our development path and the cause of painful delays in the march to our desired development destination.

Ayida goes beyond a general comment on Nigeria's military leaders when interviewed on the subject. The research team interviewing him had attempted a profiling of the military leaders under whom he had served and had obtained the following firm impressions, excluding the sometimes fascinating details:

- *Some of the military leaders were mad.* The seemingly craziest of the leaders was, strangely, the most sensible and gentle. His mad appearance was a mere façade to ward off criticism from the public. He was a complete gentleman though in his mad rush to change things made many mistakes that, as a gentleman, he owned up to and apologized when necessary. According to one Head of State, there was one truly mad senior military leader who deserved to be put behind bars, but for various reasons could not be so treated. He, too, was in a hurry to change things and mistakes were frequently made, but the mistakes were not owned up to, and scapegoats were made of others instead.

- *Some were perceived as disciplined* by the public largely on account of the popularity of their policies and actions which consisted essentially of picking up people, more or less selectively, and subjecting them to humiliation.

- *A few built their public image through patronage distribution*. As a result, they were generally liked by many, while some condemned their action as corruption.
- *Many accumulated wealth* that, in one or two cases, became rather puzzling, especially in terms of the purpose of such accumulation. Strangely for one, he maintained discipline, in spite of his primitive and gluttonous way of accumulating wealth, by instilling fear in people. He was much cleverer than people imagined; he craved power and failed only because he chose the wrong people.
- *There is no evidence of corruption with respect to one particular leader* and, indeed, he left office poor. He was honest, though naïve. Nice, but he could not enforce discipline among his colleagues. He ruled in-council, that is, he took all decisions with Council's approval, except on one occasion when he was induced to use his power as the 'first Lord of the Treasury' to give a small grant to the Supreme Council for Sports in Africa, a decision which was later ratified by the Executive Council.
- *One operated with civil servants and followed civil service procedures*, with the Federal Executive Council approving everything, after appropriate memoranda would have been submitted by Permanent Secretaries. That particular Head of State did not interfere with the procedure for awarding contracts and due process was followed to the letter.

Ayida sums up the rationale for the departure (madness) of most military rulers from laid down procedures by recalling the telling words of a Head of State who said it was impossible and unrealistic to expect that he would risk his life, carrying a gun and shooting his way to the top only to hand over responsibility for accounting to some Permanent Secretary. The same Head of State had asked Ayida incredulously, "Can you expect that I will risk my life and not control the vote [purse] and everything in the military?"

This feeling, apparently, summed up the attitude of many a Nigerian military ruler from 1966 to 1999. Another military Head of State later wanted the old system restored whereby a Permanent Secretary would be the Accounting Officer. Strangely enough, it was the same Head of State who had wanted to accumulate wealth! But more strangely, perhaps, was the opposition by some civilian Ministers to the idea. Confronting Ayida who was advising on civil service reform long after his retirement, a civilian Minister said, "it is all right if you bring back Permanent Secretaries like you, but Permanent Secretaries these days are of no use." He then pleaded that Ayida recommend that an arrangement be made to bring back Permanent Secretaries as accounting officers only after two years would have elapsed, i.e., when the tenure of the regime in which the Minister served would have been over!" Although government accepted the recommendation to bring back Permanent Secretaries as accounting officers, in practice, the Minister was still effectively in charge. Thus, the important function of Permanent Secretaries exercising effective control over the finances of Ministries and thereby providing a much-need break on government expenditure appears to have been compromised, at least for now.

In further x-raying (military) leadership in Nigeria, it is useful to examine what Ayida considers a common mistake of "practically all the military administrations in this country, [that] is, their excessive preoccupation with the economic mismanagement of their predecessors without being able to improve on their performance." This mistake appears all the more serious when it is realised that no lessons appear to have been learned from the past mismanagement by Nigerian leaders, military or civilian. This observation strengthens the feeling that such preoccupation has not been primarily concerned with bringing about improvements in governance, but more of playing to the gallery or even witch-haunting. Whichever is the case, it remains a leadership problem. According to Ayida, "Nigeria has not been blessed with charismatic leadership universally acclaimed or generally acceptable to all." Ayida further note that:

> The central missing factor in Nigeria's economic crises is good management which led to the collapse of practically all institutions. Successive Governments and leaderships may be blamed for putting the wrong men at the helm of affairs, but Nigeria must concentrate on how to restore the viability and effectiveness of these institutions before the country's economic health can be revived.

It would therefore, not be totally out of place to conclude this section on the cockpit crew with a question that may appear academic: What would have happened to the course of Nigeria's economic development if its pilot had come from the Federal Civil Service? Put more bluntly, might Nigeria's development flight have been smoother and/or faster with Ayida as the pilot?

Ayida is on record as having refused to take advantage of two opportunities to uplift his status in Nigeria's development aircraft to co-pilot. One has already been mentioned, that is, the suggestion to include some Federal Permanent Secretaries in the Federal Cabinet. To further buttress the consistent position of serving civil servants on the subject, Ayida (1989) cites a concrete example as follows:

> No civil servant wishes to discharge ministerial duties at the political level while in the Service. At the

> inception of military rule in 1966, Federal Permanent Secretaries refused to act as political heads of Ministries until Federal Commissioners were appointed early in 1967. In August 1975, a distinguished civil servant, Mr. Ime Ebong, declined the offer from the late General Murtala Mohammed as Head of State, to be appointed the Federal Commissioner from the then South-Eastern Government, and preferred to continue to serve the new administration as a Federal Permanent Secretary.

There was another opportunity which amounted to piloting the state craft, if only temporarily in a rather disguised form. In both cases, the reason for not taking advantage of such opportunities was the preference of senior civil servants to retain their traditional role as advisers to the political heads of government. When Ayida was confronted with the question of what would have happened if he had cashed in on the opportunities to pilot the state craft, he insists that it would not have changed much as most of the Heads of State he served were prisoners of some "ghosts" who were not ready to relinquish their grip on Nigeria's leaders. Explaining further, Ayida (1987) makes the following remarks:

> I am yet to see installed in Lagos a Federal Government whose Head does not feel that he is bound in chains and is not free to implement the social programmes which he feels convinced will save this country from eventual disintegration.

Paradoxically, Ayida in his lecture entitled, *Hallmarks of Labour* (1999) writes as follows:

> I still regret that the late Abdul Azeez Attah and I did not accept Colonel Gowon's invitation for us and the then Solicitor-General, Justice Kazeem to stay behind and write his take-over speech. [Perhaps if I had

> accepted the invitation] "The basis of unity is not there" would not have become the albatross of the Federal propaganda effort during the civil war and the Gowonist era of One Nigeria.

On the basis of the foregoing comments, it would seem fair to ask: Was Ayida's group of top civil servants' consistent position of avoiding the assumption of political positions the best professional judgement in an ever-changing game of musical chairs? Did Nigeria, by their uncompromising position, miss a golden opportunity to eliminate a major shackle of development and thereby stabilize a rocking aircraft? Certainly, the roles of the cockpit members cannot be expected to remain the same with the incursion of "hijackers"?

Whatever may be our verdict today on those momentous events in Nigeria's recent history, Ayida was and remains a happy purist to the core. One wonders how many more like him are left in the Federal Civil Service

Concluding remarks

We conclude this chapter by highlighting some of the learning points arising from Ayida's life as a person as well as from Nigeria's economic development, with Ayida in the cockpit (or, in the Nigerian parlance, in the corridors of power). Ayida as a person went through life with flying colours. He, therefore, flew and landed safely, in spite of the shackles. This was largely because he graduated through the 'school of roughness and toughness.' Like Joseph in the Bible, he was well prepared for the challenges ahead of him in public service. This was the clear message from his early life and record of service Reproducing more 'Ayidas' should, therefore, constitute an important, long-term objective in growing Nigeria's public service for effective national development.

One way of attaining this goal is by restructuring our educational institutions to ensure the building of a strong moral character and life-long training for self-development to ensure that graduates would be well prepared to cope with the environmental challenges of life and work. In such restructuring, training by experimentation in real-life social settings would complement the traditional experiment in the laboratory. This important component of effective preparation for a productive and fulfilling life seems to have been ignored for too long. And yet, as a Chinese saying goes, "What I hear, I forget; what I see, I remember; but what I do, I know." Put more directly, Nigerian students must be more involved in their own development by using all their faculties - brains and brawn - at all levels of their educational ladder.

As a technocrat, Ayida was definitely a flyer. In addition to the advantages of a sound preparation, his brilliant performance was aided by a challenging civil service set-up that prepared him for higher service relatively early in his career. Furthermore, successive Heads of State reposed enormous confidence in the senior civil servants by giving them onerous responsibilities. Regrettably, much of the cherished traditions of the Nigerian Civil Service seem to have vanished. There is an urgent need to re-build and re-focus the Federal Civil Service, along with other public-sector institutions that have suffered a similar fate. In doing so, it would be important to address the issue of professional training and re-training for high-level civil servants, and it is doubtful if the existing institutions in their present form, such as the Administrative College of Nigeria (ASCON) and the National Centre for Economic Management and Administration (NCEMA) can handle the professional responsibilities envisaged here.

The final lesson must revolve around what has to be done, at personal, community and national levels, to ensure that the

Nigerian economy would fly and land as planned by making maximum use of the enormous potentials in the country. The learning points have been well articulated in Part II of this book as well as the latter part of this chapter. One hardly controversial conclusion may be drawn from the various perspectives of analysis in this book: the Nigerian nation has not been as fortunate as Ayida, in the sense that despite the nation's immense resources and opportunities, its stunted flight since 1960 has been laden with all manner of shackles. In other words, one would be correct to conclude that, for Nigeria, it has been more rather than less of 'Not Flying Because of the Shackles.' The shackles have been everywhere: shackles with the identification of an appropriate destination, the design of the aircraft, the composition of the cockpit crew, the management of the external environment and the expectations of the flight passengers. Surely, all patriotic Nigerians have the responsibility of contributing whatever they can to ensure that the shackles are reduced, and eventually removed, in the shortest possible time. That resolve would be a worthy tribute to Allison Akene Ayida, Nigeria's quintessential public servant.

15

Spatial dimensions of poverty and inequity in Nigeria

Introduction

One important issue that has been a major concern to Allison Ayida, during and after his public service years, is the pervasive poverty and inequity in Nigeria. Given the country's huge resource endowment, poverty should be anathema in Nigeria. This sad paradox has provided the basis for Ayida's zealous and committed comments at every given opportunity as the widening gap between the rich and the poor remains a major obstacle to effective development management. The conclusion from his convocation lecture titled, *The Rise and Fall of Nigeria* at the 1987 Convocation of the University of Jos, summarizes his position on endemic poverty in Nigeria and the state of despair to which majority of Nigerian citizens have been reduced in the following words:

> I stand here before this audience as a sad Nigerian. I feel sad because of the sense of doom around and the shadow of doubt hanging over us. There is too much human misery around. The immiseration of the rural poor and the pulverization of urban dwellers as demonstrated in the apparent lack of collective will to

> survive, has gone too far. It is difficult to imagine how the urban poor survive today. We have to look at the human aspects of the saga in an attempt to get a true historical perspective. What does the future hold for Nigeria? (Ayida, 1988: 9).

Given the misery of the Nigerian poor and its incidence in both rural and urban areas, Ayida argues that there is an urgent need to focus attention on the increasingly unbearable sacrifice demanded of the silent majority - the have-nots in all parts of the federation. As a policy option, therefore, he stresses the need to: revive the professional and middle class as a vehicle for transmitting modern technologies and management in public and private enterprises; put an end to Nigerians continuing to live beyond their means; address urgently the present high level of graduate unemployment; and drastically reduce the inequitable distribution of development in all regions of the country. He warns that unless action is taken immediately to address these issues, the fabric of society and the ability to maintain law and order would be seriously compromised. To him development would be meaningless if the serious problems of poverty, environmental deterioration and inequitable distribution of welfare remain unresolved.

Nigeria presents a classical case of a nation in diversity; an attribute when properly managed could a centripetal force of harnessing development. That is, the diversity could provide enough potential for sustained and balanced development. Unfortunately, however, the visible distributional inequity tends to vary along ethnic lines and regions where there is abundant wealth suffering disproportionately in terms of economic and development opportunities. The Nigerian situation presents a clear case of poverty in the midst of plenty. What then is the constraint to achieving this desired goal? What is the current state of distributional inequity in the nation? While the problem of inequity is widely acknowledged, is the current solution the best option? What are the consequences of past attempts to solve this problem? What are the lessons of experience that can be learnt from other countries that have gone through such situations? How should we solve the problem of inequity henceforth based on these experiences? These are some of the issues we intend to address in this chapter.

To dutifully address the foregoing, the rest of this chapter is organized into five sections. Following this introduction is section I which deals with the evidence on the Nigerian experience on poverty and equity, and the use of equity in the development management. Section II examines the contribution of Mr Allison Ayida in the struggle to achieve equity for sustained growth and economic development in Nigeria while section III provides insights into the approaches to geographical targeting. Fostering equity in the development process is the central focus of section IV and conclusion is contained in section V.

Empirical evidence of poverty and inequity

In examining poverty and its regional dimensions in Nigeria, this section examines how the individuals and the different regions in the country have fared with respect to these four critical dimensions of poverty as espoused by Mabogunje (1999): economic, social environmental and governance. Fortunately, research on poverty and its regional distribution has been enriched in the last decade.

Nigeria made great leaps in enhancing the well being of the citizenry in the 1960s and 1970s. However, policy distortions, mismanagement of resources, corruption and entrenched ethnic interests led to colossal economic, social and political crisis that adversely affected the health of the economy. Since 1980, poverty incidence greatly accelerated. It increased from 28.1% in 1980 to 65.6% in 1996. Current estimate reveal that about

70% of Nigeria's 120 million are living under poverty (FOS, 1999). What is interesting here is the sectoral and spatial distribution of this poverty. For ease of analysis, the six geopolitical zones of Nigeria; southwest, southeast, south-south, northwest, northeast and north central which have been in use since 1995, is the central focus of analysis here.

Poverty level in Nigeria displayed distinct regional differences reflecting the different agro-climatic conditions and economic structures. While the northern zone has as much as 45% of the population leaving below poverty line, corresponding figures for the central and southern zones are 39% and 24% respectively. Further information about the geographical distribution of poverty is revealed by inter-regional or state-by-state variation.

Using three variables of life expectancy at birth, education and income, Table 1 shows a widening gap in poverty incidence in Nigeria. In terms of life expectancy, the states with the highest are Lagos and Imo (61.4 years and 60 years respectively) while the States with the lowest life expectancy were those of Kaduna (36.6 years). Bauchi (36.7 years), Borno (37.0 years). With regards to education (adult literacy) Sokoto (2.7%), Borno (10.0%) and Kano (12.1%) had the least, while the Southern States Imo (75.5%), Cross River (69.4%), Bendel (65.6%) and Lagos (65.0%) had the highest level of adult literacy.

Table 1: Components of Human Development Index (HDI) for Nigeria (1992)

S/N	*State*	*Life Expectancy at Birth (yrs)*	*Adult Literacy (%)*	*Mean Years of School*	*Educational Attainment (%)*	*Real GDP per capital (PPP$)*	*Adjusted real GDP (PPP$)*	*HDI*
1.	Bendel	53.7	65.6	4.00	45.07	5,003.4	5,003.4	0.631
2.	Rivers	50.2	51.9	3.84	35.88	4,860.7	4,860.7	0.539
3.	Cross River	57.8	69.4	3.27	47.36	2,626.0	2,626.0	0.513
4.	Lagos	61.4	65.0	3.29	44.64	2,034.7	2,034.7	0.489
5.	Imo	60.0	75.6	3.80	51.67	1,341.1	1,341.1	0.466

S/N	State	Life Expectancy at Birth (yrs)	Adult Literacy (%)	Mean Years of School	Educational Attainment (%)	Real GDP per capital (PPP$)	Adjusted real GDP (PPP$)	HDI
6.	Gongola	57.8	26.0	2.15	18.05	665.1	665.1	0.214
7.	Ondo	49.4	50.6	3.29	34.83	422.9	422.9	0.212
8.	Oyo	51.3	40.4	3.11	27.97	678.1	678.1	0.210
9.	Niger	54.9	16.0	1.04	11.01	1,262.0	1,262.0	0.191
10.	Benue	53.5	27.0	1.91	18.64	809.5	809.5	0.188
11.	Kwara	45.9	40.0	3.00	27.67	1,020.1	1,020.1	0.183
12.	Anambra	44.9	43.1	2.91	29.70	860.1	860.1	0.174
13.	Kano	57.1	12.1	0.73	8.31	692.6	692.6	0.161
14.	Plateau	39.5	36.7	2.18	25.19	1,224.1	1,224.1	0.149
15.	Sokoto	49.2	2.7	0.43	1.94	1,246.2	1,246.2	0.128
16.	Bauchi	36.7	39.8	2.03	27.21	762.2	762.2	0.127
17.	Ogun	37.4	41.8	2.18	28.80	619.3	619.3	0.126
18.	Kaduna	36.6	30.8	1.52	21.04	876.4	876.4	0 101
19.		37.0	10.0	0.55	6.85	957.8	957.8	0.042
	HDI of 1993	51.5	50.7	34.20	1,215.0	1,215.0	1,215.0	0.246

Source: UNDP (1996). *Nigeria Human Development Report*

As revealed in Table 1, all the northern states performed poorly on the HDI (i.e., below the national average) although Gongola (now Taraba and Adamawa States) is relatively better among the group. Conversely, with the exception of Ogun State, all the southern states fared much better. As aptly put by Abumere (1998a), the contrast in distributional inequity between the north and south cannot be more dramatic. The relative position of the states in 1992 were maintained in 1996 because UNDP (1996) asserted that ranking of the Nigerian states by HDI puts, for example Edo and Delta (formally Bendel State) states on the top with HDI of 0.666 while Borno has an HDI of 0.156. Were these States to be constituted into sovereign nations, Edo and Delta would rank 90th (thus falling into a medium-level developing country) while Borno State would have been the least developed state in the world. The conclusion of Abumere (1998a) reveals a similar result. All the states in the north with exception of Kano are categorized as least developed and thus poor. Lagos followed by the south eastern states are the most developed followed by the states in the south west.

Poverty also varies between rural and urban sectors. In terms of spatial distribution of poverty, rural areas exhibit higher incidences of poverty more than urban areas. The share of rural poverty rose from 49% in 1985 to 68.9% in 1996 as against urban centres, whose poverty level rose from 31% to 42% over the same period. This rural-urban poverty dichotomy also correlates with regional poverty differentiation in the country. Evidence also revealed that urban poverty was highest in the north west in 1992 while the south west had the least incidence of urban poverty. The south east region had the highest rural poverty followed by the north east and middle belt. The south west again had the least incidence of rural poverty. By 1996 however, deliberate government policy and private sector participation had caused an alteration as the south east recorded the highest incidence of both urban and rural poverty. The middle belt followed while the north east recorded the lowest rural poverty. The main conclusion from Aigbokhan (2000) is that in terms of the depth and severity of poverty, the incidence was generally higher in the southern zones in 1996 whereas, in 1992, the reverse was the case.

Abumere (1998b) while noting that from colonial times the level of income per capital has always been higher in the south compared to the north showed again that by 1988 per capita income has been rising much faster in the south than in the north. In the same vein, secondary school education has also been high for the south more than the north. In the area of industrialization, the south has also fared much better. One revealing aspect of this study is that whereas industrial efforts in the south are due to multinational and Nigeria's private sector companies, those in the north are made mainly by the federal government. Since 80% of industrial investments are made by multinational corporations (Edozien, 1968) and since these investments are mainly in the south, the gap in industrialization between the north and the south will remain for a long time to come.

The observed regional poverty and levels of development in Nigeria are not without causes, some of which dates to the colonial times. Before colonization, north Nigeria was linked to North Africa and Europe through the international trans Saharan trade routes. Cities grew up in major trade centres. However, with the coming of the Europeans to Nigeria, there was a reversal in the direction of trade and consequently prosperity. The Europeans in addition to trade established schools and hospitals, which gave the southerners an early advantage, compared to the northern region.

During colonization, trade further developed and the colonial authorities encouraged the development of export products like cocoa, rubber, palm oil, groundnut, to mention a few. The colonial authority emphasized export trade by building roads and communication networks to facilitate this trade. Areas planting food crops were neglected in the scheme of things. Coupled with this was the Township Ordinance which provided for the creation, classification and administration of all towns in Nigeria (Mabogunje, 1968). Three categories of towns - first, second and third class towns were created. Infrastructural amenities were distributed on the basis of this hierarchy. Settlements not listed were also left out of the scheme of colonial development policy.

Abumere (1998a) noted that Lagos, the only first class town is located in southern Nigeria. Eighteen second class towns were also created. Twelve of these were in the south and six in the north. While of the fifty third class towns created, thirty-eight were in the south and only twelve in the north. Whatever reasons for the township classification - ranging from ability to raise revenue, proximity to the sea, etc, - it guided the colonial administration in the distribution of amenities. The current spatial imbalance in Nigeria has its roots in colonial trade and administrative policies.

The development of modern trade with the participation of multinational corporations have only served to deepen this spatial imbalance. In terms of market, skill and raw materials (notably petroleum), which they are interested in making investments are located in the southern part of the country.

Political power in Nigeria since independence has resided mainly in the northern section. The majority ethnic groups, Hausa/Fulani, Yoruba/Igbo controlled political power at the federal and/or regional levels to the marginalization of the minorities. With the incursion of the military which has been dominated by the minorities of the middle belt. the dominance of the major ethnic groups was destroyed with the creation of more states by 1967 when twelve states were created. Ukwu (1985) pointed out that half of these were controlled by the minorities who constituted just 33.3% of the national population. Creation of more states resulted in the spread of development as the advantages resulting from access to political power and opportunities expanded. Currently, there are thirty-six such states.

One notable paradox of the political dominance of the north is that while federal investments have markedly favoured the north to the chagrin of the southerners, particularly the southern minorities inhabiting the Niger Delta where the national wealth is mainly obtained, there has been no appreciable effect on the spatial imbalance and regional poverty in the country.

Equity in development management in Nigeria

Nigeria has long recognized the danger distributional inequity of resources poses to national integration, political stability and national development. The promotion of balanced development between one part of the country and another has been stated explicitly in fixed term development plans implemented between 1962 and 1985. The fact that regional disparities were identified as been one of the causes of the political crisis that culminated in the civil war from 1967 to 1970 further invigorated the need to pursue the objective in the third and fourth development plans. The third National Development Plan went further to state that a situation where some parts are lagging behind can no longer be tolerated. The plan is, therefore, structured to generate growth simultaneously in all geographical areas of the country. The third plan aimed (therefore) to pay greater attention to regional development than its predecessors" (Aigbokhan, 2000).

In pursuit of these goals several instruments (federal government transfers, fiscal incentives, infrastructural incentives, industrial estates), development projects/programmes (River Basin Development Authorities; Agricultural Development Programmes, Oil Mineral Producing Areas Development Committee (OMPADEC), and policy of deliberate discrimination (Federal Character representation, quota system) were used to stimulate growth in the regions lagging in development. In spite of all these, distributional inequity has continued to stare Nigeria in the face and the threat to national stability is ever increasing.

Implementing national plans to foster even development, emphasis was placed more on individuals than on regional development. Thus in the political appointments as well as distribution of opportunities, individuals who benefited either do not stay in the area so that there will be no multiplier effects in the area or appropriated the benefits only to themselves. The ruling class, in many ways, implemented their programmes to achieve the goal of national integration and equity largely by looting the national treasury, sacrificing efficiency and entrenching ethnic dominance. The consequence is a badly divided nation in which most ethnic nationals are agitating for a national conference to tackle the issues of equitable distribution of political and economic resources.

People are objecting to inequity because of the belief that the country is rich enough and is capable of alleviating poverty as well as ensuring equitable development regionally. Perhaps the most important reason why inequity is most unacceptable in Nigeria is the fact that the managers and perceived beneficiaries of the oil mineral wealth are significantly different from those whose land the oil is found and who suffers the environmental, social and economic consequences of oil processing. While federal government expenditure is titled to benefit the areas and people who have political power, there is intolerable neglect, poverty and the marginalization of the oil producing communities from economic and political mainstream of the country. The consequence of this has been violent opposition to the status quo that tends to perpetuate inequity.

In fact, the underlying reason for the multi-various problems confronting Nigeria as a nation and which manifest in religious intolerance, ethnic and tribal clashes and failure in governance have their roots in the visible distributional inequities of what has come to be called the national cake. As this quest for economic nationalism along ethnic/tribal and religious lines spread, the nation suffers.

When the perceived inequity is not redressed, national unity is threatened and violent upheavals work to tear the very foundation of the nation. This manifests itself in the various civil wars, ethnic clashes and political instability that has drained human and material resources in Nigeria and other African countries to the detriment of positive development. Where the Nigerian solution of paternalistic pacification of violent/noisy groups are adopted, the nation still suffers. Efficiency is traded for equity and the moral fabric is thrown overboard in pursuit of group security. One clear case in mind here is the dual response to criminal tendencies in the Nigerian society. While a person who steals community funds are subjected to serious societal norms that punish such offenders, the same group that will not tolerate the stealing of community funds provides ethnic havens for criminals who steal government funds. Head or tail, the nation suffers.

All over the world, many countries have had to overcome the problem of inequity. Although in most developing nations, efforts have been unsuccessful and have led to civil wars as in Indonesia, Sudan, Ethiopia, Burundi and Congo. Until very recently, Nigeria paid lip-service attention to addressing the problem of inequity. It is instructive to not that while Nigeria and other African countries are still grappling with the problem of regional equity, other countries where best practices are operationalized have achieved substantial progress. Also in the latter group, there have been examples of successful bridging of the gap between the "haves" and "have-nots" and between social and ethnic groups.

One of the recent nations that have successfully overcome the problem of inequity in prosperity was a unified Germany. At unification, there was marked difference between the old West and East Germany culminating in massive migration from the East and unemployment in the West. The German government invested heavily into the old Eastern sections factories and created jobs and ensured economic prosperity. Germany did not hold the old west down while developing the East. All Germans gained from government investment but the old East more to bring the area at par with the West.

Furthermore, emphasis was in the economic institutions in the old East and not on individuals.

Malaysia presents another case of a country that has successfully used equity in managing her economy. Malaysia has three ethnic groups competing for national resources. At independence, foreign entrepreneurs came to set up plantations and also develop mines fields. They were, however, unable to attract indigenous labour who stayed glued to producing rice. Chinese immigrants came into fill the gap. At the end, a plural society of native Malays, Chinese and the European migrants developed. After the 1969 violent racial riots between the Malays and Chinese, government decided to pursue interventionist policies and assumed a vastly expanded role in running state owned companies to implement its New Economic Policy. The policy aimed at redistributing incomes and assets among the three groups the Malays, the Chinese and the foreigners in the ratio of 30%, 40%, 30% respectively of the total commercial and industrial assets of the country, with the target to be advanced over 21 years (Lal and Myint, 1996).

Malaysia pursued policies aimed at empowering the Malay peasants by modernizing the farm business through large scale irrigation, subsidies and price support programmes. She also increased expenditure on social services in health and education. She pursued land reforms and settled peasant farmers in newly opened fields where government assisted in planting rubber and oil palm plantations. This process was pursued until economic problems shifted emphasis from equity to growth through the deliberate policy of equity and openness. Malaysia has succeeded in redistributing income among the racial groups where income distribution among different ethnic groups loomed larger than income distribution between the rich and the poor.

Ayida's contribution to equity and regional development

As a man that passed through the shadow of poverty, fostering equity and regional development has been one of the major pre-occupation of Mr Ayida. This endeavour has been fully manifested in his professional career as a seasoned technocrat in the Nigerian public sector management between 1957 and 1977 and his contribution thereafter. As an unassuming technocrat, he was a key player for nearly three decades in the moulding of the Nigerian State. Even after leaving office, he has continued to be an indispensable asset to providing un-ignorable opinions on national issues. His actions and activities, while the in government, are better understood from his contributions to the national discourse after his leaving the civil service. He hardly delivered any public lectures or speeches without stressing issues bothering on poverty, equity distribution and regional balancing. He was more voracious on these issues when he realized that all the legacies his group laid in the 1960s and 1970s have been rubbished by his successors. Societal poverty eradication has been substituted by personal aggrandizement while regional balancing has been replaced by political and ethnic patronage.

My Ayida examined and attacked the problem of equity along several fronts. He was concerned most importantly with the widening gap between the rich and the poor. Any of his public discuss always provides opportunities for him to fight for the course of the common man. In fact, at some point in time, he became the vanguard or opium of the masses; an attribute he still posses till today. For instance, his National Day Lecture on "Self-Sufficiency: The Path to Virile Nationhood" in 1988, provided an opportunity for him to champion the course of the poor thus:

> It is difficult to imagine how the urban poor survive in our cities today. The survival of the rural poor has become a miracle (Ayida, 1988:17).

If the survival of the poor in 1988 was adjudged by him to be a miracle when poverty head count was just about 45.0 per cent of the population, how much more in 1996 when the poverty level was 65.6 per cent and in 1998 and beyond when it has reached 70.2 per cent. He is more of a philosopher rather than as a prophet of doom in this regard.

Prior to his earlier speech, his crusade against human misery to ivory towers through his paper titled, "The Rise and Fall of Nigeria" when he delivered the 1987 convocation lecture at the University of Jos, that there was the need for Nigeria to –

> ...focus attention on the increasingly unbearable sacrifice demanded of the silent majority – the have-nots – in all parts of the federation, especially the urban poor and the unemployed. Their deafening silence sounds to many like the gathering storm but nobody seems to listen to their cries of anguish.

In the same book, he regarded himself sad because of the emmiseration of the rural poor and the pulverization of urban dwellers, which in his opinion has gone too far. Unlike many of his peers who lived in glass houses, Mr Ayida was also close enough to have been able to see the misery of the poor and its incidence in the rural as well as the urban sectors. In the National Day Lecture he gave in 1988, he also re-emphasised his view of the polarization between the rich and the poor as well as the increasing unemployment, poverty and misery among Nigerians consequent upon the adoption of the Structural Adjustment Porgramme (SAP) in a five point agenda for Nigeria to move into the 21st century. In his fourth recommendation, he stressed that,

> The professional and middle class should not be squeezed to death since they provide the vehicle for transmitting technology and modern management in public and private enterprises. It is generally

> recognized that if Nigeria is not to continue to live beyond its means, there has to be some painful adjustment especially in our life style. But this should not sound the death knell of the professional and middle class, otherwise, Nigeria will enter the 21st century considerably weakened. The present level of graduate unemployment cannot be sustained in the long run when we are all dead. There must be an answer before the turn of the century. The increasing polarization between the "haves" and have nots" will further weaken the fabric of society and the ability to maintain law and order (Ayida, 1988).

Mr Ayida believed that to redress the problem of inequity in wealth among people in the country, there was the need for a redistribution of wealth. The point was well made in the address to the nation on its 28th independence day in 1988 when he posited that "a *country where an individual can donate over N10 nillion when the external parity of Naira was US$ 1.50... a nation where many individuals can own and operate private jets may be in the need of radical redistribution of incomes and wealth*" (Ayida, 1988:7). Unlike many people who have tasted power, he believed very strongly that there was and still is enough money to sustain a self-sufficient economy and support every Nigerian if the resources are prudently managed.

As a man that strongly believed in social justice, throughout his career, he worked hard to enthrone fairness and social justice in the country. He never believed that anything should stand in the way to the progress of any individual other than his personal ability. As a key player in the Nigerian development process, having worked with about seven successive governments at the federal level, he was awed at the way and manner the patriotic zeal for the Nigerian entity was eroded and the speed with which the same occurred. He saw how commitment to the nation changed after a few years of independence to that of narrow parochial interest. One of such institutionalized approaches used in maintaining ethnic and sectional interests was the federal character system which led to inequality in access to opportunities in the polity. In examining the fate of the nation from independence till 1987 when he presented the Convocation Lecture at the University of Jos, an address he captioned, the Rise and Fall of Nigeria he made nine proposals for Nigeria to rise again. The first of these was that there should *be equal opportunity for all, in education, employment and all matters relating to law enforcement (that federal character should not be applied only where it is convenient or beneficial to the ruling class, neither should it be used as pretext for enthroning mediocrity)*. He believed that if federal character is applied in good faith, it can bring the best form every part of the federation. He reiterated his believe that Nigeria would rise again but, only when Nigeria is led by a visionary leader who has integrity and who is fully committed to the ideals of social justice and fair play for all citizens irrespective of their state of origin, religion and/or social status.

He was also committed advocate of regional equity and this he struggled for in the areas of governance, economic development and poverty. In the area of governance, Mr Ayida believed that power cannot and must not reside in one state, one section or with one tribe in perpetuity. He believed it will not augur well for mutual trust and commitment to the nation state. The second recommendation he made in the Jos convocation lecture was that power must rotate among the various constituents of the polity. He wrote that the Nigeria cannot survive in the long run as one nation state if one section of the country has to provide the president in perpetuity. It was this believe for a Nigeria where each group is capable of being allowed to aspire to topmost hierarchy with the sole aim of fostering development that made him to change his mind to retire voluntarily from the civil service when General Murtala Muhammed was assassinated. The succession process that led to the emergence of General Olusegun Obasanjo even when majority of those who took the decision were from the north convinced Mr Ayida, that there were still sane men who believed in the corporate existence of the Nigerian entity. The reluctant acceptance of the successor with the promise of not perpetuating himself was also welcoming to him. In analyzing the power structure of the nation, he opined that never should any section of the country be made to feel perpetually enslaved like a second class citizen.

Mr Ayida's insistence in equity in terms of access to political power was not just at the federal level. He also recognized that at the state and local government levels, there will still be minorities who could be subjugated in an independent Nigeria. As a member of the committee that provided the criteria that was used to create the twelve states in 1967, one criterion which he helped in proposing but which the military junta rejected was the linguistic criteria. The criterion was aimed at creating states along linguistic lines to remove the perennial problem of minorities even at state and local levels. The reason for its rejection was that it ignores the relative sizes and population that will constitute a state. In the reconstitution of the former Bendel State, he asked that the state be reconstituted into three or four to ensure that the problem of minority is eliminated. This according to him is in the interest of future generations of Bendelites, given the current morally indefensible quota system of admission into Federal Unity Schools and Colleges, and the adverse consequences of the federal character in appointments in the federal public service. He carried this argument further by projecting as far back as 1987 that Nigeria following the example of Bendel State should be reconstituted into thirty states.

He was also deeply concerned by the deprivation of the Niger Delta area and wrote that:

> We should empathize with the silent minority, and image how we would feel if the petroleum oil produced on our soil and in the process of producing which, our waters and environment are permanently

polluted, is used to develop other places while we remain neglected.

In his own way and for more than four decades Mr Ayida has stood against inequity whether it be between the rich and the poor individuals or regions. He has always envisioned that Nigeria has the potential to develop and become a middle level world power but that distributional inequity would tear the fabric of the nation apart and prevent it from achieving this except something urgent is done about it.

Fostering equity in Nigeria's development process

One of the major wishes of Ayida is seeing an egalitarian Nigerian society with every region having equal treatment in state affairs. Arising from the seriousness with which obvious distributional inequity impact on the security and corporate existence of nations, he sees this as an urgent issue the political class must address with all seriousness. Equity in Nigeria involves sharing economic and political power: achieving distributional equity in economic and political opportunities between the rich and poor individuals, on one hand, and between rich poor regions, on the other.

Since independence, Nigeria has used a number of strategies to promote equity. Some of the methods used include fiscal transfer, economic incentives, specialized development/poverty reduction programmes, the quota system and the federal character principle. In spite of all these, the gap in distributional inequity between individuals and regions continue to widen. The irony of the Nigerian situation is that the region that has wielded political power for four decades of political independence remains the poorest. This is a unique case in the world as elsewhere, minority and deprived groups and areas in other countries seek political power to redress the wrongs of distributional inequity and, have in most cases succeeded. The simple fact is that not only has holding political power and presiding over allocation of national wealth failed to help the northern section of the country, the prescribed method of redressing equity problems have failed the nation. In fact, it has ended in entrenching ethnic hegemony and allocating resources more to the benefit of the north than the areas where the wealth of the nation is got. Clearly, this calls for a rethink of the methods of redressing equity problems in the country. The strive for equity has been an important area of Ayida's focus.

The need to redress the problem calls for a fundamental adjustment in the management of the nation stat e. a situation where a region is ruling in perpetuity with few individuals and families monopolizing political power must stop. Each of the regions should have equal claim to power. Granted that the monopoly of power by the north have not helped the north any appreciably relative to other southern regions, but, the fact remains that the north only failed to take advantage of the colossal investment diverted to the area. The prevalence of non-transparent, non-accountable and non-participatory governance is synonymous with poor allocation of resources. When all sections have equal access to political power, the national resources will be equitably distributed to ensure that no section is neglected. The issue of access to political power goes beyond sharing resources. It is recognition of the fact that no group is a second class rated one and that the federation is one of a partnership of the different groups in the polity. If power must rotate to achieve this, so be it. There is need, however, to learn from experience. Why did the north fail to use political power to redress inequity within its region? We need to pay copious attention to this for political rotation to produce results.

A growing economy is a necessary condition for dealing with unemployment and poverty with positive impact on the crime and threat to security. Policy measures must be put in place to ensure that the economy grows. It is not conceivable to hold down one group because we want to achieve balanced development in the country. This inherent goal of the quota system and federal character principle is the primary cause of inter-ethnic hatred and animosity and one of the main reasons for rejecting northern hegemony in the country. Evidence from Asia and Latin America revealed that when appropriate macroeconomic policies are combined with right institutional reforms, economic growth would be achieved which narrowed poverty and equity gaps. The literature is clear about the fact that a 2 per cent annual rate of growth in real consumption per capita often translate to a decline in the poverty index within the range of 3 to 8 percent. To this end, Nigeria has no choice but to facilitate the growth process within the range of about 7 percent as stipulated by the Summit for Social Development.

When general overall economic development is on, measures to address inequity should be pursued simultaneously through targeting of beneficiaries, whether they are individuals or regions. The existing six geopolitical zones is a good framework for redressing the problem of inequitable distribution of resources in the country. This can be achieved through several ways but three of them are highlighted here. The first approach is to inject investment funds to the regions have suffered disproportionate discrimination in the distribution of the products of economic development over the past years through massive infrastructural development. Such investments include: transportation (roads, rail and waterways), communication, health, water, and power supply. This apart from pulling industries into the areas is also capable of giving a sense of belonging to the deprived regions.

Second, the use of federal character principle should be overhauled with a view to removing mediocrity and discrimination against other individuals. It should focus more on the localization of economic and social institutions with high propensity to generating development impulse. The location of such institutions should be based on the resource endowments of each region.

The third approach is proper decentralization of resources from the national wealth to the states and the local government authorities. These other levels of governments should be empowered financially to develop their jurisdictions, which will go a long way in solving the equity problem in the country. Such funds that will be transferred should be tied to key developmental programmes with proper monitoring from the federal government and beneficiaries. This is not, however, automatic. If the present level of corruption is not tamed, it will be very difficult to make headway.

In any geographically extensive country like Nigeria, the problem of equity looms large. This is further compounded by regional jealousies which most often than not result in political crisis. Regional diversity in terms of ethnicity, language, religion, social class and even political affiliations engenders differences in the interests, needs, values, aspirations, visions and expectations. The resource endowments in such regions (physical, economic and social), also affect the access of each group to power and economic opportunities. Such an unequal access serves as ingredients of political upheavals. Thus, wishing them away is just postponing dooms day as was the case in Ethiopia, Somalia, Liberia and Yugoslavia, to mention just a few. Building on the benefits of diversity and minimizing its costs are veritable way of managing the process.

Constructive management of the ethnic and regional diversity, in Nigeria, would require measures that release the energies of the people by tapping on their sense of identity and values. The polity must be such that all sections of the national polity will develop a sense of belonging through uninhibited access to decision making process. There is need to provide for greater autonomy and empowerment of the local government system and let people debate and own decisions that will affect their relationship with other sections of the national polity. This can be achieved only through popular debate and dialogue.

Each segment of the Nigerian society should be made to participate in national development and appropriate measures put in place to ensure that people are properly mobilized and empowered to improve their conditions. This will entail substantial investment in education and health all over the country. It is crucial to invest resources in all parts of the federation to ensure economic growth and distributional equity. There is also the need to determine minimum acceptable standards of development or welfare and ensure that these are met across the country and states. Besides, the less favoured are put in a position to improve relative to the better-placed. To achieve this, framework for ensuring requisite database and continuous assessment of performance should be institutionalized.

Bearing in mind that equity is congenial to national integration, ensuring distributional and regional equity becomes sacrosanct. Mutual trust and respect will normally be achieved where perceived injustice of inequity is not very much obvious. Any positive policy move in this direction will enhance trust, confidence and loyalty, the desiderata of Nigeria's economic and political development. The interaction so generated will enhance mobility of resources across the regional and ethnic divides necessary to catalyse the required development in each region. Government also has the responsibility to remove social and ethnic prejudices by ensuring equity forms the basis of resource allocation. There is need to harness the strengths of all communities in the guest for development. The latent force and resourcefulness from within every society should be harnessed for development rather than seeing diversity as an unmanageable problem. There is a need to mobilize all segments of civil society and the private sector to ensure that the development process is all-inclusive. In addition, we must build on existing structure but allowing for creativity and enterprise development through private initiatives to ensure a more balanced and sustainable system of development, which will succeed in eliminating poverty and regional inequity.

Concluding remarks

Ayida's position on regional equity tallies with the general thrust of development literature. He strongly believes that the country's potential if well managed; Nigeria would wake up from being a sleeping giant to become a power to be reckoned with in the world. But this cannot be achieved within the present *status quo* where there is a fundamental flaw in the management of the nation state: a situation where a region is ruling in perpetually, the use of the quota system and federal character to enthrone mediocrity and foster discrimination; lopsided distribution of the country's resources; looting of public treasury, to mention a few. To foster national integration, mutual trust and confidence we must discontinue with bad side of the quota and federal character system, injection of investment funds to regions discriminated against in the areas of infrastructural development, discontinue with perpetuating rulership and always scout for dedicated and visionary leadership, as well as foster decentralized federal structure.

Bibliography

Abumere, S .I. (1998a) "Distributional Inequity and the Problem of National Integration," Inaugural Lecture.

Abumere, S. I. (1998b) "Jurisdictional Partitioning and the Poverty Gap in Nigeria," DPC Working Paper 15.

Achebe, Chinua (1958) *Things Fall Apart,* London, Heinemann Educational Books.

Adamolekun, Ladipo (1977) "Transforming the Civil Service," In: Diamond, Larry; A Kirk-Greene and Oyeleye Oyediran (Eds.) *Transition Without End,"* Ibadan, Vantage Publishers; p.408-422.

Adamolekun, Ladipo (1986) "Soldiers, Civilian Politicians and Administrators (1966-79)" In: *Politics and Administration in Nigeria*, Ibadan, Spectrum Books; pp.99-137.

Aigbokhan, E. Ben (2000) "Determinants of Regional Poverty," Development Policy Centre.

Ajayi, J.F.A. (1987) *The Land the Ancestors Built: Traditional Theories of Historical Change*, The Wiles Lectures delivered at Queens University Belfast, N. Ireland.

Ayandele, Emmanuel (1974) *The Educated Elite in the Nigerian Society,* Ibadan, Ibadan University Press; p.54.

Ayida, Allison A. (1987a) "Contractor Finance and Supplier Credit in Economic Growth," In: *Reflections on Nigerian Development,* Lagos, Malthouse Press; pp.266-70.

Ayida, Allison A. (1987b) "The Nigerian Revolution (1966-1976)" In: *Reflections on Nigerian Development* Lagos, Malthouse Press; pp.1-23.

Ayida, Allison A. (1987c) "Introduction" In: *The Rise and Fall of Nigeria: the History and Philosophy of an Experiment in African Nation-Building,* Lagos, Malthouse Press; pp.3-4.

Ayida, Allison A. (1987d) "Introduction," In: *Reflections on Nigerian Development,* Lagos, Malthouse Press.

Ayida, Allison A. (1987e) "Nigerian Enterprise for Decision Makers" (a public lecture).

Ayida, Allison A. (1987f) "The Rise and Fall of Nigeria: the History and Philosophy of an Experiment in African Nation-Building," Convocation Lecture delivered at University of Jos, January, 1987.

Ayida, Allison A. (1987g) "The Contribution of Politicians and Administrators to Nigeria's National Economic Planning," In: *Reflections on Nigerian Development Lagos*, Malthouse Press; pp.24-37.

Ayida, Allison A. (1987h) "Basic Issues in Financing Nigerian Agriculture in the Seventies" (presented to highlight the problems of Plan implementation during the *Second National Development Plan*).

Ayida, Allison A. (1988a) "Power Without Corruption: A Non-Utopian Approach," Lecture delivered at the 1988 Bendel State Public Service Forum.

Ayida, Allison A. (1988b) "Self-sufficiency: the Path to Virile Nationhood," 1988 National Day Lecture.

Ayida, Allison A. (1989) "The Public Service and the Foundation of the Third Republic," Chief Michael Ani Memorial Lecture.

Ayida, Allison A. (1990a) "Before Tomorrow Comes," 25th Anniversary Public Lecture of Academy Press, Lagos.

Ayida, Allison A. (1990b) "Notes," Talk given at Lagos Island Club.

Ayida, Allison A. (1990c) "Retirement from Public Service: Preparations and Challenges," Federal Public Service Lecture.

Ayida, Allison A. (1992) "Random Notes on the Naira Question," NIPSS Alumni Association Annual Dinner held on 3rd December, 1992.

Ayida, Allison A. (1996) "Food and Agriculture Policy Options and Plan Administration: Lessons of Experience," First Annual Lecture of the Centre for Food and Agriculture Strategy (CEFAS), University of Agriculture, Markurdi, Nigeria.

Ayida, Allison A. (1997) "The 1994 Civil Service Reforms: Review and Prospects," Distinguished Annual Lecture Delivered at the National Institute for Policy and Strategic Studies, Kuru, Nigeria.

Ayida, Allison A. (1999a) "Professionalism and Ethics in the Civil Service," Lecture delivered at the International Conference Centre, Abuja on June 22, 1999.

Ayida, Allison A. (1999b) "Hallmarks of Labour" (a public lecture).

Ayida, Allison A. (2001) "National Development Planning and the Market Economy: the Experience of Nigeria," Lecture delivered at Professor Ojetunji Aboyade Memorial Lecture at University of Ibadan on October 30, 2001.

Ayida, Allison A. (2002) "The Leader Nigeria Needs in the 21st Century," The Abuja Initiative.

Ayida, Allison A. (2003) "The Nigerian Revolution Reconsidered," Lecture delivered at Oxford University, 8 July 2003.

Borts, G.H. and J.L. Stein (1964) *Economic Growth in a Free Market*, Columbia University Press, New York.

Brown Weiss (1989) *In Fairness to Future Generations: International Property Law, Common Patrimony and Inter-generational Equity*, United Nations University, Japan and Transnational Publishers, New York.

Champernowho, D.G. and F.A. Cowell (1998) *Economic Inequity and Income Distribution,* Cambridge University Press.

Chinsmann Babasola (1998) *A Matter of People*, UNDP, Nigeria.

Crowder, Michael (1962) *The Story of Nigeria,* London, Faber and Faber; pp.255-6.

Depak Lal and H. Mint (1996) *The Political Economy of Poverty, Equity and Growth: A Comparative Study*, Clarendon Press, Oxford.

Dudley, Billy J. (1973) *Instability and Political Order: Politics and Crisis in Nigeria*, Ibadan, Ibadan University Press; p.187.

Edozien, E.C. (1968) "Linkages, Direct Regional Foreign Investment and Nigeria's Economic Development," *Nigerian Journal of Economics and Social Studies,* vol. 10, No.2.

Ekeh, Peter (1980) "Colonialism and Social Structure," inaugural lecture delivered at University of Ibadan, Nigeria.

Federal Office of Statistics (1999) "Poverty Profile for Nigeria 1980-1996," FOS, Lagos.

Isong, Clement (1985) "Spreading the Benefits of Development of all Nigerians" in E.J. Nwosu (ed.) *Achieving Even Development in Nigeria: Problems and Prospects*, Fourth Dimension Publisher, pp. 3-14.

Kayode, 'Femi (2002) *Refocusing Economic Development: The Holy Grail of Economics and Economists*? University of Ibadan, University Lecture Series, 136p.

Mabogunje L. Akin (1968) *Urbanization in Nigeria*, University of London Press.

Mabogunje, L. Akin (1999) "The Poverty Profile of Ijebu-Ode," Paper presented at the Ijebu-Ode City Consultation for Poverty Reduction, March 22, 1999.

Maxwell, John C. (1993) *The Winning Attitude*, Nashville, Thomas Nelson, p.14.

Munoz, L. J. (1988) "For the Sake of Tradition," Inaugural Lecture delivered at the University of Ibadan, Ibadan, Nigeria.

Narayan, D. R. *et al* (2000) *Voices of the Poor: Can Anyone Hear Us?* Oxford University Press for the World Bank.

Neruda, Pablo, (1964) "Lost Letters," In: *Isla Negra*, New York, Farrar Straus and Giroux; p.141.

Okojie, C. E. E. *et al* (2000) "Poverty in Nigeria - An Analysis of Gender Issues. Access to Social Services and the Labour Market." Final Research Report submitted to the AERC as part of the Collaborative Research Project on Poverty, Income, Distribution and Labour Market Issues.

Olaopa, Tunji (Ed.) (1997) *A Prophet is With Honour: the Life and Times of Ojetunji Aboyade*, Ibadan, Fountain Publications; p.99.

Olubummo, Adegoke (1985) "What Does It All Add Up To?" A Valedictory Lecture delivered at the Faculty of Science, University of Ibadan, Ibadan, Nigeria.

Oyediran, Oyeleye (1997) "The Political Bureau," In: Diamond, Larry; A. Kirk-Greene and Oyeleye Oyediran (Eds.) *Transition Without End*. Ibadan, Vantage Publishers; pp.67-95.

Pleskovic, Boris and J.E. Stiglitz(2000) "Introduction," In: *1999 Annual World Bank Conference on Development Economics*, Washington, D.C. The World Bank.

Rawls, J. (1991) *Theory of Justice*, Horwood University Press, Cambridge.

Soyibo, A.B. Alayande and K. Olayiwola (2001) "Poverty Alleviation in Nigeria," in S.I. Abumere and A. Soyibo (eds.) *Development Policy and Analysis* in Honour of Akinlawon Ladipo Mabogunje Development Policy Centre, Ibadan: pp 173-212.

Soyinka, Wole (1983) "Del Renacimiento Cultural Africano," In: Barcelona (Ed. Serba) 'La Afirmacion de la Identidad Cultural.' (Cited by L.J. Munoz (1988) In: "For the Sake of Tradition," Inaugural Lecture delivered at the University of Ibadan, Ibadan Nigeria.

Soyinka, Wole (2003) "Soyinka Replies Obasanjo," *The Guardian* on Sunday, August 3, 2003; pp. A4, A12.

Spender, Stephen (1986) "A Question of Identity," In: *Collected Poems: (1928-1985)*, New York, Oxford University Press; p.166.

Teriba, Owodunni (1978) "Illusions and Social Behaviour," an Inaugural lecture delivered at the University of Ibadan on 9th March, 1978; 27p.

Udoji, Jerome (1995) *Under Three Masters: Memoirs of an Administrator*, Ibadan, Spectrum Books; pp.88-91.

Udoji, Jerome (1999a) "The New Style Public Service," In: *Which Way Nigeria?* Ibadan, Spectrum Books, pp.123-129.

Udoji, Jerome (1999b) "The Civil Service in the Year 2000 and Beyond," In: *Which Way Nigeria?* Ibadan, Spectrum Books, pp.173-81.

Udoji, Jerome (1999c) "Political Neutrality of Civil Servants," In: *Which Way Nigeria*? Ibadan, Spectrum Books, pp.84-97.

Ukwu, I. Ukwu (1985) "Even Development in Nigeria: An Overview," in E.J. Nwosu (ed.) *Achieving Even Development in Nigeria: Problems and Prospects,* Fourth Dimension Publishers pp 15-58.

UNDP (1996) Nigerian Human Development Report, UNDP, Nigeria.

World Bank (1999) World Development Report 2000/2001, Consultation with the poor, Nigeria: Voice of the Poor; Country Synthesis Report, Nigeria.

Young M.D. (1992) *Sustainable Investment and Resource Use: Equity, Environmental Integrity and Economic Efficiency,* Man and the Biosphere Series VI. 9, The Pantheon Publishing Group, Melbourne, Australia.

Index

www.ingramcontent.com/pod-product-compliance
Lightning Source LLC
Chambersburg PA
CBHW011828020426
42334CB00025B/2970
* 9 7 8 9 7 8 0 2 3 1 8 5 9 *